MW00782406

The Privateers

The Rivals

The Privateers

*How Billionaires Created a Culture War
and Sold School Vouchers*

JOSH COWEN

HARVARD EDUCATION PRESS
CAMBRIDGE, MASSACHUSETTS

Copyright © 2024 by the President and Fellows of Harvard College

All rights reserved. No part of this publication may be reproduced or transmitted in any form or by any means, electronic or mechanical, including photocopy, recording, or any information storage and retrieval systems, without permission in writing from the publisher.

Paperback ISBN 9781682539101

Library of Congress Cataloging-in-Publication Data

Names: Cowen, Josh, author.
Title: The privateers : how billionaires created a culture war and sold
  school vouchers / Josh Cowen.
Description: Cambridge, Massachusetts : Harvard Education Press, [2024] |
  Includes bibliographical references and index.
Identifiers: LCCN 2024005627 | ISBN 9781682539101 (paperback)
Subjects: LCSH: Privatization in education—United States. | Educational
  vouchers—United States. | Education and state—United States. |
  Educational equalization—United States.
Classification: LCC LB2806.36 .C69 2024 | DDC 379.1—dc23/eng/20240401
LC record available at https://lccn.loc.gov/2024005627

Published by Harvard Education Press,
an imprint of the Harvard Education Publishing Group

Harvard Education Press
8 Story Street
Cambridge, MA 02138

Cover Design: Jackie Shepherd Design
Cover Image: Suprun via Getty Images

The typefaces in this book are Minion Pro and ITC Stone Sans.

Contents

The Privateers: A Directory

Alliance Defending Freedom (ADF): A right-wing organization focused on anti-LGBTQ+ legislation and litigation, repealing reproductive rights, and mandatory public spending on private/homeschool. Seed funders include the DeVos family.

American Federation for Children (AFC): The national voucher advocacy group, with state-based chapters, cofounded by Betsy DeVos. Parent organization of AFC Victory Fund, a Super PAC devoted to political organizing on voucher issues.

American Legislative Exchange Council (ALEC): The national coordinating group for sample right-wing legislation and policy templates. A major recipient of Bradley Foundation funding.

The Lynde and Harry Bradley Foundation: The Milwaukee-based funding juggernaut devoted to conservative and increasingly right-wing causes. Seed funder of early voucher advocacy in Wisconsin and of early and ongoing litigation defending vouchers in federal court. Major funder of State Policy Network organizations—a group of conservative state-based think tanks. Funder of all voucher research, as of this book's publication, showing positive impacts on voucher users.

The Council for National Policy (CNP): A secretive national policy advocacy network, whose members have included the DeVos family and groups affiliated with Charles and David Koch. Modern members

viii THE PRIVATEERS: A DIRECTORY

have included Heritage Foundation and Bradley Foundation leadership, as well as major right-wing donors.

EdChoice: Formerly the Milton and Rose D. Friedman Foundation. A policy advocacy group and clearinghouse for—and funder of—pro-voucher research. A Bradley Foundation funding recipient.

The Heritage Foundation: The right-wing think tank and CNP mainstay running political operations on voucher messaging, book bans, and anti-LGBTQ+ reports. Also a founding backer of Moms for Liberty, a Bradley Foundation funding recipient, and organizer for Project 2025—the set of enabling acts proposed for a second Trump administration.

Institute for Justice: Founded with a personal donation from Charles Koch, serves as legal operation for voucher litigation. Coordinated multiple Supreme Court cases, served as training ground for voucher defense lawyers. Kenneth Starr was an affiliated attorney. Major recipient of Bradley Foundation funding.

Moms for Liberty: A national network of political activists that began in Florida. Affiliated with Florida GOP, backed by The Heritage Foundation and CNP affiliate The Leadership Institute. Major advocate of book ban, anti-LGBTQ+, and voucher legislation.

Preface: On Facts, Freedom, and Faith

I did not want to write this book.

Much of my career as a researcher, writer, and teacher has been built on the idea that evidence should inform public policy. What works, why, and for whom? As a specialist in the particular area of education policy, I accepted from an early professional age the idea common in policy circles at the end of the twentieth century that a scientific approach to answering these questions had largely been missing from education—that teaching, learning, and decision-making about both had, until then, been more art than science. The entire funding stream that I was fortunate enough to benefit from as a doctoral student, beginning in 2004, was devoted to training a new generation of scholars on that very idea: that science, data, *evidence* can and should determine new approaches to reforming American schools. That training program was housed by no less than the US Department of Education and funded by Congress.

This was the view with which I leapt, as a young scholar, at the chance to join large research projects concerning the extraordinarily controversial issue of school vouchers: programs that use tax dollars to fund private school tuition and expenses. Even before my doctoral training, I had served while a master's student at Georgetown on what I thought was an exciting new evaluation of a privately funded trial version of those programs. And by the time I began that doctoral work at Wisconsin, an expanded version of the nation's oldest publicly funded version offered a new opportunity to extend that interest. I felt lucky to work on a federally supported grant with the express purpose of training young analysts to use evidence-based research, while also joining a team that would examine Milwaukee's famous voucher system anew.

Looking back two decades later, I think that my youthful enthusiasm for evidence-use in public policy seems misplaced—optimistic, for sure, and probably naïve. For in the years leading up to the COVID-19 pandemic, some of the largest academic declines ever apparent in the education research record, on any topic, have been attributable to school vouchers. And yet the drumbeat to devote more and more resources to these voucher systems after years of failure according to any standard used to evaluate public schools, remains louder than ever. I imagine that, like most people with more than a casual stake in education—teachers, school leaders, theorists of learning, or civil servants in state and local agencies—I've known that both the intellectual and political origins of voucher programs have always been ideological. But a sense of why one should do something does not by itself preclude a commitment to how to go about doing it nor a reevaluation of whether to continue doing so when one has clearly made a mistake.

Dating back to the late 1990s, many of the same luminaries in the debate over education policy in the United States were the same people demanding accountability for public schools: data-informed decision-making, standards of excellence, and more attention to outcomes and not just to inputs. And many of these in turn were among those calling for expansions of school choice; new methods to hire, evaluate, and retain teachers; and the centering of market approaches to persistent problems in educational opportunity. The federal training program that opened the doors to my career began during the first term of the George W. Bush presidency. It was a line item in one of the first budgets created under the No Child Left Behind initiative that turned the federal effort in education from a framework originating in the 1960s War on Poverty to a politically right-of-center agenda for efficiency and production. Insofar as political coalitions went at the start of the twenty-first century, the evidence folks and the market folks were often very much the same.

There was something else occurring at the federal level as the Bush administration launched this new, supposedly evidence-based educational effort. Bush signed the very first federally funded school voucher program, for Washington, D.C., schools, into law in January 2004. That was ten months after the US invasion of Iraq. And it is important for readers of this book to understand that I came of age professionally in the immediate aftermath of what is officially known as Operation Iraqi Freedom. After an early stint as a graduate assistant on a voucher evaluation in 2002, I took a pause in my studies to work as a research-producer in CNN's political unit. My entire employment at the network coincided with the Bush Administration's rollout of the case for war: the purported evidence for Saddam Hussein's weapons of mass destruction, the claims from the highest levels of government that freedom itself was at stake, and that in the post-Saddam era the Iraqi people would greet American troops as liberators. All day, every day, my job as a young twenty-something staffer was to help prepare the show's on-air talent to interview members of congress, journalists, and advocates for and against invasion to debate that case. From the beginning, doubts about the evidence on Saddam's arsenal and doubts that US troops would avoid a high-casualty occupation, gave way in the mainstream of D.C. thought to the fervor of a war-bent government.

"We're here for your fucking freedom, now *back up*," yells an armed marine quoted in one history of the Iraq War.[1] For a scholar of American education, the words *freedom* and *liberty* come loaded with both affirmation and caution. Alongside voting booths and bus rides the effort to desegregate American society began in American public school districts, launching the civil rights era in which freedom summer and "free at last" became storied moments. But those were organic, community-driven movements—a national historical campaign, to be sure, but rooted in the traditions and in the power of the Black American experience. On the other hand, the decades since and, in particular, more recent years have seen a more paternalistic claim to freedom brought to bear in education policy-making. School choice, for example, the policy domain on which this book is focused, is often proposed by both conservatives and not a few progressives in something resembling an offer. Consumer-driven markets for education—including those proposed in early days by intellectuals like the economist Milton Friedman—are very much intended as race-neutral propositions toward freedom, up from a marginalization that is paradoxically bound by race. These are offers of, rather than claims toward, a limited educational emancipation. At the same time, school choice arguments are unmistakably energized in recent years by white conservatives demanding a kind of nationalist vision of freedom for themselves.

By both the coincidence of my personal formative years and by professional orientation I am deeply skeptical of any policy initiative—especially one pushed by the American Right—based on the pretense of liberating other people. That is true whether the issue is sending soldiers my age to war on the other side of the world or diverting vast new resources away from schools attended by children the age of my own toward a narrow, often radically religious form of educational change. All the more so in either case when these nation-building activities abroad and dismantling of church-state walls at home are not only infused with the language of freedom but also the language of evidence. How many think tanks, briefings, reports, and testimonies were inflected with crusade-minded ideology while insisting that Saddam Hussein had weapons of mass destruction? How many times in the last three decades of education reform has the revolutionary notion of funding dogmatic religious education in place of a civic minded public good been infused with the language of "data?"

It is toward an answer to that second question that I set out in this book. I did not want to write it because I still do believe in the importance of rigorous policy analysis, program evaluation, and evidence in decision-making at all levels of government. But that belief has become far more of a guide for best practice, so to speak, than a driving spirit itself. And because, more to the point, the evidence against vouchers is actually overwhelming. Yet the persistence of those programs, alongside even more pernicious elements of what their adherents jingoistically call "education freedom"—book bans, marginalization of LGBTQ+ families, censored curricula on issues of race and diversity—has never been stronger.

Perhaps this reads as cynicism, but what I actually intend, more carefully, is skepticism. What I hope this book does is make it impossible for any open-minded reader to encounter claims about school choice, school vouchers, parents' rights, or any other tenet of that conservative "freedom" agenda with any but the strongest doubt and deepest hesitation. Who has funded the work? Who has distributed its contents? Which organizations and which public figures are associating themselves with those claims, whether they are stakeholders in the education space or not? And not to put too fine a point on it: where do the people lining up to march for education freedom line up on other questions like environmental protection, health care access, immigration, elections and voting, marriage equality, and reproductive rights?

My fear is that the weight of evidence against the schemes I write about in this book is already so heavy—and yet seemingly to no avail—that the answers to the questions above are really more for history now than for active public policy. I hope not. I would not have written even a page of this book had I truly believed so. In any case, if this book succeeds in raising doubts and fueling skepticism about any of the claims toward either freedom or facts put forward by people bent on dismantling public schools, that will allow more time and more resources to come to bear on solving truly difficult problems in American education. Those include persistent inequality, a science of learning that proceeds only in fits and starts, and a long-standing lack of urgency among most political leaders to really prioritize the well-being of children.

Much of this book points in one way or another toward deliberate efforts to manipulate public policy toward the politics of exclusion and isolation using, first, the language of free markets and then—and especially today—the language of religious faith. If I am professionally conversant in the language of economics, I am personally fluent in the language of faith. I was raised in a devoutly Catholic home, which until my teen years was also a household within a Christian community nationally networked to a movement that rose during the late 1960s and known more broadly as the Charismatic Renewal. Our community, located near the University of Michigan, was a sister community to a group called the People of Praise, which was located near the University of Notre Dame. People of Praise became famous when its then-member, Amy Coney Barrett, rose to the US Supreme Court.[2]

Nothing about the free exercise of a faith tradition demands that we subject to it our intellect, or our spirit of shared humanity, when we decide to engage in public policy. A person has to want to be such a subject. During the drafting of this book, for example, Pope Francis signaled openness to creating same sex blessings for LGBTQ+ couples.[3] Such moves have placed the Pope at odds with many of his leading Catholic cardinals in the United States, who have pushed for a more stringent conservative interpretation of Church dogma just as right-wing organizing around issues of gender and sexuality has become more hostile in American politics. Francis has called such politics "backwardness" and warned American Catholics not to let "ideologies replace faith."[4] That school vouchers and the larger push toward so-called education freedom—of which vouchers are but one part—have become so engulfed in that religious radicalism was neither foreordained nor theologically required.

The politics of exclusion and isolation, and the education policies resulting from and within them, are as strategic and willful as they are heavily financed by some of the wealthiest people on the planet. They are, one might say, a choice.

Notes on Sources and Funding

This book is the product of personal experience and professional expertise. The implied critiques apparent in these pages concern the insular nature of the case for school vouchers and the vast, tightly networked and well-financed political operation on which that case is dependent.

To meet the standard set by the first critique myself, I have abstained from anecdotal or observational accounts I might otherwise have provided as a form of hearsay. Instead, I rely on specific studies, journalism, public statements, or events as the source material for this book. I have written nothing that cannot be footnoted.

To meet the second, I note for the record that I have received no financial or other in-kind support for this book save a one-semester sabbatical granted to me by Michigan State University during the final months of writing. More generally, and over the course of my career, most of my grants leading up to this writing have fallen squarely within what many public school advocates critically call the neoliberal education reform network. These include funding from Arnold Ventures, the Smith Richardson Foundation, and nearly $500,000 from the Walton Family Foundation. This last organization appears several times in later chapters. All told, I have been a principal investigator or co-investigator on nearly $14 million in grants from these and other sources—most of which to large multi-institutional research teams spread over many years and on which I have been honored to serve.

All but one of these grants, or at least my role in them, ended prior to the start of my writing. The last open grant is scheduled to end in 2024 and is a $1,962,613 portion of the $10 million total awarded to Tulane University from the US Department of Education Institute for Education Sciences (Award Number: R305C180025) to create the National Center for Research on Educational Access and Choice (REACH), a research and development institute devoted to the empirical study of school choice policy.

Although the research I conducted as part of that funding has ended and played no part in this book's creation, I remain, as of this writing, one of the five members of the REACH National Board of Directors. The REACH grant was awarded in 2018 by the US Department of Education while Betsy DeVos was in her second year as secretary.

TIMELINE: Key Events in This Book

1990s	2000s
1990: Wisconsin creates a pilot school voucher system in Milwaukee for nonsectarian schools.	**2000:** Betsy DeVos-backed voucher ballot initiative is defeated by Michigan voters 69 to 31 percent.

1990: *Politics, Markets and America's Schools* is published, with Bradley Foundation funding.

2002: The US Supreme Court rules in *Zelman v. Simmons Har* that vouchers do not violate the federal constitution; voucher defense is organized by Koch ar Bradley-funded Institute for Justice.

2002: *The Education Gap* is published, with Bradley, Walton, and Milton and Rose D. Friedman (today, EdChoice) Foundation funding.

1995: Wisconsin expands vouchers to religious schools.

2004: President Georg W. Bush signs first federal vouchers into l in Washington, D.C.— first students enroll.

1996: Ohio creates a school voucher system in Cleveland.

2005: The Wisconsin legislature reauthorizes vouchers; the new legislation names the School Choice Demonstration Project at the University of Arkansas as official evaluator.

1998: Wisconsin Supreme Court upholds state vouchers for religious schools.

2005: Hurricane Katrina devastates New Orleans and t city's school distri

1998: New York City (privately funded) voucher data are first released.

2005-2012: The School Choice Demonstration Project provides official evaluations for Milwaukee and Washington, D.C., voucher systems.

TIMELINE: Key Events in This Book

2010s	2020s

2011: Indiana creates statewide vouchers.

2020: US Supreme Court further expands voucher scope in *Espinoza v. Montana Dept. of Revenue.*

2012: Louisiana vouchers go statewide

2016: Donald J. Trump is elected President.

2022: Moms for Liberty holds first major national convention with Heritage Foundation and Leadership Institute as primary sponsors.

2017: Betsy DeVos becomes US Secretary of Education in Trump administration.

2022: US Supreme Court overturns *Roe v. Wade* in *Dobbs v. Jackson Women's Health Organization;* further expands voucher scope in *Carson v. Makin.*

2017: Large negative voucher results officially released in Indiana, Louisiana, and Washington, D.C.

2017: US Supreme Court further expands voucher scope in *Trinity Lutheran Church v. Comer.*

2023: Seven new states pass voucher systems; twelve states expand existing vouchers.

2018-2019: More negative Indiana, Louisiana, and Washington, D.C., voucher results confirmed.

2005-2012: The School Choice Demonstration Project provides official evaluations for Milwaukee and Washington, D.C., voucher systems.

Introduction

What Voucher Research Really Says

*"Trump Administration Advances School Vouchers
Despite Scant Evidence"*

—*SCIENTIFIC AMERICAN* HEADLINE, AUGUST 2017

As I write this, the state legislature in Texas is opening a special session to consider a bill that would provide public funding for private school tuition. The plan is the latest iteration of a school vouchers program with origins dating back to the 1950s. As an expert on school choice who spent formative professional years working with and around leading voucher advocates, I am fielding phone calls at all business hours from reporters, stakeholder groups, and even legislative staff asking for comment or advice. They are reaching out because I have spent the two years leading up to this day publicly warning about the harm vouchers cause, particularly to already vulnerable children. The evidence against school vouchers notwithstanding, dozens of states have introduced voucher bills, and more than ever before have passed them. I have testified formally, spoken, and written against these plans, bringing my unique perspective of once working within voucher advocacy evaluations and later partnering with state policy makers' data-informed decision-making.

1

My hope as a result of speaking out is that more people now know about the way that modern vouchers prop up struggling private schools, underwrite tuition for existing private schoolers, and cause almost unprecedented academic loss for the few children who do leave public schools for the empty promise of voucher success. I also hope my efforts have helped to add new attention to the discriminatory barriers many publicly funded private schools raise to curate their enrollment if they do accept voucher payments. All of these are patterns identified by the data over the last ten years. But the facts, it would seem, are no match for big-dollar investments—many of them opaque contributions from extraordinarily wealthy individuals that have been pushing these plans forward for more than thirty years. Voucher programs are expanding, while the evidence against them is mounting. To understand why is to ask not only about policy or politics, tax dollars or private spending, history or current events but also about the other story being told by the ideologues behind these plans. Faith without works is dead, or so the saying goes. What are the works—whence came the appearance of miracles—behind the radical faith in the wisdom of dismantling public schools?

EDUCATION AND "EDUCATION FREEDOM"

Education is personal. In both the social and the neurological senses of the word *learning* we are adaptive creatures, processing and attempting to make sense of the world around us before we are conscious. Education is also about memory: the way we build identity and outlook based on the information our minds collect and retain, often whether we know we have done so or not. And our memories are evocative: we experience emotion when we recall our own histories as we position ourselves within the events of our lives around us. When the event concerns schooling, whether for our own children or for our fellow citizens, our experiences weigh heavily on the measure we take of our responsibility to teach, prepare, continue to be taught ourselves, and contribute to a shared knowledge and understanding of our worlds broad and local. Whether we believe the children we have helped usher into the world are ours, belong to a God of our understanding, or belong utterly to themselves with us only as caretakers for a time are consequences, too, of the stories written by our pasts.

These personal histories live. Whether we attended an American public school, a private religious or secular school, an international equivalent of either, an isolated or networked homeschool, or some combination or variation of any directly determines at least part of the way we evaluate the choices we face as parents, voters, and participants in the lives of young people living around us. Are our homes the centers of our communities? Or are our churches? Where do our libraries, our recreation centers, and our local providers of food and health care fit in to our understanding of what it means to be from a place and to live within it? How much to these organizations do we give, and what do we expect in return?

The slogan "education freedom" joins two abstract concepts that are fundamentally relational into a phrase loaded with meaning. As a matter of public policy, the first of those words begins, as I have just argued, with the personal. And freedom? The questions of freedom of what and for whom well predate the American experience. How many republics, democracies, and not a few authoritarian governments began by claiming the mantle of liberty as the mark of authority and power? I study the American political and policymaking processes, and I do believe there is something special and exceptional in the American experience. But that does not make our nation immune to pretenses to freedom. If anything, we are uniquely vulnerable to a weaponized freedom growing inside our wide, expansive borders. Because within the American expression of freedom remains a strain of fundamentalism—religious, racial, and violent orthodoxy around the right to carry lethal weapons—that simply will not countenance the existence of any alternative with which it comes into social contact.

Too often in American history, the ones who suffer when that fundamentalist notion of freedom dominates are our children—especially those at risk because of their race, gender, family income, or religious traditions. This makes the role of public education in American history and American life more than just a technical matter for policy analysis. Education is more than an economic market for goods and services or a sociological construct in which different groups of people are stratified from the earliest of ages. It is in a very tangible way the place—schools, themselves, are the grounds—for many of the most intense struggles over more abstract concepts like freedom, justice, and, ultimately, human rights.

In the narrowest sense, school vouchers are a policy mechanism. Seemingly, vouchers are a vehicle to promote education—a means to an end. But crucially, and almost paradoxically, vouchers *as* policy have from their earliest days been pushed by their most vocal adherents as an *end to* policy—at least insofar as education itself is concerned. As a theory of action, vouchers position parents as consumers: speculators in an educational gold rush, each for themselves apart from how each bands together as a church, a shared economic venture, or some other organizing force. There is one kind of freedom in that vision, surely, but it comes at cost to the liberty of others whose entire being may be an affront to whatever ideology binds together some of the more aggressive speculators in that free-for-all landscape of shared American life.

Of course, I mean some of the religious radicalism so influential in American politics today. In a larger genre of writing on the topic, this book joins other work about that radicalism.[1] The contribution here is to highlight the way that vast wealth, virulent ideology—usually Christian nationalist in nature, but also a powerful strand of economic libertarianism—and an insular network of intellectuals, lawyers, and lobbyists have advanced an agenda from the rightward fringes of education policy into the political median. Given my own background and experience, I single out sectors of the professional research community as responsible for establishing what passes as both a theoretical and empirical rationale for not only school vouchers but also the broader push toward education freedom. That push includes all strands of the so-called parents' rights movement from book bans, re-education on issues of race in American history, and a new marginalization of LGBTQ+ families.

The work of conservative professors, fellows, analysts, and advocates toward these ends, whether as adherents or merely accomplices, has been necessary to that push from the very beginning. An essay by a professor at the University of Chicago in 1955, proposing school vouchers, was seized by integration opponents in the months after court-ordered desegregation as a means to avert that decision. More than three decades later, two more professors repurposed that idea to set forward a rationale for education reforms in two impoverished US cities. And it was a fourth professor who bent the tools of social science to motivate vouchers not only in those cities but in jurisdictions across the country, in cases all the way up to the US Supreme Court. And it is that fourth professor's acolytes—his students and his students' students—who maintain the rapid-response, campaign-style war room responsible for nearly every white paper, policy brief, report, and book-length polemic supporting the expansion of these policies today.

That effort is more than proactive. It is, at crucial moments, defensive. For as school vouchers have expanded, so too has the evidence-informed case against them. Voucher advocates have managed to spread privatization plans in states across the country despite a growing number of data-backed arguments against those schemes—results that are the consequences of what amounts to bad social science theory. Vast sums of money have supported the academic and other research-focused adherents to voucher ideology as policy entrepreneurs. That support—what amounts to industry funding of research to support a product—has successfully countered the empirical reality of the voucher scheme in many places. But those dollars have not been able to change that basic reality.

Strip away advocacy research on either side: no conservative advocacy groups disguised as think tanks, no research shops set up by teachers' unions, no freelancing bloggers or social media stars with a hundred thousand followers and a hot take. Expert analysis, independent, and investigative journalism and a handful of transparent state and federal accountability audits show that policies diverting public funds for private school tuition have some of the worst outcomes in the education research record to date.

Here is that evidence in seven straightforward results:

1. Today's Voucher Programs Primarily Support Students Who Were Never in Public School

As the number of states with vouchers has grown in the years leading up to this book's publication—and in particular over the months leading up to the "year of universal choice" heralded by voucher advocates—the typical voucher recipient had never been in public school. Either these students were already enrolled in private school without taxpayer support, were in homeschool, or were enrolling in private kindergarten from the start. Estimates uncannily hover around the same figure—roughly 70 percent—of students in the most recent programs coming from private schools in states that have released the data: Arizona, Arkansas, Florida, Indiana, Iowa, Missouri, New Hampshire, Ohio, and Wisconsin.[2] And we know from similar reporting that many of the private schools serving such students raise tuition once vouchers become law.[3]

2. The Larger and More Recent the Voucher Program Is, the Worse the Academic Results

Between 1996 and 2002 a series of academic papers and other reports by one team of pro-voucher researchers showed small positive voucher impacts on standardized tests. Between 2005 and 2010, two major evaluations—one in Milwaukee and the other in Washington, D.C.—found no impacts, whether positive or negative, on student outcomes. Since 2013, as voucher programs began to nevertheless expand in the number of states and the number of students served, studies from multiple evaluation teams have found that vouchers cause some of the largest academic declines on record in education research. In Louisiana, for example, the results from studies modeled as randomized control trials—conducted by two separate research teams—found negative academic impacts as high as –0.40 standard deviations.[4] A second, federal evaluation in Washington, D.C., using that randomized design, and research in Indiana using statistical methods to measure student outcomes over time, both found impacts closer to –0.15 standard deviations.[5] Results in Ohio using similar methods to the Indiana research found academic loss up to –0.50 standard deviations.[6] To put these recent, negative impacts in perspective, current estimates of COVID-19's impact on academic trajectories hover around –0.25 standard deviations, while Hurricane Katrina's impact on New Orleans students was roughly –0.17 standard deviations of academic decline.[7]

Similarly, although earlier studies—including one for which I was the lead author—found evidence that vouchers may modestly improve educational attainment (high school completion or college enrollment), more recent research has found no attainment impacts in either direction.[8] Moreover, the mechanism behind any improvement is ambiguous, especially in the face of substantially negative test score results. If a small voucher advantage is apparent, it may be due to pipeline impacts—religiously affiliated high schools sending students to their counterpart religiously affiliated colleges nearby. And that research is clear that the attainment advantage exists primarily for students who don't leave voucher programs—a major source of potential selection bias in even the randomized studies.[9]

3. Financially Distressed Private Schools Explain Negative Student Results

Research shows that vouchers create new markets for pop-up school providers, opening specifically to cash in on the taxpayer subsidy.[10] The schools that existed before—if they accept vouchers at all—tend to be financially distressed, with the voucher program acting as something of a bailout.[11] Research from Milwaukee, the country's oldest program, has shown that 41 percent of private schools accepting vouchers closed during the program's life span.[12] The average time to failure was four years for pop-up schools opening after that program expanded, and eight years for pre-existing schools. Financial distress is one reason that academic research predicted what media reporting has shown in newer voucher programs: that private schools raise their tuition when taxpayers begin subsidizing costs via vouchers.[13]

4. The Most Vulnerable Kids Suffer High Voucher Turnover—Or Are Pushed Out of Voucher Schools

When it comes to vouchers, the decision is as much about the school's choice as parental choice. Much of the early debate on school vouchers—and about school choice more generally—concerned the concept of "cream-skimming." The idea behind that unfortunate phrase was that private schools had incentives to simply admit relatively advantaged students over comparably disadvantaged peers. The income limits on early programs found little to suggest that cream-skimming fears played out—at least insofar as they related to family resources.[14] Instead, the evidence shows high rates of student turnover within and between school years for voucher-using children. In two studies, my own research team found not only that rates of student exit from Milwaukee's voucher program approached 20 percent annually but that those former voucher students saw academic improvements once they returned to public schools.[15] Who were those children who gave up their voucher? They tended to be students of color, lower-income students, and those performing comparably poorly on test scores.[16] Reports from Florida, Indiana, and Louisiana have found annual exit rates from the program similarly high.[17] Investigative reporting has also identified student pushout as one way that voucher schools manipulate the enrollment to get the students they want. Reports show that students with disabilities and students who identify (or whose parents identify) as LGBTQ+ have been asked to leave voucher programs after a more transparent admissions process has let them into the school.[18]

5. Oversight Improves Voucher Performance

Since the dismal voucher results began appearing more than a decade before this book's publication, a major talking point among voucher advocates has been attributing that academic harm to "overregulation."[19] The idea largely concedes that, in past programs, voucher-accepting private schools were financially distressed, lower-quality providers. But that concession holds that government oversight on issues like admissions standards (which include enrollment rules against discrimination) or standardized testing kept out more effective providers. The problem with the "overregulation" theory is that it's untested. In fact, to this day, the only empirical evidence of the effects of accountability on a voucher program comes from our team in Milwaukee, which found that, once a new law requiring No Child Left Behind–style performance reporting applied to the voucher program—and once private school outcomes were listed by school name, as in the public sector—voucher academic outcomes rose dramatically.[20] It is partly through oversight programs like Wisconsin's that we have some explanation for negative voucher impacts: there, for example, many of the lowest scoring students in STEM subjects on the state exam were using vouchers to attend schools teaching creationism as their science curriculum.[21]

6. Parents Looking for Academic Quality Struggle to Find Room in Private Schools

The pattern of recent academic loss for voucher students raises the question of what parents actually want. Studies from New Orleans are especially useful, because researchers at and affiliated with Tulane University have been able to use actual school application data to study how parents make priorities.[22] Those results indicate that, although parents do consider school features like demographics, safety, size, and distance to home, the academic performance of the school remains a determining factor in the way they rank preferences.[23] Similar results have been found in Washington, D.C., as well.[24] Unfortunately, that evidence also suggests that there simply are not enough effective private schools to go around—perhaps a more practical explanation for dismal voucher results than ideological arguments about regulation.[25]

7. Voucher-Induced Competition Raises Public School Outcomes Somewhat—But the Evidence for Directly Funding Vulnerable Schools Is Stronger Instead

Finally, for those hoping for a bright side to vouchers, there is modest evidence that voucher programs compel small improvements in public school achievement outcomes through competitive pressures. Such results have been found in Louisiana and in Florida in multiple versions of the latter's voucher program.[26] In these papers, statistically significant impacts of competitive pressure are most apparent in low-income communities that stand to lose substantial funding from voucher programs. However, if the goal is to simply improve public school outcomes, studies showing the impact of directly funding public schools are far more prevalent.[27] Providing more resources to begin with, in other words, helps students more than pitting vulnerable communities against each other to compete for scarce dollars.

A ROAD MAP FOR THIS BOOK

This case against school vouchers is not one sided, but it is as one sided as social science gets. The evidence presented here was uncovered across multiple fields of academic expertise, using multiple methodologies, and across many different cities and state locations. To this research has been added, especially in recent years, investigative reporting from media outlets as broadly focused as the *New York Times*, to regional newspapers and magazines, to specialty press like *Chalkbeat* and *Education Week*. This journalism has been necessary in the face of increasingly opaque and often nonexistent public reporting requirements for new or reauthorized voucher programs.

This book is the story of the counternarrative to that research and reporting: how a small band of interconnected and insular groups of conservative advocates, tightly networked to some of the wealthiest and most influential players in right-wing US politics, invented a rationale for school privatization largely from nothing and out of nowhere. How that network of scholars, lawyers, donors, and activists assembled themselves to push for a particular policy item in a larger agenda can be described only as religious nationalism.

Chapter 1 focuses on the origins of the voucher idea and the links between its founding father, Milton Friedman, and the libertarian and religious nationalism strands of US politics responsible for enacting that idea alongside other components of "education freedom" today. It is in those first pages that we meet Charles Koch, Betsy DeVos, and the little-known network called the Council for National Policy that bands many of the ancillary actors in these pages together.

Chapter 2 introduces the Lynde and Harry Bradley Foundation—the main funder of the right-wing "counter-intelligentsia" originating all of the voucher policymaking since 1990. Beginning with the nation's first voucher program in its home city of Milwaukee, the Bradley Foundation has had a critical role in the three central columns of every voucher push since then: research, policy advocacy, and litigation. Here we meet the key figures spanning each of those columns, including Harvard's conservative voucher guru Paul E. Peterson and a legal foot solider named Clint Bolick, both of whom entered the fray at key places with Bradley dollars to do their work.

Chapter 3 builds from the early victory for vouchers at the US Supreme Court, in 2002, where Bolick, Peterson, and the infamous Kenneth J. Starr all played major defining roles. This chapter documents the aftermath, in which the nation's first federally funded voucher scheme in Washington, D.C., followed as a direct result of both the Court's ruling and of Peterson's own efforts in the late 1990s. Chapter 3 also introduces other ancillary figures who would feature in the policy development of these plans moving forward.

Chapter 4 provides an in-depth examination of what voucher advocacy research looked like on the ground in those early days, using my own experience working for a demonstration of that form of advocacy scholarship headed by one of Peterson's former trainees. Here we see that advocacy research is subtle: it is the product of tight networks, second chances for failing programs, redefined research questions, and entirely new lines of inquiry—anything, *anything* that will provide vouchers a new edge of forward momentum.

Chapter 5 documents the flip side of that process: the utter, empirical disaster that became school vouchers in the decade that began in 2010 and ended just before the COVID-19 pandemic. These results, noted previously in the research summary and detailed further in this chapter, posed something of an existential crisis for voucher advocacy. These negative data appeared across different states, different legislative and regulatory frameworks, and for the first time apart from the carefully controlled settings of voucher advocacy research.

Chapter 6 describes the retrenchment, or the ways in which voucher advocacy was saved both by the vast right-wing donor network whence it began and by the larger political current defining "education freedom" through the policy successes of Christian nationalism during the presidency of Donald J. Trump. Chapter 6 shows how, far from damaging the voucher movement, the events described in chapter 5 served to make the movement even more dangerous, binding it once and for all to right-wing ideology and the politics of Trump and post-Trump America.

Chapter 7 brings vouchers into today's political moment, greeting names from the book's earlier pages alongside new names like Rufo, DeSantis, and Moms for Liberty. If the thirty-year march documented in chapters 1 through 6 was always fueled by some of the uglier and more caustic features of the "parents' rights" agenda, it is in chapter 7 where they burst open into the narrative.

And then I conclude. I structure the final chapter as an epilogue, glancing backward but mostly looking forward, weighing warnings about discrimination, exclusion, and human rights alongside very practical threats to democracy on issues like voting and the peaceful transition of electoral power. One need not be fluent in every democratic theory of education, I argue, to look aghast at the role of Bradley Foundation officers in Donald Trump's election-denial activities, of Council for National Policy members in voter suppression tactics, and ongoing efforts to degrade the freedom of some Americans—and their children—in the name of religious values and free exercise. There must, I insist, be a reckoning.

IT'S ALL POLITICS, ALL ALONG

I wrote about many of these themes, and even some of the details, in an essay published by the *Hechinger Report* in July 2022.[28] I covered my own background on a five-year evaluation of Milwaukee's program (the subject of chapter 4 here) as well as a larger comment about the funders of voucher research, and their ties to culture wars and election denial (chapters 6 and 7). I thought I was making a largely stand-alone public comment about the extraordinary evidence against school voucher programs and about the political background behind them. What I could hardly have known was that over the months that followed, the *Hechinger* piece was about to change my professional presence from a largely behind-the-scenes evaluator of state and local programs to a more public role warning of the dangers of educational privatization. These warnings appeared as columns in more than a dozen major media outlets under my own byline and countless more in news and syndicated reports as on-record quotes. The editor of *Time Magazine* reached out and asked for one thousand words more.[29]

What I bring to this story is not simply years working in and around voucher research. I have also worked as the editor of a journal called *Educational Evaluation and Policy Analysis*. I am one of five members of the national board of directors for the Center for Research on Education Access and Choice (REACH) based at Tulane University. My title is Director of Planning/Oversight Research, and that center is the research and development affiliate on school choice issues for the US Department of Education.[30] My work has been funded with several million dollars by organizations devoted to education reform. I, or teams on which I've been a member, have served as outside evaluation partners with state educational agencies, budget offices, and school districts. Because of the very insular nature of school voucher research—a topic I discuss in the pages that follow—there are very few researchers or writers with voucher evaluation experience who have also worked with state and local governments on entirely unrelated questions. And there are very few other experts with experience in those other education policy partnerships who came of age professionally within the voucher research network.

What this means is that I have seen the voucher push play out from multiple sides and while wearing multiple professional hats. And it is with the full weight of that experience—eighteen years now and counting—that I say emphatically: there is nothing in education policymaking today that comes close to the conservative political apparatus accessed by and indeed influencing and even driving, at times, the creation of evidence on behalf of school vouchers. Because of the fundamental link in this present time to broader culture war battles centered around religious nationalism fights over the meaning of freedom, I believe today that voucher advocacy is fundamentally damaging to American civil society. Years ago, I was more involved in this creation than most, and less involved than many. I would like to think my small part was something less than as an accomplice. But certainly, I have been a witness.

Much of the story I have to tell is something like the machinations of one big metaphorical family. There is deep, old money involved. There is a venerated historical patriarch, who bequeathed a legacy to the clan's elders today. There are uncles who made their billions in oil and gas and now, as they approach their earthly demise, are spending it to buy permanence for their life's objectives. There is the rich aunt with her own inherited billions to spend on pet projects and enthusiasms—the facts and results of those works be damned. There are tentative, largely sympathetic younger siblings who can never quite buy in to the family business but can never quite leave it, either. And there is a new generation of prodigals: the young hucksters on the make, unrestrained by the norms and values and discipline that even the most aggressive of the older generation stopped short of abandoning.

What you will not find in these pages is the story of a grassroots movement. Although the backers of these school voucher schemes have seized on the language of civil rights—choice is "the civil rights issue of our time!" they insist—you will find no bridge to Selma.[31] And even among the advocates whose hearts and intentions are known, as it were, only to God, who claim to center the lives of historically marginalized children in their plans and proposals, there is the unescapable reality. That reality is that vouchers as a "solution" to problems associated with income, gender, or especially racial inequality come from anywhere but the communities to whom those activists say they direct their thoughts and prayers. It is as if these foundational inequalities in American life are only worth addressing, in this construct, when purported solutions come of, and by, an overwhelmingly white and male intellectual framing.

One thing is certain: the case for vouchers, whether by scholars, writers, lawyers, lobbyists, or billionaire heirs has always been a deliberate construction. It is the architecture of an assault on public education as a defining American institution. This is no movement, it is rather more a coup, and it has been a right-wing political operation from the start.

1

"The Right of Parents"

Under such a system, there can develop exclusively white schools,
exclusively colored schools, and mixed schools.

—MILTON FRIEDMAN, 1955

Every story has its own beginning.

For early twenty-first century efforts to divert tax dollars toward private schooling, the origin story starts in the middle of the twentieth century. However broad its modern aims may be up to and including contemporary culture war targets, the intellectual framework for the contemporary school choice movement began alongside massive resistance to *Brown v. Board of Education* in 1954. Less than eight months after the Supreme Court's historic decision ordering the integration of American public schools and with them whole sectors of public life, the economist Milton Friedman published his first version of *The Role of Government in Education*, the work that "launched the modern school choice movement."[1]

Milton Friedman's personal views on segregation were complicated, by the standards of the day.[2] By modern measures, however, those views rest firmly in opposition to government oversight of any kind, including on the issue of race. In a lengthy second footnote to *Role of Government*,

Friedman conceded both that his idea was quickly "suggested in several southern states as a means of evading" *Brown* and that such appeal was "a possible defect" and a "count against it."[3] Although he personally "deplor[ed] segregation and prejudice," he also argued that it was not "an appropriate function of the state to try to force individuals to act in accordance" with integration. Friedman opposed "forced segregation" and "forced nonsegregation" equally, he explained, although if forced to choose within a public education system, he would generously choose the latter consistent with *Brown*. Friedman also argued that his voucher proposal could obviate choosing "between these evils" of either segregation or mandatory integration imposed by the Court: "The fact that I must make this choice is a reflection of the basic weakness of a publicly operated school system. Privately conducted schools can resolve the dilemma. They make unnecessary either choice. Under such a system, there can develop exclusively white schools, exclusively colored schools, and mixed schools. Parents can choose which to send their children to."[4]

FRIEDMAN DURING *BROWN*

The *Brown* decision has taken its rightful place in American history as the symbolic first stride in civil rights marches of the 1950s and 1960s. It also replanted schools in American political culture as the grounds for social change—or for conservative redoubt—seeded by the Scopes trial about the teaching of evolution in Tennessee some thirty years earlier. That theme of schools as battlegrounds in the culture war is a theme we will return to throughout this book. The modern "education freedom" push goes well beyond school choice. It gathers book bans, the marginalization of LGBTQ+ children and families, attacks on equity and inclusion initiatives, and bans on critical race theory under a broad banner of so-called parents' rights.

But as a starting place for that push, it is important in the context of both legal theory and public policy to remember that the unanimous *Brown* decision by the ultimate judicial authority had profound and yet very specific implications for activity in every area of public life: who to sit, eat, and learn beside. "Massive resistance" to the decision was geared as much to those areas of public life as it was to anything more existential. For all the confrontational declarations of "segregation now, segregation tomorrow, segregation forever" that amounted to philosophical—if demagogic—objections, what marks the resistance to integration was the very calculated steps taken to identify particular strategies for evading it.[5] As the locus of the *Brown* decision in the context of public schooling rather than another public space, such as the train car in 1896's *Plessy v. Ferguson*, which *Brown* functionally overturned, schools were the immediate concern of those specific efforts. That urgency was heightened by the pernicious myth of white children—especially white girls—as victims of Black aggression, all the more framing the issue as a matter of parental responsibility, even instinct, to respond.[6]

As Duke University economic historian Nancy MacLean shows through analysis of media reporting at the time, it is impossible to imagine a lay consumer of news—much less an intellectual of Milton Friedman's standing at the University of Chicago—to be unaware of the strategic resistance to integration characterizing public policy in southern states while Friedman was writing his initial manifesto.[7] His editor, Professor Robert Solo, was assembling the volume in which that essay first appeared and called Friedman to attend specifically to the utility of his nascent school vouchers proposal for avowed segregationists looking to avert *Brown*. What appears as footnote 2 in the final *Role of Government* manuscript was a result of prior correspondence between Solo and Friedman on the implications of that connection.[8] Solo implored Friedman to reflect that the racist context of *Brown* opposition could not be "changed by individual action," and was instead "alterable only by collective action" through the government.[9]

Although his published *Role of Government* footnote stated that forced desegregation as an evil was lesser than forced segregation, it was nevertheless an evil. In their personal correspondence, Friedman's replies to his editor leave little room for interpretation. Comparing Court-ordered desegregation to the Nazi state vanquished by the Allies a decade earlier, he wrote: "How in principle" was there any difference between "forcing this particular change [integration] in the context of tastes and values and those which, for example, Hitler wanted to enforce?"[10]

This does not necessarily put Milton Friedman personally on par with the political leaders organizing directly against *Brown* through massive resistance. Certainly it is possible to write a broad history of that resistance without including Friedman. What is impossible, however, is to write a history of the school-based response to *Brown*—or indeed of parents' rights politics—without noting that Friedman was developing what became the idea for school vouchers at precisely the same time that Thurgood Marshall was arguing *Brown* at the Supreme Court. Further, Friedman was putting pen to paper while political leaders were reacting to the Court's decision. Fundamental to that reaction in the sphere of public education was the appeal of Friedman's idea to those intending to fight integration in public schools.

Friedman was willing to overlook that appeal, and perhaps even exploit it, as a catalyst for realizing his idea to use the tax code to subsidize private tuition. It was this idea—what became school vouchers—that allowed segregationists to frame a racist response to the Court's desegregation orders as an issue of markets and what we would today call parental choice. The instructive example comes from Virginia, the state closest to the national capital and home to the capital of the Confederacy. Resistance to *Brown* in Virginia moved quickly from a loosely organized and rowdy activity of rallies and protests to policy proposals emphasizing publicly funded "allowances" for private school tuition—a design closely resembling Friedman's newly published voucher framework.[11] And the curious appearance of Friedman-esque language in letters to the editor for local Virginia newspapers—couched in the terms of the esteemed University of Chicago economist—measures the speed at which *Brown* opponents transmitted his ideas through words like "choice," "government monopoly" and "competitive education industry."[12]

VOUCHERS AND POST-*BROWN* RESISTANCE

Southern legislatures enacted a variety of voucher-like programs in the years following *Brown*, and Friedman was hardly a passive observer.[13] In the days before Twitter and Facebook could broadcast a few words instantly to the eyes and ears of local organizers on the lookout for new tools in their campaign, Friedman was sure to transmit his ideas through the means available at the time. He sent copies of his newly published *Role of Government* to a politically connected acquaintance in Northern Virginia, who dutifully distributed them further to local papers "in the philosophy of freedom and free enterprise."[14] He spoke at Southern conferences paid for by conservative donors, where his lecture notes affirmed his published work by arguing that the "appropriate solution" to tensions rising from integration mandates was a "privately operated school system with parent choice of schools."[15] And, perhaps most tellingly, Friedman worked directly with a second influential Virginian, Leon Dure, who was assiduously constructing and then coordinating an effort to prevent desegregation through policies framed as questions of individual liberty and "the freedom of the marketplace" rather than overtly racist intent.[16] Beyond language and framing, Friedman provided Dure with a political network, including introductions to the American Enterprise Association, which later became the American Enterprise Institute—an organization that will appear again in this book's later pages.[17]

At least five states across the South followed the general example in Virginia. In Texas, Governor Allen Shivers created an advisory committee with the express goal of finding practical efforts to maintain segregation in public schools and meet the letter of the Supreme Court's order. That committee explicitly cited Virginia's efforts in its report and lamented that by 1956 Texas had fallen behind all other southern states, except for Arkansas and Tennessee, in creating legal plans to resist school integration.[18] The report called *Brown* "clearly wrong" and listed the key problems of the committee's focus as the following:

- the prevention of forced integration;
- the achievement of maximum decentralization of school authority;
- the ways in which the State government may best assist the local school districts in solving their problems.[19]

The Texas committee followed that problem statement with an extended review of what it purported to be public opinion, and the proposition that the state encourage districts to create dual-enrollment systems with "white" and "negro" schools permitting voluntary transfer between those primarily segregated bodies. The committee's reasoning cited a number of legal interpretations that held that only discrimination—not segregation—was illegal under *Brown*. Recognizing that the combination of compulsory attendance laws and the possibility that Black parents might select integrated schools for their children meant a type of "forced integration" on white children, the committee proposed its school vouchers plan, quoted in full here:

> The abolition of compulsory education in such a situation gives the parent a choice, the choice of integrated education for his children or no education. We do not believe that this is a satisfactory choice, and accordingly we recommend that the Legislature give serious consideration to some sort of tuition grant plan, whereby a parent who does not wish to place his child in an integrated school may receive State funds to have the child educated in a segregated, non-sectarian private school. Such aid should be given only upon affidavit that the child was being withdrawn from the public schools *due to the parents' dislike of integration* [emphasis added]. Needless to say, the child could not then be enrolled in an integrated private school.[20]

The Texas committee's voucher proposal was, therefore, a direct response to *Brown v. Board of Education*, to subsequent school integration, to Virginia's lead in resisting those efforts, and in particular to the possibility that white parents would require tax-subsidized private tuition because—and in the committee's view *only because*—the parent wished to avoid racial integration. That bill never passed, and indeed Texas's opposition to school vouchers remained steadfast for decades, not in solidarity with civil rights but through efforts of rural legislators protecting the economic interests of their constituent school districts—often their area's largest employers.[21] But the original Texas proposal—mere months after *Brown*—followed the larger efforts first in Virginia and then across the rest of the old Confederacy to avoid the practical results of the Supreme Court order.

It was as a direct result of that resistance, caught up in the larger struggle for and against civil rights in the United States, that Milton Friedman's voucher proposal solidified its place among the libertarian tenets of American public policy. Like a business venture or technological innovation—think Zoom or food delivery phone apps during the COVID-19 pandemic—Friedman's initial vision for school vouchers used by parents-as-consumers flourished with segregationists' need after *Brown* to find ostensibly race-neutral solutions to their perceived problem of racial integration. It is important to note too, both in the effort to be thorough and in anticipation of the later pages in this book, the overt appeal of the Friedman idea to religious educators. A Milwaukee priest named Virgil Blum, for example, working where decades later a school voucher program would fall under a national microscope, had been arguing at roughly the same time for tax subsidies for religious education. Blum saw, like Friedman, that the idea had immediate consequences for the issue of racial integration. Vouchers, wrote a conservative columnist assessing Blum's arguments, were "plainly applicable to such disputes," and that "any discriminating done would be by the parents and the schools they chose to support."[22] Such a claim could be found on any number of conservative messaging platforms today.

As Milton Friedman built his academic career, winning praise and eventually the Nobel Prize for his work on monetary policy, he maintained a close and even dogmatic adherence to the original voucher proposal he outlined in *Role of Government* during the aftermath of *Brown*. And while his importance to public policy in the twenty-first century remains likewise linked to that effort near and dear to his heart, his instinct for aggressively placing his economic work into the political moment went well beyond his efforts to distribute his work to anti-integration activists in Virginia after *Brown*. Friedman was "an ideologue," in the words of fellow Nobel Laureate Robert Solow, "a True Believer, not giving to skepticism or self-doubt." He was "relentless, plausible, tactical, convincing, good with an audience." His fame peaked during the Ronald Reagan and Margaret Thatcher years, riding "a more profound and pervasive Right-wing surge" and "deeper forces than mere free market ideas."[23]

ENTER THE KOCHS

Riding that surge with Friedman, and perhaps in fact helping to guide its libertarian direction behind an almost unlimited reserve of financial resources, were the billionaire industrialists Charles G. and David H. Koch, who became the preeminent financial force for conservative politics at the turn of the twenty-first century. The Koch brothers, especially Charles, embody the link between the Friedman-style approach to school privatization and the other great right-wing movement of the time: the growth of the Religious Right broadly, and evangelical political activism more specifically. Friedman's *Role of Government* voucher manifesto provided intellectual (and in southern states, potentially legal) cover for resistance to integration; this makes it significant not only in the histories of public education and civil rights but also in the political development of the United States. There is no theoretically necessary link between libertarian orthodoxy and conservative social ideology. But what Friedman's voucher manifesto did a half century earlier, beyond providing race-neutral language for segregationists to avert *Brown*, was provide a blueprint for making common cause between libertarian economics and what we now call culture war issues.

Milton Friedman was old enough to influence the Kochs—Charles's son Chase has joked about hearing Friedman's work read aloud in the family home—but young enough to know them personally.[24] The Kochs founded their libertarian economic think tank, the Cato Institute, in 1977, one year after Friedman won his Nobel Prize. In the years before his death in 2006, Friedman was an active contributor to Cato's prolific publishing agenda, while the Kochs spent more than $35 million on the institute before separating from the center in a nasty split in 2012.[25] Cato retains a "Milton Friedman Award for Advancing Liberty," whose prize inscription calls Friedman *"perhaps the greatest champion of liberty in the 20th century"*—a telling depiction of a man whose work provided aid and comfort to *Brown v. Board* resistors and who was a contemporary of Martin Luther King, Jr.[26]

There is little in the public record of direct alignment between the Koch brothers' personal, social, or religious views and those of other wealthy collaborators like west Michigan's billionaire DeVos family, who are also central to this book. Indeed, as David Koch himself said toward the end of his life, "I'm a conservative on economic matters and I'm a social liberal," perched as he was as a major benefactor of the arts and medicine on the outskirts of New York City high society.[27] Charles's own views—like those of Friedman around race—are more muddled on contemporary issues like abortion or gay marriage, but where they meet is on government policy. For the Kochs, the original *bete noire* was and remains economic regulation, especially around issues pertaining to the environment, the oil and gas industry in which the original Koch family holdings began, and education policy.[28]

THE "DOERS AND THE DONORS": THE COUNCIL FOR NATIONAL POLICY

Economic libertarians like Friedman and the Kochs were willing and often enthusiastic opportunists when it came to filling a breach in the social or cultural life of the country—around race, abortion, gay marriage, and more recently transgender rights—with libertarian principles they purported to be a balm. The economic politics of Charles Koch quite literally meets the religious politics of groups like the DeVos family, the Family Research Council, the Southern Baptist Convention, and the Christian Coalition through an organization called the Council for National Policy (CNP): "a little-known club of a few hundred of the most powerful conservatives in the country," representing members from media organizations, think tanks, political strategists, and extraordinarily wealthy donors focused on fundamentalist policy goals.[29] The CNP membership list, including its first president, Christian fundamentalist and Left Behind series author Tim LaHaye, reads in journalist Anne Nelson's exhaustive reporting like a who's who of the last fifty years of conservative donor activism.[30] Other members or attendees reportedly include Wayne LaPierre of the National Rifle Association, Leonard Leo of the Federalist Society, Ginni Thomas (the political activist wife of Justice Clarence Thomas), and former Vice President Mike Pence.[31] Pence's public efforts after leaving the Trump administration have included school vouchers and other conservative education priorities.[32]

What they have in common is a shared progressive enemy (usually but not always the Democratic Party), antipathy toward regulatory government, hostility toward labor unions, and a wariness of demographic change they believe to come at a cost to their economic interests and social values. Education is an intersection for these ideological pathways because— as with *Brown* and broader desegregation efforts—it is in education that social values form. And so, above all, members of CNP and its affiliate groups connect through an active, even aggressive, approach to the use of wealth to further their aims in the political arena, particularly in state legislatures and executive offices. It is at the state level, after all, where much of the mechanics of education policy form and function. Reporting on the CNP describes a "merry-go-round of reciprocal funding" around these shared priorities in an almost incestual network of celebration and citation.[33] Charles Koch himself once received the "Richard DeVos Free Enterprise Award" at a CNP biannual meeting, indicating further alignment between Koch's organizations and the more religious bent of CNP energized by DeVos cash and other influential partners.[34] As reporter Jane Mayer noted in her history of Koch's operation, quoting family patriarch Richard DeVos, the CNP joined "the doers with the donors."[35]

Apart from aligning their individual networks with CNP activities and other national policy gatherings, the Koch and DeVos families jointly conjure the spirit of Milton Friedman through a variety of 501(c)(3) and increasingly 501(c)(4) groups like Americans for Prosperity, Stand Together, Yes Every Kid (Koch), and the American Federation for Children (DeVos). The full activity behind those donations and activities are covered in Mayer's and Anne Nelson's separate, book-length journalism, as well as that of numerous political scientists and other scholars.[36] In addition to her work

specifically on Milton Friedman's link to segregation, Duke's Nancy MacLean has her own book on the Kochs and recent American political history.[37] But the key point for the present volume is that the CNP and similar,
smaller groups in that larger network function as a kind of central, ongoing
meet-and-greet for wealthy conservative exchange. It is through that exchange that Milton Friedman's broad framework for fully privatized education moved from a political expedient against racial integration in the
1950s to a key policy priority for some of the wealthiest and most influential political actors in the Religious Right. Friedman's language of markets
and individual liberty that gave cover to segregationists requiring a
race-neutral lexicon to resist *Brown* still exists aplenty in the modern
voucher push, through the CNP and its affiliates using economic dialogue
as the accent of modern-day culture war and religious nationalism. It is
as if Milton Friedman walked into one of the posh, luxurious hotel ball-
rooms of the Koch network's annual gathering spaces and walked out as
Betsy DeVos.[38]

DEVOS-ISM

Like a password for entry into those halls that has remained unchanged
for years, the word *parents* persists through the transfiguration of Friedman's once-fringe idea into modern school voucher mobilization. Recall
the 1955 footnote in *Role of Government* that "there can develop exclusively
white schools, exclusively colored schools, and mixed schools. Parents can
choose which to send their children to."[39] Consider the central rhetorical
role of parents in recent politics, both in education and beyond. Betsy De-
Vos's personal website summarizes her own vision for school choice as "to
give parents freedom to find the best option and fit for their children."[40]
Officially, DeVos served as the US Secretary of Education—head of the federal Department of Education—during the (as of this writing) single term
of Donald Trump's presidency. But unofficially she has been a key funder
of and political activist in the CNP and its affiliates for decades. As far back
as the early 1990s DeVos cochaired a lobbying group called "Of the People,"

whose goal included amending state constitutions to include the phrase "The right of parents to direct the upbringing and education of their children shall not be infringed."[41]

"In financial terms," writes the journalist Katherine Stewart, "the Christian Right today is to a substantial extent the creation of the Michigan wing of the American plutocracy."[42] Betsy DeVos, alongside her husband, Dick; her late father-in-law, Richard Sr.; and her own fabulously wealthy parents, Edgar and Elsa Prince, and brother Erik Prince, has built a fortune in west Michigan while maintaining a deep affinity for conservative religious politics.[43] Erik Prince attended CNP meetings while building his private security company, Blackwater, the mercenary group that became infamous in Iraq.[44] Fully apart from her role in the Trump administration, through two terms as chair of the Michigan Republican Party and in national GOP finance circles, Betsy DeVos has been, to borrow her father-in-law's depiction of CNP, both a donor *and* a doer. By 2023 her network mustered more than $250 million over the years to lobby for school choice initiatives—the "most deployed resources" nationally, according to a leaked slide deck from American Federation for Children, the group she founded.[45]

In her home state the DeVos doing and donating included serving as the driving force behind Michigan's for-profit charter school system in 1994; a failed school vouchers ballot initiative in 2000 on which the DeVoses split from Republican Governor John Engler, only to earn 31 percent of the vote despite a $4 million contribution from the family (Betsy quit her first stint as state GOP chair via angry voicemail after Engler withheld his support); and a sustained effort to turn Detroit's famously struggling public school district into a charter school marketplace.[46] Michigan's for-profit charter school system—a diffuse array of individual schools, more than eight in ten of which are managed by companies that earn revenue from state school aid funds—remains the largest by market share in the United States.[47] Apart from its lack of funding to religious schools, Michigan's charters most closely resemble a privatized education system: a consolation prize for the DeVoses' inability to pass full Friedman-style vouchers. It is also among the least regulated in the country, with one influential critic—the head of a large Detroit-based philanthropic organization also active in public education causes—complaining that DeVos "is committed to an ideological stance that is solely about the free market, at the expense of practicality and the basic needs of students in the most destabilized environment in the country."[48]

That Friedman-style free market dogma marks the portfolio of the entire DeVos family agenda and the basis for the ideological connection to the Kochs and others. In commentary written for the *Detroit News*, Betsy DeVos once demanded that the state "liberate all students from this woefully under-performing district model" of education and allow parents to "use state education funds at the public or private school of their choice." The DeVoses preached that gospel throughout other mainstays of the CNP, notably at the Heritage Foundation, the right-wing think tank founded by political operative Paul Weyrich, who would also create the American Legislative Exchange Council (ALEC). Both Heritage and ALEC will appear throughout later chapters to this book. But it was at Heritage in 2002 that Dick DeVos outlined what became a common strategy for voucher advocates and other conservative activists in CNP to achieve policy goals: focusing on state-level elections, including Republican primaries, to advance not only unrestrained educational markets but also new limits on labor unions (especially, for the DeVoses, teachers unions)—another priority of the Kochs.[49]

"FREEDOM" FROM "REGULATION"

Emphasis on deregulation in the education space fit nicely—sometimes overtly—with CNP emphasis on private enterprise. During her second stint as Michigan GOP chair, Betsy DeVos once issued a statement all but insisting that Michigan workers were overpaid: "Many, if not most, of the economic problems in Michigan are a result of high wages and a tax and regulatory structure that makes this state uncompetitive," she wrote.[50] And an account of DeVos's first months as Secretary of Education notes, "In perhaps her most mystifying move to date . . . [DeVos] posted plaudits for Trump's withdrawal from the Paris climate accord on the Department of

Education's website, an international concern far outside her jurisdiction."[51] These instances of emphasis on deregulated private enterprise more broadly aside, the religious zealotry of the DeVos version of free markets is what particularly animates the school choice movement and broader culture war struggles today. Recorded in 2001 at a meeting called "The Gathering" of the National Christian Foundation, whose wealthy members overlap with CNP, Betsy DeVos explained that school choice could "advance God's kingdom."[52] Her husband elaborated, "The church, which ought to be, in our view, far more central to the life of the community, has been displaced by the public school as the center for activity. . . . We just can think of no better way to rebuild our families and our communities than to have that circle of church and school and family much more tightly focused and being built on a consistent worldview."[53]

The Heritage Foundation maintains a DeVos Center on Life, Religion and Family, and the DeVos family has always seen its extreme wealth as reflecting their Dutch reformed, prosperity gospel faith tradition. In that, theirs is a more personalized and self-serving view of the intellectual link between the family's Calvinist roots and the spread of capitalism first articulated by sociologist Max Weber more than a century ago.[54] The senior Richard DeVos was particularly known for a lavish lifestyle that he interpreted as God's gift and which he transmitted into his political and economic views by saying, "Being a capitalist is actually fulfilling the will of God in my life."[55] His daughter-in-law's version remains squarely fixated on parents, and on religious parents in particular. Her early-days push to add state constitutional protections for parental choice also included strong denunciation of the notion that "it's the school's job to hand out condoms, to psychologically test children, to give them a version of history that's contrary to what their parents teach, to emphasize self-esteem and other fluff over reading, writing, and arithmetic," as her spokesperson put it. Those rights of religious parents, to quote one profiler, "obliterated all other social concerns."[56]

The tension for the DeVoses, the Kochs, and other holders of both extreme wealth and unyielding libertarian, market-oriented ideology is in the imposition of their own will on states and local communities. Although a very real grassroots network of parents, business owners, and religious fundamentalists does exist, it is to a remarkable degree cultivated and maintained by the small network of CNP "donors and doers" that mimic a major political party.[57] As will become critical in later chapters, these include clear and often verbatim transmission of model policy and sample legislation from DeVos and Koch affiliates—for the purposes of this book, so-called parental rights, school choice, and in particular school voucher legislation—through organizations like ALEC, the group founded precisely to do so by Heritage founder and CNP member Paul Weyrich.[58] Thus, the DeVos and Koch approach to individual liberty and freedom extends only to a point, and whether the issue is religious dogma or laissez-faire economics, groups like CNP and ALEC exist in part to leave little room for local implementation, variation, or deviation from the vision their members have in mind. As Betsy DeVos put it in the 1990s, "I have decided to stop taking offense at the suggestion that we are buying influence. Now I simply concede the point. They are right. We do expect something in return . . . We expect a return on our investment."[59]

UNDER INTELLECTUAL COVER

In 1959 a group of St. Louis Catholics founded Citizens for Educational Freedom with the statement that could appear on any number of websites six decades later: that there exists a "God-given and inalienable right [for] parents to direct and control their children's education."[60] The next year, as part of his effort to provide contacts and materials to conservative organizers fighting desegregation in Virginia, Milton Friedman introduced Leon Dure—the activist former newspaper editor—to Citizens, which was focusing on receiving its "fair share" of tax dollars for area parochial schools, and which would soon claim thousands of members in more than twenty states.[61] Dure and Citizens leaders began to correspond, with the organization distributing his Friedman-inspired articles on voucher concepts to its broader constituency. Although Dure's primary objective was providing parents in his state a legal off-ramp for sending their children to integrated schools, and Citizens was primarily concerned with obtaining financial support for their sectarian schools, they met at the mutual goal of diverting public spending into private education. And key to both approaches into that common end was the language of individual liberty, articulated by Milton Friedman: liberty, above all, for individual parents—either rights as consumers or as personal clerics in their children's theological development.

In that way, Friedman's efforts to link academic, even prestigious, scholarly pedigree to an ideological objective are a necessary feature of the birth story for modern efforts to privatize education and wage a more fundamental culture war around children, parents, and families. It is not just that Friedman's voucher framework provided inspiration for more specific policy proposals. Indeed, as histories of massive resistance show, segregationists had independently come to a similar practical conclusion that they might manipulate state policy to fund alternatives to integrated schools.[62] What Friedman did was give that movement a cadence and a theme—an alternative beat to counter the rhythm of the civil rights marches around him.

From Friedman's example, the modern push by Charles Koch, Betsy DeVos, and other holders of extreme wealth to move funding away from public education into private schools depends on and is inextricably linked to a conservative intelligentsia that provides theoretical, legal, and, in recent years, legislative and policy support. For all of their billions, the Koch and DeVos networks have been unable to simply buy a desired outcome without grounding that goal in an idea—what political strategists call a "message." That message begins and ends with a narrow concept of parents: overwhelmingly white, Christian, married, and heterosexual. But in between is a scaffolding of policy platforms connecting state and federal tax code, the legislative and budgetary processes, administrative law, and finally constitutional theory. The purpose was and is to do away with schools existing as a core function of democracy and stand up instead a privately held, sectarian, and theocratic version of publicly funded education.

2

"Soldier-Scholars"

They must be given grants, grants, and more grants
in exchange for books, books, and more books.

—WILLIAM SIMON, OLIN FOUNDATION

It is no accident that Milton Friedman, Charles Koch, and Betsy DeVos each created their own think tanks.

The Milton and Rose D. Friedman Foundation (today, EdChoice), the Cato Institute (formerly the Charles Koch Foundation), and the American Federation for Children (AFC) may have different classifications for Internal Revenue Service tax identification—the former two are 501(c)(3) and the latter a 501(c)(4)—indicating different limits on direct lobbying and advocacy, but their underlying purpose is the same.[1] Although Cato is devoted to a number of libertarian economic policy areas, EdChoice and AFC are organized primarily around expanding not only school choice per se, but publicly funded private school choice in particular. We saw in chapter 1 how Milton Friedman and a variety of political actors in the 1950s worked symbiotically to both spread Friedman's school vouchers gospel and create an intellectual basis for conservative education priorities—notably resistance to *Brown v. Board of Education* but also tax support of Catholic schools. So too do more recent efforts to expand vouchers across the United States depend directly on policy development, model legislation, and above all the distribution of a narrow and politically directed set of facts to support those goals.

The first modern publicly funded school voucher program began in Milwaukee, Wisconsin, in 1990. One imagines the DeVos family looking wistfully across Lake Michigan—Milwaukee is almost exactly due west across the lake from the family capital near Grand Rapids—but if their home state was not to inaugurate a voucher vision, it was at least their ideological cousin, regional neighbor, and sometimes collaborators in the Council for National Policy (CNP) who would secure that ideological distinction. Years of patient networking, financial and political investment, and the establishment of new institutional pillars—Koch's Cato, but also the CNP cornerstone Heritage Foundation—and the mobilization of the Christian Right alongside the rise of Ronald Reagan, made the 1970s and 1980s the maturation period of Milton Friedman's privatization idea. In these two decades, the mixture of libertarian policy priorities with religious cultural conservatism began to take shape.[2] By the late 1980s the politics were ripe for action.

THE MILWAUKEE PROJECT

Milwaukee's voucher program—formally, the Milwaukee Parental Choice Program—was, by its conception, the product of a number of locally based groups that included prominent Black Democrats representing primarily communities of color. These activists included Democratic state legislator Polly Williams as well as former Milwaukee Public Schools chief Howard Fuller, who would go on to become a prominent national voucher advocate. But the real driving force behind the voucher program was the Lynde and Harry Bradley Foundation, a far-right Milwaukee-based foundation seeded with money its founding brothers had reaped through defense contracts during the two world wars.[3] The foundation's president, as of this writing, is also on the CNP governing board.[4] Although Lynde and Harry were both dead by 1965, and their eponymous foundation remained a small regional organization during the formative years of the Koch and DeVos family fortunes, a merger between its corporate sponsor and defense contractor, Rockwell International, in the mid-1980s substantially increased the foundation's assets and its ability to attract top political talent. In 1985, almost overnight, the Bradley Foundation became one of the largest philanthropies in the country, "swimming in cash," as the journalist Jane Mayer has noted, and with new leadership at the helm.[5]

Michael Joyce moved to Milwaukee to take over the newly flush Bradley organization after years as executive director of another conservative philanthropy with seed funding in the energy industry, the John M. Olin Foundation, and influential stints such as membership on the first Ronald Reagan presidential transition team in 1980–1981.[6] Early investments by both the Bradley and Olin Foundations during the 1980s included organizations tied to religious fundamentalism, such as the Institute for Religion and Democracy, "which was created to oppose the social justice positions and liberal theologies of mainline Protestant churches."[7] On the secular side, while at Olin, Joyce had helped create an infrastructure of conservative intellectual policy development—an effort that included Charles Koch's own funding initiatives—to establish what Olin's then-president, William Simon, called a "counter-intelligentsia," opposing the influence of progressive intellectuals on public policy and supporting free enterprise and libertarian thought.[8] At Bradley, Joyce would build off that "beachhead" established during his Olin years to place the foundation as what Jane Mayer, in her chronicle of Koch-related dark money, called "a righteous combatant in an ideological war."[9] Its primary contributions were to think tanks and research fellowships organized around that objective. Beneficiaries of early Bradley research funds at that time included Harvard and Yale, as well as Charles Murray, whose notorious 1994 book, The Bell Curve, argued that low IQ scores and race are closely correlated.[10]

Closer to home, Michael Joyce focused the Bradley effort on school vouchers in Milwaukee. The foundation "helped to legitimate vouchers as a school reform strategy, helped establish a climate necessary for the [original voucher] bill's passage, and contributed to the program's legal defense."[11] That included the setup of yet another policy think tank, the Wisconsin Policy Research Institute (WPRI), which led local research on vouchers and other priorities.[12] Now called the Badger Institute (as of this writing), WPRI remains part of the State Policy Network, established with heavy funding from the Kochs, DeVoses, and other members of the CNP.[13] Critical to the counter-intelligentsia that Michael Joyce helped build at the Olin Foundation were reams of writing: white papers, policy briefs, and reports to bolster the development of conservative legislative priorities. Intellectuals and policy advocates alike were to be given "grants, grants, and more grants in exchange for books, books and more books."[14]

The Milwaukee voucher program was a major realization of this strategy. As the program made its way first through stakeholders and then the Wisconsin legislature, almost as if on cue a book arrived on the national scene that purported to show a new direction for publicly funded education. *Politics, Markets and America's Schools*, by John Chubb and Terry Moe, reoriented and updated the Milton Friedman framework for the 1990s.[15] Both authors were fellows at the conservative Hoover Institution—a major recipient of Olin Foundation funding during its heyday and of Bradley funding more recently.[16] The Olin and the Bradley Foundations, among others, funded *Politics, Markets and America's Schools*, adding Chubb and Moe to a long line of other notable Olin recipients, such as William F. Buckley (whose *Firing Line* television program was a direct Olin beneficiary), Dinesh D'Souza, and a then-conservative named David Brock, whose book *The Real Anita Hill* attacked the famous witness in Clarence Thomas's Supreme Court confirmation hearing.[17] *Politics, Markets and America's Schools* was first released in June 1990—two months after Republican governor Tommy Thompson signed vouchers into law in Wisconsin, and two months before the first students began using vouchers to attend Milwaukee private schools.[18]

To the Bradleys, Olins, and other large-dollar conservative foundations behind the development of voucher policy, the 341 Milwaukee schoolchildren in seven private schools became something of a demonstration project for the voucher idea. Eligibility for the Milwaukee Parental Choice Program (MPCP) in those early years was limited to low-income families who had never been in public school and who intended to enroll in nonsectarian private schools. The program grew slightly to 830 students attending 12 schools by fall 1994 and, in its first 2 academic years, required annual academic testing and outside research evaluation, to be overseen by the Wisconsin Department of Public Instruction (DPI).[19]

As the first students arrived in private schools, the State Superintendent of Instruction, a critic of the voucher program, appointed University of Wisconsin professor John F. Witte as its official, independent evaluator. Witte later wrote that, because the superintendent was "an outspoken critic of vouchers, some pro-voucher supporters assumed I was a voucher opponent from the beginning." Despite evidence from his previous work "that would actually indicate [he] might have leaned the other way" in his personal views, voucher backers' beliefs that Witte's eventual finding was incorrect in concluding that the program had little overall impact on student outcomes, and that the state's evaluation was biased, both "played a role in the political history of the voucher movement."[20]

That charge of political bias around a less-than-desired finding from one of their social policy objectives was part of what led the Kochs, the DeVoses, and groups like the Bradley and Olin Foundations to fund their own research in the first place. Witte couldn't have known it in 1990, but by becoming Wisconsin's official evaluator of the first voucher program in the country, he was putting a target on his back that others after him would carry over the decades that followed. Witte was in essence entering into what became known later as a "research- practice partnership" in education: in practical terms, the outsourcing of an evaluation or audit to an independent analyst acting on behalf of a state agency, legislature, school district, or other governmental entity.[21] The advantage of such an arrangement is, at least in theory, some separation between the goals of the government partner—which could include political objectives—and the scientific matter of review. The research partner brings that separation of interests, along with expertise, while the government side sets the priorities, specific questions for research, and where appropriate, the legal authority to conduct the analysis. These partnerships are the opposite of what in the business community would be called industry-funded research: in-house reviews of a product's quality or safety intended to motivate and justify that product's existence on the open market. What the research-practice model fails to solve for, and what the first, official voucher evaluation asked, was what happens when findings from the independent review clash with those of industry-style research funded and distributed by political advocates.

The technical details around Witte's official evaluation were published in annual reports beginning in the spring of 1991, as well as subsequent academic papers, book chapters, and an eventual summary monograph published in 2000.[22] Although the evaluation found that parents of voucher users indicated greater levels of satisfaction with their children's educational experiences over time, Witte also found little consistent evidence that vouchers improved test scores or attendance rates and found that students gave up the vouchers at high rates to return to Milwaukee Public Schools. These were hardly a ringing confirmation of the promises made by political champions of the program itself, the expectations of backers like the Bradley Foundation, or of the libertarian Friedman-style approach to education prioritized by Charles Koch, Betsy DeVos, the Heritage Foundation, and other ideologues.

"REAL POLITICAL ISSUES"

The Milwaukee voucher evaluation was a big national education and political story. The New York Times covered the story, running a summary article in 1995, after the last official Witte report, under the headline "In Test of School-Voucher Idea, the Sky's Not Falling, But Neither Is Manna."[23] The article noted that local advocates such as final bill sponsor Rep. Polly Williams found the official Witte results "unduly negative" and that the state's Legislative Audit Bureau had reviewed the Witte report and determined no final conclusion could be drawn for or against vouchers. The Times also reported Williams's concerns that the program could one day open to religious schools (which she opposed) and that neither the most dire critiques of vouchers nor the brightest promises had come to fruition.[24] In other words, both the Times coverage of Milwaukee vouchers and the official Witte evaluation for the state depicted the program as a mixed bag of outcomes. And the *Times* gave the last word in its write-up to a pro-voucher advocate.

But a week later, in response to that article, a Harvard professor named Paul Peterson sent a letter to the *Times* editor, angrily denouncing the official state evaluation and implying the *Times* coverage had made its conclusion worse. "You uncover a strange incongruence," Peterson wrote, "Parents are enthusiastic about choice," yet the state's evaluation found little academic benefit. Faced with such results, Peterson lectured the editor:

> Your readers are well advised to rely more heavily on parental experiences than on a flawed evaluation. The [Witte] study does not take into account parental education, occupation, welfare dependence, whether or not the household is headed by one parent or two, a student's native language, and whether a student has severe social problems. The control for family income is woefully imprecise . . . That students from particularly disadvantaged backgrounds did as well in choice schools as did public school peers, despite the fact that the cost of the program was approximately half as much, is a sign these schools must be doing something right.[25]

Peterson had, up to that point, limited research experience evaluating education policy, though he had written widely on political education issues like school reform and busing. Nearly thirty years removed from his PhD in political science at the University of Chicago, Peterson had made his way through the academic ranks focusing on such topics as federalism and the social safety net. He was known primarily for his 1990 book, *Welfare Magnets*, which argued critically that states with generous welfare programs became "magnets" attracting impoverished new residents.[26] But in 1995 he also was a recipient of both Olin and Bradley Foundation funding.[27]

Peterson omitted a key detail from his letter to the *Times*: that he had launched his own reevaluation of the Milwaukee voucher program, partly with support from the Olin Foundation.[28] He had already blasted the Witte evaluation in drafts reports delivered in the two months prior to his *Times* letter and would, upon release of the original Witte data on the nascent World Wide Web, begin to circulate a paper in academic and other circles.[29] Along with his then-graduate student Jay P. Greene (now at the Heritage Foundation) and a rotating list of other junior collaborators, Peterson wrote of the Witte evaluation's "egregious" errors and flaws, ignoring the "highest quality evidence," which they claimed to show large academic benefits to the voucher program.[30] In what would become a recurring theme for voucher research advocates over the next two decades—and which will reemerge in later chapters of this book—Peterson and Greene also blamed the original authorizing voucher statute, which they implied set the program up for failure through its income limitations and in particular its prohibition on religious school participation. According to Peterson and Greene, it was not simply that the state's official evaluation of the program had failed by neglecting to show positive results, it was that vouchers themselves "suffered from severe legislative restrictions that made it difficult for the program to succeed."[31] That Peterson and Greene were nonetheless able to wring positive results from such a "hard case," as they put it, supposedly showed the promise of school vouchers after all.[32]

The full detail of Peterson and Greene's salvo is detailed in a final version of that critique published in 1999, after years of back-and-forth with Witte and colleagues.[33] Witte's own summary rejoinder is published in his book about the project.[34] On the surface, the debates between the two teams would be familiar to any researcher engaged in social science peer review and/or public distribution of their results: arguments about sample selection, design, and specification of analytical models, or which outcome best reflects the program's original intent.[35] What was unique to the fury over the official Wisconsin voucher results was its vitriol and the special ferocity with which Paul Peterson and Jay Greene attacked those results. Also salient was the close alignment between that attack and the policy priorities of the voucher advocacy coalition.

The main points of the Peterson critique were laid out by Daniel McGroarty in a piece called "School Choice Slandered" published in 1994 in *The Public Interest*, a neoconservative magazine with ties to both the Olin and Bradley Foundations—and former head of both, Michael Joyce—through its cofounder, Irving Kristol.[36] McGroarty called Witte a "hired gun" of the state government, which he suggested had fixed the evaluation to fail, noting that the Witte results were cited by critics in multiple anti-voucher articles—including those distributed by teachers' unions.[37] The trade publication *Education Week* covered the hostility, and Peterson's particular role in it, noting that Peterson's findings "endeared him to voucher advocates hungry for the credibility that his name and his university affiliation bring." The article described Peterson's penchant for making his arguments first in newspaper opinion pages and fast-tracked reports rather than peer review. The piece quoted Greene's defense of his mentor by explaining the goal: "it's important to continue to release information without going through a lengthy review process when you're addressing real political issues that occur in real time." *Education Week* also noted that Peterson's colleagues within his home professional field raised concerns about his relationship with the Olin and Bradley Foundations— relationships that Peterson brushed off as inconsequential to his results.[38]

Jay Greene's comment that "real political issues" required "real time" influence without "a lengthy review process" acknowledged perhaps more than he intended. In what will become a familiar theme in later chapters here, the timing of the original 1994–1995 Peterson-Greene attack on the official evaluation occurred precisely against the backdrop of the push during that same timeframe to renew and expand the Milwaukee voucher program.[39] That push was led again to a large degree by Michael Joyce and the Bradley Foundation, which had over the prior year been working to coalesce local business support for the reauthorization.[40] Albeit in early form, previewed in the 1994 McGroarty *Public Interest* article, the Peterson-led pushback to the state's official results thus served to support the voucher program's renewal at exactly the right time. The particular Peterson-Greene charge that the original voucher program was doomed to fail because of legislative restrictions excluding religious schools was especially on-message to the Bradley coalition's aims in late 1994 and early 1995.[41]

Correspondingly, the successful renewal of Milwaukee's voucher program in the spring of 1995 included religious schools, and a huge cap increase of up to fifteen thousand seats for voucher students.[42] The religious provision immediately ran into legal challenges, which made their way up and down the state court system—with an eye toward the US Supreme Court—for the next three years. Legal aid for voucher supporters in those cases was organized by an attorney named Clint Bolick, cofounder of the right-wing Washington, D.C., legal advocacy organization Institute for Justice, which would become something of a litigation cousin to the more prominent Federalist Society, sharing many of the same goals and funders.[43] Bolick had been an aide to Clarence Thomas and created the Institute for Justice after a direct pitch for seed money to Charles Koch himself, who personally committed $1.5 million to the group's startup.[44] At one point, Bolick was aided by Kenneth Starr, who would soon become nationally famous for the Whitewater and Monica Lewinsky-related investigations of President Bill Clinton. Starr's firm charged the state of Wisconsin more than $300,000 for a month of work in 1998, but the bill was picked up in its near-entirety by a grant from the Bradley Foundation.[45]

They were successful. In 1998 the Wisconsin Supreme Court eventually approved expanding the program to religious schools by a vote of 4–2.[46] But on the policy side, the legislature's expansion prevented the state from conducting a new evaluation of the voucher program. Therefore, it was in a new city and a new state that the test of school voucher funding for religious schools occurred. While Milwaukee's voucher expansion to religious schools was making its way through state courts, a coalition of advocates in Cleveland, Ohio, had been working for several years to bring a voucher program to the shores of Lake Erie, building from the example in Milwaukee. These leaders included Republican Governor George Voinovich, the city's Catholic diocese and lay leaders, and City Councilwoman Fanny Lewis, who was influential in statehouse politics when it came to Cleveland issues.[47] Lewis had actually traveled to Milwaukee on a fact-finding trip, where she met voucher sponsor Polly Williams and the Bradley Foundation's Michael Joyce after making an earlier connection with the

Koch-funded Clint Bolick, who was then preparing to defend Milwaukee's religious component.[48]

ON TO CLEVELAND

Intended by Governor Voinovich and other supporters be a voucher "model for the country," the Cleveland Scholarship and Tutoring Program began funding vouchers to low-income students attending fifty-two schools— nearly all Catholic—in 1996.[49] Two of these schools were brand new and had opened specifically to receive voucher funding. These two schools, the so-called "Hope Schools" for the first word in their names, were seeded with startup money from the Walton Family Foundation, which, with vast resources from the Walmart fortune, was fast becoming another major national player on the school choice advocacy scene.[50]

As in Milwaukee, an official evaluation on behalf of the state's Department of Education occurred. And as in Milwaukee, that state evaluator— in Cleveland's case, a team led by Kim Metcalf of Indiana University— ultimately found few overall differences in student achievement.[51] And again as in Milwaukee, there to counter those null results were Paul Peterson and Jay Greene, who once more with Olin Foundation funding would provide research demonstrating a city's voucher effectiveness, dismissing the Metcalf reports with language similar to the words they used in Milwaukee: "The research design for this study has many flaws, casting serious doubts on the accuracy of its reported findings."[52] In the Cleveland case, however, the Peterson-Greene team did not wait on the official results to begin promoting the voucher program and were, within a year, circulating a report showing "large gains" for voucher students.[53] The entire basis for their claim of achievement impacts for Cleveland voucher users came from test scores from just two schools that happened to be "made available," in their words, to their research team.[54] Those two schools were the so-called Hope Schools noted previously and were funded by the Walton Family Foundation. Despite that connection, and despite that Walton subsequently joined the Olin Foundation in funding Peterson's work on the Hope schools, the Peterson-Greene team only disclosed Olin and Walton funding—not Walton's additional role in setting up the two schools themselves, on which the Peterson-Greene team based their favorable report.[55] Thus the "lessons from the Cleveland Scholarship Program," as the Peterson-Greene team would call them, would be based largely on two schools set up specifically to receive voucher funding, to provide a demonstration case for pro-voucher researchers to study, and for voucher backers to then *ipso facto* circuitously as a justification for yet more vouchers.[56]

At the time, neither the Peterson-led research-advocacy for school vouchers nor a sense that those efforts would always arrive at the pro-voucher position consistent with the position of his funders were particularly secret. The *Education Week* profile of Peterson noted previously, for example, was titled "Researcher at Center of Storm Over Vouchers," and centered around Peterson's pro-voucher research and its funders. "Wherever he has gone," the article notes, "he and his colleagues have come to the same conclusion: Private school choice works."[57] The piece described "Mr. Peterson's penchant for bypassing scholarly journals to make his case in newspaper editorials," in addition to his research studies, noting this tactic against both the Milwaukee and Cleveland evaluators. "Even when he has limited data, he's always squeezing out whatever data he can to arrive at a predetermined answer," said Professor Bruce Fuller, an early voucher critic at University of California, Berkeley. Fuller noted that with Olin and Bradley funding Peterson's work, "That's like the tobacco companies sponsoring studies on the effects of smoking."[58] A later textbook for future evaluators would cite the Peterson Milwaukee work as a cautionary example of ideologically predisposed research and "a hidden agenda," particularly in Peterson and Greene's willingness to use lower-than-conventional standards of statistical inference to make their case.[59] Even Paul T. Hill, an otherwise prominent school choice supporter, singled out the Peterson Cleveland work as "not a persuasive study."[60]

But research quality was hardly the point, despite the pretense to analytical rigor. The real stage for their effort in Cleveland was the courts. Apart from a collection of reports issued by a Peterson-run center at Harvard, and chapters in an Olin-funded, Peterson co-edited book called *Learning from School Choice*, the Peterson-Greene research from Cleveland makes only a limited appearance in the historical record of voucher scholarship.[61] What it did do was become—alongside their Milwaukee efforts—part of a case making its way through the judicial system that would eventually become *Zelman v. Simmons-Harris*: the 2002 US Supreme Court decision that approved public funding for private school tuition at religious schools, with Cleveland vouchers at the center of the specific case. Justice Sandra Day O'Connor cited Peterson and Greene's report in her concurrence to *Zelman*, and Paul Peterson himself filed what the voucher program's defense attorney called "very lengthy affidavit that describes the different kinds of options available and what their benefits are."[62]

NEW CONTROVERSIES

By then, Paul Peterson was well on his way to establishing a site for new demonstrations of the school vouchers idea. The Children's Scholarship Fund, an organization cofounded by John Walton (of the Walmart Walton family) had established private school scholarships in cities across the United States. These funds mimicked school vouchers in the sense that they offset the cost of private school tuition, but unlike the Milwaukee and Cleveland programs, were not supported by taxpayers. As a charity program, there was nothing remarkable about conservative support for private school enrollment. But in collaboration with Paul Peterson, the funds could provide a proof-of-concept for voucher impacts, in part because the private nature of the program allowed Peterson and team to set their own rules for evaluation free from the sort of "severe legislative restrictions that made it difficult for [vouchers] to succeed" that he had fretted about in Milwaukee.[63]

And in three cities—first and foremost, New York City (the School Choice Scholarships Foundation), but also Dayton, Ohio (Parents Advancing Choice in Education), and Washington, D.C. (the Washington Scholarship Fund)—similarly structured and related funds provided tractable research sites for the voucher demonstration project.[64] If the team's research on Children's Scholarship recipients nationwide was to provide broad, generalizable motivation for vouchers on questions such as who used vouchers and why, the smaller, three-city sites could at least in principle become field experiments of voucher impacts on student outcomes: policy interventions organized much like a randomized control trial in a laboratory test of a new pharmaceutical product. Peterson and team described the theoretical importance of such experimental designs as "the best research design for evaluating social science interventions," a methodological view shared by many nonideological scholars.[65] But such a high-quality standard exists only when a number of other conditions are met, most notably high rates of intervention take-up, low rates of program exit, and—perhaps above all—impact estimates robust to different models of analysis. The absence of each condition was to plague the Peterson and colleagues' three-city voucher trials.

Peterson was still in the middle of debates on Milwaukee and Cleveland voucher impacts in 1998, when his team released the first of three annual reports on the first of those privately funded voucher programs.[66] That evaluation report on New York City scholarships, coproduced by Mathematica Policy Research, Inc. (a policy analysis firm), found positive test score impacts and parental satisfaction increases after one year of voucher usage. In addition to the usual support from the Olin and Bradley Foundations, the New York report was also directly funded by the Milton and Rose D. Friedman Foundation and the conservative Achelis and Bodman Foundations (which would later merge), the Smith Richardson Foundation, and several others.[67] The Peterson team found similar results in the next two waves of New York data, as well as in the Dayton and Washington, D.C., sites.[68] Those positive impacts were covered again by the *New York Times*, which noted the links to conservative funding sources and critics' concerns about high rates of student exit from the voucher program.[69] Two weeks later, however, the *Times* ran a follow-up under the headline "New Doubt Cast on Study That Backs Voucher Efforts."[70]

The evaluation company Mathematica, which had originally partnered with Peterson, had distanced itself from his results. Mathematica, as the *Times* reported, said the results

> were overstated by the lead researcher [Peterson], a Harvard professor
> known within the academic community for his exuberant support of

vouchers. In fact, the company says, in New York there was no significant test-score difference between students who attended private school on vouchers and those who stayed in public school. Bothered by what it describes as the report's exaggerated claims, the company, Mathematica Policy Research of Princeton, N.J., has now taken the unusual step of issuing a statement that cautions against leaping to any policy conclusions. Mathematica calls the original finding "premature."[71]

At issue this time were limits to New York City's positive results. Although positive results were present in the other sites and for some students, the third-year New York results were limited to African American sixth graders, with students in other grades realizing no impacts. More than half of those offered the voucher also turned the offer down. As Mathematica's David Myers, who had collaborated on earlier reports, told the *Times*: "If you ask the question, 'When I offered students vouchers, did I make a difference in their test scores?' right now you come away saying, 'No, there's no impact.'" Commenting on the results, Henry Levin of Columbia University noted the timing of the release during the fall 2000 election season, while Texas Governor George W. Bush was campaigning in part on the success of other conservative educational reform efforts: "The pressure to get something out at election time was a much more dominant theme than the idea of letting it go through review."[72] Although Levin was a voucher skeptic, his speculation was little different than Peterson acolyte Jay Greene's own comments explaining the Peterson approach they had collaborated on in Cleveland: to "release information without going through a lengthy review process when you're addressing real political issues that occur in real time."[73] For his part, the *Times* reported, "Professor Peterson dismissed the criticism, saying his work 'was looked at by lots of people lots of times'" for review.[74]

BRADLEY: THE TIE THAT BUYS

The debate over Peterson's New York voucher results would continue and will appear again in the following pages. Taken alongside his efforts in Cleveland and earlier in Milwaukee, they mark a decade of strenuous research advocacy on behalf of school vouchers. From the reauthorization of the Milwaukee program, the jump start coinciding with the Cleveland program, the legal challenges to both voucher plans, and the launch of the nationwide Children's Scholarship Program and its sister sites on the eve of the presidential election of 2000, the Peterson-led research had a knack for appearing at opportune political moments for the voucher cause. Indeed, as we have seen, members of that team made no secret of that synchronization.

But the key point is that the Peterson team was hardly an isolated group of conservative scholars shouting their views from the ivory tower. They were part of the tightly connected network of funders and right-wing activists introduced in chapter 1 who were pushing tax support for private education for years. Peterson's own aggressive, at times dismissive, tone documented in *New York Times, Education Week,* and even academic textbooks, itself recalls Milton Friedman's own notoriety as a condescending and even aggressive debater.[75] But that mimicry was more than mere flattery. With so many names of scholars, political actors, and big-money players, the critical role of research-advocacy in the policy agenda of the Friedmans, the Kochs, the DeVoses, and other conservative influencers could appear at once obscure and overwhelming.

So, to review: establishing a "counter-intelligentsia" to push conservative social priorities and libertarian economic policy was a key priority of Charles Koch and his network.[76] That network has, over time, grown to include the DeVos family and other major Republican Party donors in the CNP. The John M. Olin Foundation and the Lynde and Harry Bradley Foundations, like the Koch family organizations, grew from energy industry fortunes, sharing with Koch and the broader CNP hostility to government oversight, to organized labor, and to public education and other social policy areas. Richard Graber, president of the Bradley Foundation as of this writing, is also on the current CNP board of governors.[77] First the Olin Foundation, and then increasingly the Bradley Foundation, drove the school privatization agenda. It is no accident that the first voucher program in the United States arose in Bradley's home city of Milwaukee. As Koch network chronicler and *New Yorker* reporter Jane Mayer put it, "The Bradley

Foundation virtually drove the early national 'school choice' movement, waging an all-out assault on teachers' unions and traditional public schools. In an effort to 'wean' Americans from government, the foundation militated for parents to be able to use public funds to send their children to private and parochial schools."[78]

As such, Bradley was the key political driver behind the Milwaukee voucher program, which opened in 1990. Just three months before the first voucher students enrolled, the Bradley and Olin-funded *Politics, Markets and America's Schools* by John Chubb and Terry Moe, of the Bradley and Olin-funded Hoover Institution, was published. After the state's evaluator released results showing that vouchers had no impact on student outcomes, Harvard's Paul Peterson—who had received Olin and Bradley money in the past—began a multiyear effort to discredit those reports, publishing his own, more favorable, results in reports newly funded by the Olin Foundation, which also began funding Peterson's results showing similarly favorable evidence from the nascent Cleveland voucher program. Central to Peterson's critique of the initial Milwaukee voucher program was its exclusion of religious schools, which were subsequently included in the 1995 reauthorization of the voucher program, on the heels of Peterson's first published reports. The Bradley Foundation also funded the legal defense of public funding for those religious schools, which was coordinated by Clint Bolick of the Institute for Justice—the libertarian legal group founded with $1.5 million in seed funding from Charles Koch. Among the attorneys receiving Bradley funds to defend Milwaukee vouchers was Kenneth Starr, whose firm received more than $300,000 for one month of work.[79]

Bradley and Olin were then among the backers of Peterson's most ambitious voucher project, a study of three privately funded scholarship programs in New York City, Dayton, and Washington, D.C. Also funding Peterson's new work was Milton Friedman's personal foundation, and a relatively new player on the voucher stage, the Walton Family Foundation. That work included research on the Children's Scholarship Fund, cofounded by John Walton, son of the Walmart founder.[80]

Over the following two decades, the Bradley Foundation would appear alongside organizations created and maintained by Charles Koch and the

DeVos family, to underwrite much of the political advocacy around school vouchers and school choice more broadly.[81] Increasingly, these donors direct that funding toward organizations engaged in direct advocacy like American Legislative Exchange Council (ALEC), the Heritage Foundation, and various members of the State Policy Network and other CNP affiliates. But none of these local think tanks have the pedigree or mainstream national prominence of a professor with appointments at both Harvard and Stanford Universities. Ensconced in Cambridge and at Stanford's Hoover Institute—itself still a major recipient of Bradley donations—Paul Peterson remains the most decorated of the CNP-adjacent researchers and the embodiment of the reciprocal relationship between voucher policymaking and voucher evidence. From the very earliest years of school voucher existence, political advocacy was linked to and dependent on an ongoing set of demonstration studies whose financial backers had explicit intent to use that intellectual pedigree to support conservative ideological objectives.

That stepwise strategy of funding the creation of voucher policy, funding reports on that voucher policy, and then using those to justify more school choice again was established by the Bradley Foundation and its allies in the 1990s. In Paul Peterson, the Bradley Foundation and its broader network of conservative allies found an enthusiastic partner to carry out that strategy. And in Peterson's student Jay Greene (now at the Heritage Foundation), on to a new generation of acolytes in the first years of the twenty-first century, there exists a ready-made network to distribute more funding and extend that strategy. As one Bradley profiler noted, "Typically it was not just the same university but the same department, and in some cases the same scholar." The result was a kind of "intellectual cronyism" for "soldier-scholars."[82] Further, Koch profiler Mayer stated, "The anointed scholars were good ideological warriors but 'rarely great scholars.'"[83]

Without knowing it at the time, and as an early-career analyst on one of Peterson's studies and its follow-up, I myself appeared on the list of Bradley-funded scholars.

3

Implementation

These are people who have connections . . . who have friends. Without them I think it is fair to say this wouldn't have gone anywhere.

—CONGRESSMAN TOM DAVIS (R-VA)

As controversial as they were at the time, the Paul Peterson–led studies of privately funded vouchers in the three cities of Dayton, New York, and Washington, D.C., persist more than twenty years later as the best available evidence that school vouchers might improve student achievement. In that sense, the Lynde and Harry Bradley Foundation, the James B. Olin Foundation, and the Walton Family Foundation got what they paid for: the academic pedigree of Harvard and Stanford stamped on proof-of-concept studies of private scholarships that—at least in the Walton case—they also helped to fund on the front end.

Further, the fact that Peterson and his protégé Jay P. Greene were so deeply involved in earlier controversies about Milwaukee and Cleveland results—debates that made national education news—should not obscure the fact that the three-cities voucher trials in New York City, Dayton, and Washington, D.C., began a new era of pro-voucher research. The private funding of vouchers in these three sites was itself unremarkable. As we saw in chapter 2, after all, Peterson and Greene's Cleveland work was heavily based on the two private schools created by the Walton Family Foundation to both receive incoming publicly funded students and to provide data sources for the researchers' voucher demonstration study.[1] The three-cities trials were, however, the first major voucher projects launched directly by Peterson without first condemning another study. And as such they were the first major voucher projects over which the lead researcher had more or less full operational control. These New York City, Dayton, and Washington, D.C., studies created the template for beginning, controlling, and then distributing pro-voucher findings through a tightly connected and insular network of advocates that still exists.

The Bradley Foundation is the funding thread that connects that work from its role creating the Milwaukee voucher program that Peterson defended years earlier, through Peterson's Cleveland research, to the three-cities voucher trials themselves, and onward into the next two decades.[2] Chapter 2 documents the particular controversy over the New York–specific results—that the Peterson team overstated those results—as well as the belief among other experts that Peterson was "always squeezing out whatever data he can to arrive at a predetermined answer."[3] But that tendency, and its role in shaping both law and public policy, goes well beyond an academic debate. For in the four years that Peterson was creating, distributing, and defending his three-cities voucher research, he was continuing to work with supporters of Cleveland's religious voucher program as it made its way through the federal courts. What, in 2002, culminated in the Bradley-funded book *The Education Gap*, summarizing that three-cities research, has to be understood in the context of the Bradley-funded defense of the Cleveland voucher program in *Zelman v. Simmons-Harris* at the US Supreme Court the very same year. It was in *Zelman* that public funding for religious private schools was first blessed by William Rehnquist and concurrences in a 5–4 decision.[4]

EYES ON THE ZELMAN PRIZE

Still fresh from his Clinton impeachment notoriety of 1998 and 1999, Kenneth Starr led the pro-voucher attorneys in *Zelman* before and during the

2001 Supreme Court term.[5] Starr was backed by the Institute for Justice in those efforts—just as he had been while defending Milwaukee's religious vouchers in state court. Recall that the Institute for Justice was cofounded by Clarence Thomas staffer and voucher advocate Clint Bolick after a personal plea directly to Charles Koch, who gave $1.5 million to the effort.[6] The Institute is a close cousin of the more famous Federalist Society, but where the latter is something of a convener and clearinghouse, the former provides on-the-ground trial support. As one analyst wrote, "The Federalist Society serves as an intellectual forum for debate, deliberation, and the vetting of judges, [while] the IJ [Institute for Justice] has actualized many of the society's (and the network's) goals through litigation, often in state and federal courts that embrace shared jurisprudence."[7] The Bradley Foundation gave $4.3 million to the Institute for Justice through 2021— $750,000 of which between 1998 and the *Zelman* decision alone.[8] The Foundation still crows about its *Zelman* role, noting in the citation to its annual Bradley Prize award to another Institute cofounder, William Mellor: "In *Zelman v. Simmons-Harris*, the Institute for Justice successfully defended Cleveland's school choice program from a lawsuit brought by the teachers' unions and other school choice opponents to establish the constitutionality of school vouchers."[9]

That defense relied heavily on Paul Peterson's Cleveland research and on the notion that Cleveland public schools were failing the city's children. Peterson himself submitted a sworn affidavit, as did Kim Metcalf, the evaluator whose work Peterson had said was littered with "many flaws."[10] But where Metcalf's statement was brief and tentative (three pages), Peterson's affidavit was insistent and urgent, spread over twenty-three pages in the case appendix. Judith French, the attorney actually appearing before the justices, made a point of calling it a "very lengthy affidavit," while arguing at the bench, as if to demonstrate the evidentiary power of the case.[11] From start to finish, Peterson's statement reads more like a manifesto.

Peterson's affidavit began with a general history of school choice and of the Friedman voucher proposal.[12] He claimed that Friedman's idea languished in academic obscurity for decades, ignoring the efforts Friedman himself made in the wake of *Brown v. Board of Education*—covered in chapter 1 in this book—and crediting Chubb and Moe's *Politics, Markets and America's Schools* (the Bradley and Olin-funded volume) with restarting the voucher conversation in 1990. In the document, Peterson sets the tone for what would become a standard expositional framing (among pro-voucher researchers) and message development (for political professionals). His brief insists that school choice generally, and school vouchers specifically, are an idea whose time has come: a response to crisis in public education; the natural result of parental uprising to demand response to such a crisis; and vouchers as an evidence-based response to meet that demand. The preponderance of that evidence was provided by Paul Peterson and team.

On key policy questions—who chooses vouchers and why, voucher effects on student outcomes, parental satisfaction, racial demographics of schools, and the religious orientation of families and their educational providers—the twenty-three-page Peterson affidavit not only is directed to the specific issues at hand in Cleveland but also rests heavily on Peterson's evidence from Milwaukee and from the emerging three-cities studies he was conducting at the time (the affidavit was entered in 1999 as the case began its long route through the US judiciary system). The effect of the document is to show the benefits of not only the Cleveland program but the Milwaukee vouchers before it, and of new purportedly cutting-edge voucher plans in New York and its sister sites in Dayton and Washington, D.C.

Nowhere in the affidavit does Peterson note that research had been underwritten by conservative donors, including the Olin and Bradley Foundations, or note that the latter of which was also supporting the Starr-led legal team defending vouchers before the same Supreme Court. Nowhere does Peterson note that the New York, Dayton, and Washington, D.C., programs in particular were funded by Bradley in an ongoing demonstration of voucher effectiveness. Or that Chubb and Moe's book, which Peterson highlighted, was itself a Bradley-Olin product that Moe later credited Peterson with mentoring.[13] The closest statement of disclosure actually appears in a research paper by his acolyte Jay Greene, as a stand-alone appendix, written for the Buckeye Institute and presented at an academic conference. The point of the Greene contribution was to show "the evidence on racial integration suggests that access to a choice program that includes religious schools makes a significant contribution to promoting racial integration in Cleveland schools."[14] The Buckeye Institute was then, as now, a member of the Koch-DeVos–affiliated State Policy Network introduced in chapter 2, with both entities recipients of substantial Bradley funding, along with Ken Starr and the lawyers at Institute for Justice.[15] Years later, in an interview with the State Policy Network's promotional materials to celebrate the twenty-fifth anniversary of its founding, Robert Enlow, president of Milton Friedman's own namesake organization (now EdChoice), gushed that he was "proud of our work with the Institute for Justice on legal cases, especially *Zelman v. Simmons-Harris . . .* The case set the precedent that school choice is legal."[16]

By then the Friedman Foundation was also directly funding Peterson's three-cities studies, which, along with his Cleveland work, were key to the *Zelman* case.[17] They formed nearly the entire evidence base for the merits in the Starr team's petition to the Supreme Court, and a key part of the oral argument once they had their day in court. They also provided documentation for the communications strategy both before and after. In their petition to the Supreme Court, Ken Starr and company began their Statement of the Case with a detailed description of what they called the educational "crisis in Cleveland" and the presentation of vouchers as the resolution to that crisis.[18] In oral arguments before the Court, Judith French, the Assistant Ohio Attorney General, explicitly pointed to Paul Peterson's research, as did Justice Sandra Day O'Connor in her concurrence with the majority Rehnquist opinion.[19] Standing on Court steps for a press briefing following the oral arguments, first Judith French then Kenneth Starr alluded to the performance record of various voucher programs and then to the underlying point previewed by Peterson years earlier in his angry letter to the *New York Times*: that regardless of policy impact, what mattered were parent opinions above all.[20] Quizzed by a reporter about whether vouchers were "ineffective," French insisted:

It's totally unfounded by the record. Now it is true that this is a pilot project, and you would get results as you might expect from a pilot project. I think the fairest way to say it is that the scholarship students are doing at least as well as the public school students. And in many cases are doing better. Another way of looking at it, though, is what the parents think. The parents love this program. The parents love the scholarship program. They see it as a very viable option, and they are probably in a better position to judge whether the program is working.[21]

After taking the microphone from French, Ken Starr pointed directly to the preferred Milwaukee voucher results and to parents, exclaiming:

The question that you just asked was well, what about this program, some say some pretty bad things about it. Ask the parents. . . . Why would people oppose the right of parents to choose for their child? Why? Why? Why would people want to defend a system that Justice Scalia today said—there's a monopoly—Why can't we in fact now in fact especially with the Milwaukee experience have Ohio follow in the context of this very, very difficult situation in Cleveland.[22]

From the standpoint of legal maneuvering it is unremarkable for scientists, academics, and other researchers to participate as experts in Court proceedings, including under oath. It is also common for those efforts to be compensated. I myself have done so—though not while producing research at the same time, or with the same financial support as those providing compensation for that expert consulting. Paul Peterson's efforts in *Zelman v. Simmons-Harris*, and his research in Milwaukee and then in Cleveland, depict his involvement as a curious, even dispassionate observer of natural trends in public policy and public opinion. The presentation both in the affidavit and in the books, papers, and reports referenced in that document, is that of an erudite, endowed Harvard scholar peering out from the paneled walls of his ivory tower office to observe a phenomenon before going back to his books. But, as we have already seen, Peterson's role in the voucher story—from the results he found to the politically advantageous timing of those results—was anything but accidental, beginning with the Bradley Foundation as a driving hand behind both the voucher studies and the voucher legal defense. Peterson was no more an outside, unbiased observer to *Zelman* than that case's chief counsel Kenneth Starr was an objective inquisitor of Bill Clinton.

A VOUCHER VICTORY LAP

But even after their 5–4 *Zelman* victory in June 2002, such a pretense continued with the three-cities voucher trials that (especially New York) helped both to defend vouchers in *Zelman* and to propel their adoption forward. By the time the Court released its opinion, the three-cities research had appeared for several weeks in book form as *The Education Gap*.[23] The book depicts a number of research patterns related to civic participation, discipline, and, above all, parental satisfaction. But at its core is the proposition that vouchers address the academic "gap" between white students and historically marginalized communities. That result is based on test score advantages realized by voucher students primarily in New York but also in Dayton and Washington, D.C. Those results, however, are limited only to Black students in New York—the only group to see test score gains in all three years and sites.[24]

The preface in *The Education Gap* hits the same ambiguous passive-tense notes as Peterson's *Zelman* affidavit, explaining that "a group of philanthropists in New York City was considering a private voucher initiative" and "when Peterson proposed that a research team carefully evaluate the intervention, the group agreed to cooperate" so long as Peterson "could quickly raise the necessary funds. Fortunately, several foundations supplied the funds necessary" for the project.[25] Soon after, other "philanthropists" began private voucher programs in Dayton and Washington, and "they, too, were interested" in the plan. In D.C., this was the Washington Scholarship Fund, an entity with ties to the DeVoses and Waltons that would soon play a major role in a new, publicly funded voucher program.[26] "What began," *The Education Gap* notes, "as a mere secondary analysis of a small voucher program in Milwaukee blossomed almost overnight into a massive research enterprise."[27]

In essence, then, the *The Education Gap* book tour became a *Zelman* victory tour. The Court decision inaugurated the principle of state tax support for religious schools as a constitutional policy option, while *The Education Gap* began a run as the summary compilation of the best empirical case for vouchers in the United States. With both supported by the Bradley Foundation, it was a one-two, legal-policy punch to mark 2002 as a banner year in voucher policymaking. The randomized designs of the three-cities private voucher plans in New York, Dayton, and Washington, D.C., supplemented by data from the Walton-funded Children's Scholarship Fund and a small program called CEO-Horizon outside San Antonio, formed a formidable methodological approach that voucher advocates would point to for years to come: not only, as *Zelman* found, could vouchers exist, but *The Education Gap* purported to show that they should.

Three months after *Zelman*, Paul Peterson convened a group of like-minded scholars and lawyers to discuss the ruling and its implications moving forward. The meeting was directly funded by the Olin Family Foundation, and its proceedings were published a few months later by the Hoover Institute under the title *The Future of School Choice* as part of a larger "Initiative on American Public Education" funded by the Bradley Foundation and other donors.[28] In Peterson's introduction to the volume, he alternated between dispassionate scholar and giddy activist, quoting George W. Bush's public response to *Zelman*, which compared the decision to *Brown v. Board of Education*, and musing "but is it?" Peterson then enthusiastically framed the discussion with Clarence Thomas's concurrence in a passage he called "stirring."[29]

Peterson published the comments of Kenneth Starr himself as the first chapter, "The Equality Principle"—a defense against what he called discrimination against religious institutions and parents.[30] Other attendees and contributors included Terry Moe, of the Olin-Bradley funded *Politics Markets and America's Schools*; Peter Berkowitz, a conservative academic from Hoover and George Mason University who would later win a Bradley Foundation Prize for his work on conservative campus speech; C. Boyden Gray, the former White House Counsel for George H. W. Bush and founder of the Committee for Justice, a group that helps vet conservative judicial appointees; and the ubiquitous Clint Bolick, of the Institute for Justice. Bolick's chapter, "Sunshine Replaces the Cloud," served partly as a celebration of the *Zelman* majority, and partly as a screed against the dissenting justices, who he called on "the verge of panic," taking "up the role of lobbyists" for public education, and "shrill."[31]

Between *Zelman* and his own closely aligned evidence in Milwaukee, Cleveland, and then the three-cities research in *The Education Gap*, Peterson had cause for what he called "implied optimism" and "a sense that this movement, unlike past school reform fads, [was] likely to press forward, simply because choice, once granted, is seldom withdrawn. Once parents exercise it, they love choice dearly, all but ensuring its perpetuation."[32] Quite correctly, his post-*Zelman* gathering and the resulting essays assumed that vouchers would begin to expand beyond sites Peterson himself had studied. He could hardly have known, however, that the evidence he compiled in *The Education Gap* during the run-up to *Zelman* would remain the best case for vouchers for more than twenty years. Despite vehement criticism upon re-analysis of the New York portion of the book by other scholars, that was as good as voucher results were ever going to get.[33]

A NEW POLITICAL OPERATION: THE D.C. VOUCHER PLAN

In the months that Peterson and his conservative colleagues were discussing and compiling their post-*Zelman* celebratory volume, the US Congress was moving quickly as well. With the Republican George W. Bush in the White House and, after November 2002, the GOP back in control of both legislative chambers on Capitol Hill, the time was ripe to take advantage of the Supreme Court's recent blessing by bringing vouchers to the nation's capital, whose education system was ultimately under federal control. The Washington Scholarship Fund, studied by Peterson's team for *The Education Gap*, was connected enough to be singled out by no less than President Bush himself during a 2003 press event at a D.C. charter school to publicize the White House's support for school choice. Bush declared: "The Washington Scholarship Fund is an interesting idea where people came together, I presume from the business community, and others, and put up money to help children. There are a thousand applications last year for a hundred slots. It's a measurement, a data point, a measurement of demand where people are interested in doing something differently."[34]

At the same event, Bush singled out an affiliated group, D.C. Parents for School Choice, which "became the public face of the District of Columbia voucher movement," and its founder, Virginia Walden Ford, a major hero on the Right for her compelling story as a mother desperate to provide quality education for her children.[35] But this was no neighborhood group of concerned parents. Supported by John Robert, a local real estate mogul who had contributed millions to voucher causes, the group enlisted a network that included Dick and Betsy DeVos, John Walton, and Clint Bolick's Institute for Justice to pull the voucher bill over the finish line.[36] "These are people who have connections on the Hill, who have friends. Without them I think it is fair to say this wouldn't have gone anywhere," said Republican Congressman Tom Davis, the bill sponsor.[37] In one ad, D.C. Parents for School Choice attacked Edward Kennedy, comparing the Massachusetts senator to infamous Birmingham Police Chief Bull Conner, saying, "Senator Kennedy, your brothers fought for us. Why do you fight against us? Are the unions really more important than these children?"

The School Choice Incentive Act of 2003 became law in early 2004, creating the D.C. Opportunity Scholarship, a new voucher program that, for families at or under 185% of the federal poverty limit, offered up to $7,500 per student to attend a local private school.[38] The law mandated an annual evaluation, to be conducted under the auspices of the US Department of Education, which contracted with a team led by Patrick J. Wolf, a Georgetown professor of public policy who, like Jay Greene, was a former doctoral student under Paul Peterson. Wolf had recently led the D.C. site of *The Education Gap* research studying the privately funded vouchers administered by the Washington Scholarship Fund. It is at this point that I note that, in 2001, I was hired by Wolf while myself a graduate student at Georgetown, to assist with data collection and analysis. That work is acknowledged by the Peterson team on page xix of *The Education Gap*. Soon after Wolf began the D.C. voucher evaluation for the US Department of Education, he would move to the University of Arkansas to join the new Department of

Education Reform headed by Jay Greene. He would also begin a new evaluation of Milwaukee's voucher program—a subject of chapter 4.

Wolf's evaluation of the D.C. Opportunity Scholarship program never
encountered the criticism or doubt that both internal and external researchers had raised about the positive findings from Peterson's New York City
voucher, presented in *The Education Gap* and other papers.[39] In a more
proximate sense, I myself never encountered anything during my research
assistance under his direction, or later in the new Milwaukee study I describe in chapter 4, that would suggest anything beyond appropriate methods of data analysis. But the rigorous methods required by the voucher
program's authorizing statute were only as sound as the data to which the
researchers applied them. If Wolf's team followed the mandate given to
them by US Department of Education, the same can hardly be said for the
Washington Scholarship Fund, which won the contract to administer the
new, publicly funded version of what it had done for the Peterson team to
study in *The Education Gap*. That implementation involved day-to-day recordkeeping and financial documentation, as well as recruiting students
and private schools to admit them.[40] The Fund was assisted in those implementation efforts by none other than D.C. Parents for School Choice,
the lead group behind voucher passage in the first place.[41] The Washington
Scholarship Fund was also supported, with more than $400,000 in dona-
tions earmarked for private school participation in the first years of the
program, by the Lynde and Harry Bradley Foundation.[42]

In a detailed, ninety-eight-page audit conducted over the first two years
of the D.C. voucher program, the US Government Accountability Office
(GAO) singled out the Washington Scholarship Fund for its poor financial
recordkeeping, noting that the Fund's history as a small advocacy
organization during *The Education Gap* years had ill equipped it to rap-
idly meet the requirements of running a large government contract: "WSF
greatly expanded its operations from $150,000 in federal and foundation
grants in fiscal year 2004 to $12.9 million in 2006 without sufficient ac-
countability mechanisms to govern the use of the funds."[43] One problem,
the GAO explained, was that: "WSF did not develop the comprehensive and

detailed fiscal policies and procedures needed for internal control over its financial and programmatic operations. WSF's draft policies and procedures lacked key control activities and did not detail procedures for approving scholarship payments or require documentation that procedures were carried out as required."[44] And, the GAO continued, that "WSF's accountability over OSP scholarship payments was further weakened by a lack of comprehensive and detailed policies and procedures to guide its processing of receipts and payment of scholarships and administrative expenses."[45]

The other issue was that students of struggling public schools—the main ostensible target for the "opportunity" implied by the voucher program's name—were especially unlikely to gain entry into the disproportionately religious number of private schools that the Fund recruited with help from D.C. Parents for Choice and other entities:

> WSF faced challenges recruiting students from schools in need of improvement, ensuring private school placement opportunities and quality, and providing parents with accurate information regarding private schools [emphasis author] . . . While students from schools in need of improvement had priority for receiving scholarships, for each year the program has operated, the percentage of students from schools in need of improvement who were offered scholarships has been smaller than the percentage of students in District public schools who attended such schools.[46]

Recruiting private schools to participate in the voucher program by accepting low-income students was the activity the Bradley Foundation's financial support to the Washington Scholarship Fund, according to Bradley's IRS forms, intended to energize.[47] For those particularly needy children—the proverbial poorest of the poor even among a target population of lower-income students—the results would eventually be correspondingly poorest, an outcome that Wolf himself implied in an academic essay several years later.[48]

The Fund took issue with the GAO's report, but the federal watchdog agency stood by its findings, noting that the issue was hardly trivial and went to the heart of the voucher program's ability to function with taxpayer dollars: "While WSF implies that the deficiencies noted in this report are minor in nature and disagreed with our conclusion that the Act prohibited payments to schools that customarily charged no tuition, we stress that the issues we identified are indicative of potential problems and if not addressed could have a material, detrimental effect on WSF's accountability over federal funds."[49]

After implementing the D.C. voucher program during the first five-year portion outlined in legislation—the same years of the Wolf evaluation for the US Department of Education—the Washington Scholarship Fund withdrew from its contract, and the responsibilities transferred to a new third party, D.C. Children and Youth Investment Trust Corporation. In 2013 the GAO would find similar problems with that vendor's handling of taxpayer dollars, in particular one issue it had flagged regarding the Washington Scholarship Fund: a lax verification process to confirm that voucher users' income met the eligibility criteria. It also singled out the new vendor's trouble advertising the program to a broader pool of potential applicants. The GAO concluded, "The Trust's policies and procedures lack detail in several areas related to school compliance and financial accounting, which may result in little overall accountability for program funds."[50] We will encounter the results of a newer independent evaluation of the D.C. voucher program during those years in later pages of this book.

NAMES NEW AND OLD

Two names, already introduced, warrant a further greeting here before they reappear in later chapters. The first is Virginia Walden Ford, the activist founder of D.C. Parents for School Choice, the group that compared Senator Edward Kennedy to Bull Connor during its push for vouchers and that later assisted the Washington Scholarship Fund in implementing the first program.[51] At the same charter school event in which President George W. Bush praised the Washington Scholarship Fund and suggested it as the model for the federal voucher plan, Bush singled Ford out for praise as well. Bush said:

Virginia Walden-Ford, who I met, is the executive director of the D.C. Parents for School Choice. . . . Virginia is a good person to be running the program. She—mom of three. Her youngest son looked like he was a—I guess the best way to describe it would be a train wreck. He wasn't doing well in the public school system. He might say, the system quit on him, but he certainly quit on the system. And Virginia pulled him up and got him into a Catholic school. . . . It's a wonderful story about a mom who never gave up. So she's taking that experience and is now trying to help other parents who are frustrated and other parents who are looking for different options for a particular child.[52]

Bush's remarks paint the same picture that voucher activists would use to promote the cause later in both D.C. and throughout the country. Born in Arkansas, Ford would return there in later years as a home base to both lead education reform efforts and to personify the results of school choice—the devoted mom described by Bush. Her story could have come from Hollywood, along the lines of the films *Stand and Deliver* or *Lean on Me*. But as far as movie rights went, Hollywood itself passed. Instead, it was the conservative education reform community that seized select features of Ford's story for a made-for-the-movies moment.

Years after Bush signed the D.C. voucher program into law in the wake of *Zelman*, Ford's role in that process and her broader biography were depicted in a movie called *Miss Virginia*, produced by a group called The Moving Picture Institute. In the film, Ford is a modern-day civil rights activist, and her group's well-funded political activity—the ads, for example, against Senator Kennedy—is missing from the script. But like the efforts of D.C. Parents for School Choice, *Miss Virginia* was little more than another political operation. The Moving Picture Institute is an affiliate of the State Policy Network, and its funders—including the Mercer family, DonorsTrust, the Scaife family foundations, the Bradley Foundation, and various Koch affiliates—are reportedly still mainstays of the Council for National Policy (CNP) outlined in chapters 1 and 2.[53] The rollout of *Miss Virginia*, which was also financed by the Walton Family Foundation and the Searle Freedom Trust, resembled the announcement tour of a political candidate, complete with traditional and social media targeting.[54] Milton Friedman's own foundation (now EdChoice, on which Ford remains a board member) arranged special screenings, as did the Institute for Justice.[55] Betsy DeVos keynoted an event honoring Virginia Walden Ford and celebrating the D.C. voucher program in the buildup to the film's release, hosted by the Heritage Foundation, at which the program's first evaluator, Patrick Wolf, also spoke.[56] Before funding *Miss Virginia*, the Moving Picture Institute had underwritten films by the Documentary Foundation, an outfit run by a filmmaker-activist whose name was soon to become synonymous with attacks on public schools: the name Christopher F. Rufo.[57]

The second name is that of Dr. Howard Fuller. Like Ford, Fuller was a major force in a key voucher bill passage—in Fuller's case, the original Milwaukee bill in 1990.[58] Unlike Ford, however, Fuller came not from the so-called parents' rights movement but out of the education stakeholder community as a former superintendent of Milwaukee Public Schools. What they share is a deep connection to members of the CNP—the Koch-DeVos-Bradley combination at the core of school vouchers politics—with some Walton Family Foundation and other broader school choice support as well. Fuller's work in Milwaukee both prior to and after the voucher program's initial passage is well documented elsewhere, and his own autobiography details that effort from his point of view.[59] In his book, Fuller details a personal journey from the Black Power movement of the 1960s to supporting vouchers and other forms of school choice. What is important at this juncture is that Fuller, like Ford, was at first a regional, city-based leader who, almost from the beginning, was also a collaborator of the deep-pocketed backers behind the national push for school privatization.

Also like Ford, Fuller hardly rested upon his laurels after bringing vouchers to his own city. Indeed, Fuller's activism can be seen as the template for Ford and others for future political activity after the initial period of local legislative success. Fuller was instrumental in the Bradley-led efforts to expand Milwaukee's original program to religious schools, and in forming the advocacy group School Choice Wisconsin with the

husband-wife duo George and Susan Mitchell, to continue lobbying on behalf of the city's (now state's) voucher program.[60] Fuller was also among
the Milwaukee-based leaders along with Bradley's chief Michael Joyce,
whom Institute for Justice founder Clint Bolick arranged to meet with
Fanny Lewis in the run-up to Cleveland's voucher push, and in defending
both cities' voucher programs in state and federal court.[61] Along with
George Mitchell, Howard Fuller wrote his own series of reports on Milwaukee vouchers and racial integration, to follow up on Paul Peterson's
studies of the program.[62] And like Peterson, Fuller was directly quoted in
Zelman oral arguments by lawyers arguing for the program.[63] His affidavit assured the Court that, while his testimony was "specific to Milwaukee, the conclusions are equally applicable to Cleveland," and in that cyclical
way voucher advocates would come to cite each other in later years, Fuller
drew as much on Peterson's work in both cities as on his own experience
as an urban education leader.[64]

At the time of *Zelman*, and until his retirement, Fuller occupied a Bradley Foundation—endowed chair at Marquette University, and founded
and directed the Institute for the Transformation of Learning there, a center also heavily financed by Bradley.[65] In that capacity, he also founded the
Black Alliance for Educational Options, a school choice advocacy group
also heavily financed by Bradley, as well as by the Walton Family Foundation and the Olin Foundation, whose board also included the ever-present
Virginia Walden Ford herself.[66] In a later interview, Fuller acknowledged
his close relationship with the Bradley Foundation but claimed that, apart
from its funding priorities around school choice, their relationship with
him was hands-off:

> For a lot of people, taking money from the Bradley Foundation was con-
> sidered to be a betrayal. For me, it was an issue of trying to get resources
> to do the work that I wanted to do. . . . People get mad at me for saying this,
> but it's like a group of Black people get in a room and have a discussion
> about which White people's money is okay. Like Soros' money is okay, not
> Bradley. How do you make those decisions? I make them based on princi-
> ple, strategy, and tactics.[67]

Although he has said he personally opposed Donald Trump's presidency later, Fuller made a video of support for Trump's nomination of Betsy De-Vos to the US Department of Education, "based on our personal relationship, based on the fact that she supported work that I had been doing."[68] At a retrospective celebration of his sixty-year career in 2023, Fuller posed with other leading education reform activists in front of a backdrop of celebration sponsors, including the Walton Family Foundation, City Fund, the Yass Prize, EdChoice, and Stand Together, one of the cornerstones of the Koch network.[69]

Long before that, however, and before Koch affiliates would make a film about Virginia Walden Ford's voucher advocacy, both Fuller and Ford would play outsize roles in the ever-growing capacity of voucher advocates to conduct and distribute research on the programs they had made their lives' work.

4

Demonstration

*Wisconsin's creation, implementation and expansion of a
private school voucher program in Milwaukee has resulted
in a dual system of education in the city.*

—AMERICAN CIVIL LIBERTIES UNION, 2011

When Betsy DeVos's younger brother, Erik Prince, won a contract to gar-
rison his private security force, Blackwater, alongside US armed service
members in Iraq, it was as far as any public record has since shown, a
legitimate—although no-bid—contract.[1] From its origin as a small private
training group for soldiers of fortune and former military personnel,
Prince's mercenary firm received its wartime deals through a record of
quickly accrued experience after 9/11, and his own family political connections that included attendance at the Council for National Policy (CNP).[2]
But for all of the infamy Prince's firm earned for civilian deaths and arms
sales overseas, and for all of the congressional and criminal proceedings
investigating those deals, there is little to suggest the firm was unqualified
at the time of its contract to do what the George W. Bush administration
had paid for it to do.[3] There are only so many private security forces with
global experience to go around. In the same way, when Vice President
Dick Cheney's former firm, Halliburton, won no-bid contracts to provide

logistical support to the troops in Iraq and Afghanistan, it created a public relations nightmare, but the administration justified the contract because, as an oil and gas company, Halliburton had already established its own presence in the region.[4]

The process for evaluating school voucher programs, and for using the evidence from those evaluations to both defend them in court and to justify future voucher policies, has worked in a similar, cyclical manner. Well-networked conservative groups and individuals provide key policy services at critical developmental moments and then build off that experience to offer even more services. In previous chapters, we saw how Harvard professor Paul Peterson created a scaffolding of voucher evidence to propel individual policies (Milwaukee, Cleveland, and then Washington, D.C.), and an evidence base from which to build litigation all the way to the Supreme Court. We also saw how that evidence arose at the same time as the funders of that research—in particular, the Lynde and Harry Bradley Foundation—were also supporting the legal defense of school vouchers through the Koch-seeded Institute for Justice. And we saw how all of these groups were also organizationally connected to the DeVos family and other members of CNP. What Peterson had done, in effect, was not only create an evidence base for vouchers in legislation and in court but also establish a track record for himself and for his acolytes to eventually win and manage new projects toward the same future ends. This is the education locus of the conservative counter-intelligentsia "beachhead" prioritized by the Bradley and John M. Olin Foundations, among others.[5] Once established with an early track record, the efforts would only grow.

A NEW LOOK AT MILWAUKEE

In 2006 I joined yet another wave of that work. Earlier that year, blessed by both state and federal courts, Milwaukee's voucher program expanded up to a 22,500-pupil limit on enrollment. The authorizing legislation, Wisconsin Act 125 of 2005, also required a new, five-year evaluation of the Milwaukee Parental Choice (voucher) Program that included standardized testing for what the statute called "a representative panel" of voucher-using students.[6] The original program, implemented in 1990 and described in chapter 2, required the state superintendent of public instruction to "monitor the performance of the pupils."[7] It was on that authority that Superintendent Herbert Grover first appointed University of Wisconsin's John Witte as the state evaluator for the original program. Recall that Grover had subsequently been ridiculed by voucher advocates for his opposition to the program and that Witte's evaluation was the target of Paul Peterson's direct attack within Peterson's own, more favorable, reports on vouchers' success.[8] In the 2005–2006 reauthorization of the program, the legislature gave the evaluation not to the administrative discretion of the state superintendent but directed by statute for it to be under the auspices of an entity called the School Choice Demonstration Project.[9] The founder and director of that project was Patrick Wolf, the former Peterson student, collaborator on the three-cities *Education Gap* studies, and evaluator for the new federal D.C. voucher program introduced in chapter 3.

Patrick Wolf was at that time an associate professor at Georgetown University, where I had met him and worked as a graduate research assistant in the final year of his work with Peterson and the Washington Scholarship Fund. Wolf was in the process, however, of moving both his faculty appointment and the nascent School Choice Demonstration Project (hereafter, the Demonstration Project, or just Project) to a newly established Department of Education Reform at the University of Arkansas. The new department was chaired by Peterson's other former student, Jay P. Greene, with whom the former had written the pro-voucher Milwaukee and Cleveland reports. The circumstances of the founding of the Department of Education Reform at Arkansas have never been publicly clear in full, but what is established is that at least $10 million in seed money, to be matched by the university general fund and other donations, originated from donors affiliated with Wal-Mart's Walton family.[10]

Wolf's evaluation of D.C.'s voucher program was already underway when, as a doctoral student at the University of Wisconsin, I joined the Milwaukee version when it began in the summer of 2006. He had been tenured at Georgetown only two years earlier, and although his move to Arkansas in the 2006–2007 academic year came with the new "21st Century

Endowed Chair in School Choice" in Greene's new department, he was by any standard of the academic profession an early career researcher, now leading not one but two brand-new inquiries into perhaps the most controversial and well-watched education issue at that time. Unlike his mentor Peterson, Wolf maintained cordial relationships with many voucher skeptics, and, although I had worked for him in D.C., it was actually through John Witte that I joined the new Milwaukee evaluation.[11] Wolf was the principal investigator for the evaluation. By statute his School Choice Demonstration Project would act on the state's behalf, but he brought in Witte for his "veteran leadership" to serve as co-principal investigator, along with Jay Greene himself.[12] Peterson retained a role on the evaluation's research advisory board.[13]

Witte's primary responsibility on Wolf's new Milwaukee evaluation— and the one for which I had day-to-day responsibility as a doctoral fellow— was for the study of student academic outcomes outlined in the legislation. There was an irony to this: Wisconsin Act 125 expressly required that the "representative sample of pupils" using vouchers be studied for five years alongside "the scores of a comparable group of pupils enrolled in" Milwaukee Public Schools.[14] This is what social scientists call a matched comparison group design, which considers outcomes of interest after accounting for observable characteristics that might influence both the outcome and participation a treatment condition—in this case, vouchers. The method is in many ways similar to the method Witte used more than a decade earlier, and what Paul Peterson and Jay Greene had directly criticized.[15]

But from the standpoint of creating a post-*Zelman* evidence base on which to build new and expanded school vouchers programs, the real centerpiece was the D.C. evaluation Wolf was leading at the same time in the nation's capital, discussed in chapter 3. The federal government's requirement to create a randomized control trial of the program there outdid, from the standpoint of methodological rigor, the matched comparison requirement in Wisconsin Act 125. But the new evaluation in Milwaukee provided several advantages to voucher advocacy research that Wolf's D.C. study did not. First, Milwaukee retained important symbolic value as the first voucher program in the nation and as the site of Peterson's vehement attack on the state evaluator. If that state evaluator, Witte, could be seen breaking bread with Peterson's protégé on a new study in the name of rigorous research, it would give the voucher program a kind of cross-the-aisle appearance that earlier Peterson-affiliated work had not shown. Second, the five-year interval for the evaluation was longer than Witte or Peterson had been able to do—three years was the typical maximum—in either Milwaukee itself, in Cleveland, or in the three-cities *Education Gap* work on which Peterson and Wolf had collaborated. It was thought, and is still argued, in the voucher advocacy community, that these programs need time to mature and their beneficial impacts become clear.[16] Five years of study would allow that time.

Finally, and above all, Wolf's group, the School Choice Demonstration Project, was named explicitly in statute. That carried enormous weight in the city apart from the precise language used to guide the work. And in a relationship that was becoming common among researchers focusing on public school outcomes through what are known today as research-practice partnerships, the Project's funding came from private foundations even as it engaged in research activity on behalf of a government entity.[17] This arrangement saves taxpayer dollars, and if the funders maintain a distance between their organizational priorities and the integrity of the research process, this can result in a scientifically sound, and from the standpoint of official agencies, optimal and efficient arrangement. The Demonstration Project's funders for the Milwaukee voucher evaluation were the ever-present Bradley Foundation, the Walton Foundation, a conservative philanthropy called the Kern Foundation, and a politically neutral Annie E. Casey Foundation.[18]

In 2006, when I joined the Demonstration Project, the statutory guidance from Wisconsin Act 125 to create and track a representative panel of voucher students alongside comparable public school students—Witte's main role—was the urgent priority. Not only did the law require that data collection, but as in previous studies the impact of vouchers on student achievement was always going to be under close scrutiny. To do so with some semblance of scientific fidelity for five years meant that the Project had little time to waste between spring 2006, when the law took effect, and the fall testing window that public schools followed. The mechanical difficulty was that, although Wisconsin Act 125 required all voucher-receiving schools to begin or continue testing students in grades 4, 8, and 10 with a nationally normed exam—and to then report those results to Wolf's Project—private schools could select any nationally normed exam to meet that requirement. To meet the other requirement, the representative panel, the Project had to select a subset of voucher users to take a specific exam: the Wisconsin Knowledge and Concepts Exam, a criterion-referenced test that the state required of its public schools to meet federal accountability obligations.[19]

As the named evaluator in statute, the Demonstration Project had uncommon authority to conduct its evaluation. But while at the program level, the Milwaukee voucher expansion and its funding were tied at least at the outset to the existence (though not the results of) the Project's role, individual private schools had little requirement to participate apart from sending anonymous student results for the Project to process. In other words, for us to meet the "representative sample" piece of the statute's mandate, the Project would have to depend essentially on the extent to which individual private schools felt the need to comply. In theory, if the Project drew a particular school's enrolled voucher-using student at random into the representative sample, the spirit of Wisconsin Act 125 implied that the school should administer the Project's test to that student. But the statute gave no explicit demand for individual schools to do so.

It was up to stakeholders in the program—especially George and Susan Mitchell at the Bradley-funded School Choice Wisconsin, which had helped launch the program more than a decade earlier, and Howard Fuller, by then in his Bradley-endowed chair at Marquette University—to bring private schools into the fold.[20] As early investors in the voucher idea, it was in their interest to meet the terms of the new expansion. And it was through their encouragement, particularly that of Susan Mitchell and School Choice Wisconsin, that Milwaukee private schools became willing subjects of the Project's research. In that sense, these groups played an important administrative role not unlike the private school recruitment by the Washington Scholarship Fund, funded by Bradley as well, and D.C. Parents for Choice, described in chapter 3. George Mitchell in particular claims credit for

Demonstration Project's evaluation in the first place. In an angry email that he sent to me in September 2023, after I had made public comments to Wisconsin media that were critical of a 2023 School Choice Wisconsin voucher report, Mitchell wrote that the Project's evaluation was "in the planning stages long before Act 125" and that "the relevant language in Act 125, which [he] helped draft, facilitated the work of the study team by requiring schools to provide the team with test data."[21] It is significant that, in Mitchell's telling, the Demonstration Project's involvement preceded its official designation in statute and that he himself helped craft that authorization.

VOUCHERS: A DATA-GENERATING PROCESS

As the point person on Witte's team at the University of Wisconsin that was to supervise the data analysis for the "representative sample" outlined in statute, I and the other project personnel simply depended on the intercession of the Mitchells, Fuller, and individual private school directors to execute the state's requirements. Also key were personnel at Milwaukee Public Schools and the Wisconsin Department of Public Instruction.[22] As with individual private voucher-receiving schools, the state statute implied but withheld explicit compulsion for these entities to fully participate in the creation of the sample of students it mandated for study. At early meetings with private school leaders in church halls and basements at which our Project team outlined the terms of the state-mandated evaluation, some school leaders were enthusiastic—they were eager to show their prowess— while others exhibited resistance to the new study. I remember being approached by representatives of a Waldorf-style school that wanted no part of administering standardized tests at all. In other instances, I and other Project team members had to proctor exam sessions ourselves, for private schools that would not devote staff time to do so. But in the end, the efforts of School Choice Wisconsin in particular prevailed, as did the research-based goodwill of the Milwaukee Public Schools staff, and we were able to administer the state-required exams, and collect the results, in a timely way both in the fall of 2006 and in subsequent years.

Wisconsin Act 125 created a rare redundancy for transparency and accountability, in that not only did the legislation directly authorize the Demonstration Project to act on the state's behalf in collecting and analyzing
voucher school and student test scores but it also required the legislature's
own research arm, the Legislative Audit Bureau, to do a follow-up analysis—
a replication, as it were, of our data analysis. The Act was ambiguous on
the scope of the Audit Bureau's task, apart from language stating, "The
legislative audit bureau shall review and analyze the standardized test score
data received from the School Choice Demonstration Project."[23] As the analyst with day-to-day responsibility for the testing data, it was my job in
each of the five years to transmit the information confidentially to the Bureau and to work with their staff on any follow-up questions they might
have about our research choices. The law neither authorized that bureau
to demand, nor prohibited the Project from giving, information on which
private schools each voucher user was actually attending. But both Wolf
and the voucher advocacy groups assisting the Project's work interpreted
that ambiguity as preventing specific school names from entering the audit. As a result, while the Audit Bureau broadly confirmed our results—
that no academic difference between voucher users and public school
students were attributable to the voucher program over the years we studied it—it was limited in what it could report on specific private schools.[24]

But if the creation of the "representative sample" for comparison to public school performance on the state's official exam, and the ancillary delivery of other testing materials in select grades to Wolf's Demonstration
Project were the legislative goals outlined in the voucher program's reau-
thorizing statute, the Project itself represented a new opportunity for school
choice advocates. For dating back to Paul Peterson's own work in Milwaukee, in Cleveland, and especially in the three-cities *Education Gap* study,
standardized testing outcomes could only be part of the "demonstration" for choice effects. From the beginning, parent satisfaction, school
safety, competitive effects on public school outcomes, and other measures
were as, if not more, important to the voucher case. And although Wisconsin Act 125 did not convey authority to the Project to collect those
data, the authority the Project did have—and its endorsement and aid

from the Mitchells, Fuller and others—spoke volumes for its credibility in the local voucher community.

As a result, by far and away the scope and volume of the Demonstration Project's efforts in Milwaukee were located away from what the authorizing statute had made the centerpiece of the evaluation—the public-private testing comparison. Of the thirty-six reports published by the School Choice Demonstration Project in the five years that I served as the lead analyst for the matched comparison-group study actually required by the state, only ten made up the annual reports outlined in Wisconsin Act 125. The bulk of the documents were focused on parental satisfaction, school participation, or the impact of voucher competition on public schools. An additional three reports—on the voucher program's impact on character, effect on crime, and a study on how "Parent Religiosity or Private School Choice May Reduce Crime and Paternity Disputes in Milwaukee"—were released long after the portion of the work required by statute had ended.[25]

Whether intended or not, these ancillary studies served as insurance for the investments made by the Bradley and Walton Foundations in, and the support given by local voucher advocates to, the Demonstration Project. No one involved in the Project—not Wolf, Witte, myself, or other analysts—could have predicted that in the five years of our tracking of test score differences, per state law, we would find none attributable to the Milwaukee voucher program. That was, of course, not what Paul Peterson's earlier research in that city, or in Cleveland, or Peterson's three-cities *Education Gap* study (that Wolf helped lead) had found when presenting positive voucher impacts. That was, however, the pattern indicated by Witte's original state evaluation, and by the state evaluator in Cleveland—as chapter 2 of this book summarizes. In my role as the analyst of the test score data for the Project, I saw no proverbial "thumb on the scale" from the voucher-backing foundations related to our data collection or results. And, even if I had, the Audit bureau's own check of the data should have caught it. But evidence can be created in part by the questions that are asked, and by what social scientists call the data-generating process. As we saw in previous chapters, the role that the Bradley Foundation in particular has played in voucher research has been not only to fund the analysts like Wolf or Peterson on one end but also to incentivize private schools to participate on the other end. This does not include the other political and legal activity associated with the legislative creation and judicial defense of the programs in the first place.

What is critical to understand about the specific questions of focus in voucher advocacy research, beginning with Paul Peterson's work, is their origin in the need to inform actual and potential litigation, or legislative proceedings. Many of the twenty-six reports issued by the School Choice Demonstration Project's Milwaukee study not required by Wisconsin Act 125 were specifically focused on questions arising in the *Zelman* case and in the Ken Starr–led defense (also, as we have seen, partly funded by Bradley). Among these were "The Milwaukee Parental Choice Program's Effect on Integration," "The Fiscal Impact of the Milwaukee Parental Choice Program," "Family Voices on Parental School Choice in Milwaukee: What Can We Learn from Low-Income Families?" and "Parent and Student Experiences with Choice in Milwaukee, Wisconsin."[26] The latter focus, on parent satisfaction with vouchers regardless of the empirical impact of the policy—a trade-off articulated specifically by Starr on the Supreme Court steps after *Zelman* arguments—were also appearing in Wolf's concurrent D.C. voucher study: "Family Reflections of the D.C. Opportunity Scholarship Program," for example, or "Satisfied, Optimistic, Yet Concerned: Parent Voices on the Third-Year of the D.C. Opportunity Scholarship Program."[27] And a number of the authors—many graduate students and staff under Wolf or Jay Greene in the new Walton-funded academic department at Arkansas—became future activists in their own right in the voucher policy space at places like the Heritage Foundation and EdChoice, formerly the Milton and Rose D. Friedman Foundation.[28]

VOUCHERS ON THE DEFENSIVE

Taken together, with the Bradley Foundation funding these research projects, funding the Demonstration Project's partner organizations like School Choice Wisconsin and Howard Fuller's Institute for the Transformation of

Learning (which, notably, was also authorized by Wisconsin Act 125 to accredit voucher schools) as well as the recent *Zelman* defense from the Institute for Justice, the Project represented an important piece of the scaffolding for ongoing and future voucher policy formation. The "demonstration" in the Project's name was the creation of evidence to summon for advocacy, litigation, or the creation of a narrative in mainstream media.[29] In that, this was a natural development for what Jay Greene called "addressing real political issues that occur in real time" in defending his old Milwaukee and Cleveland work with Paul Peterson[30] and for the "counter-intelligentsia" objective to promote conservative public policy more generally.[31] The activity is more subtle than the manufacturing of data or falsification of results. It comes instead from that data-generating process determining everything from which private schools participated, which questions get asked, and—even back to the passage of Wisconsin Act 125 itself—which are asked, by whom.

Another example of this cyclical form of research advocacy comes from the Demonstration Project's "Report #35: Special Education and the Milwaukee Parental Choice Program."[32] The report was prompted by a federal complaint filed by the American Civil Liberties Union and disability advocates against the Wisconsin Department of Public Instruction (DPI) that ultimately had authority over the voucher program, and against two voucher-receiving schools, for extraordinarily low rates of voucher enrollment by students with special academic needs or disabilities.[33] The report was an add-on to the annual batch of testing and summary reports issued by the Project and appeared only in the final year of the evaluation—soon after the disability lawsuit against the state was filed. Report 35 took the unusual step of criticizing DPI head-on for what it called the agency's "error in reporting a flawed measure of disability" that the report insisted was an undercount of the voucher program's true rate of disability enrollment that had prompted the lawsuit.[34] Because voucher-receiving schools are not actually required to label students with special needs as public schools are, the report contended, the true measure of student disability rates in the voucher program was likely much higher. Based on proprietary access to voucher schools facilitated by School Choice Wisconsin, and proprietary access to surveys of parents by the Project, the report argues "we strongly advise readers to instead focus upon our more reliable estimates of the disability rate in MPCP."[35]

In that way, the entire existence of Report #35 was a defense of the voucher program against the complaint by disability advocates. The complaint itself, filed at the Department of Justice in 2011, argued that "Wisconsin's creation, implementation and expansion of a private school voucher program in Milwaukee has resulted in a dual system of education in the city" and alleged that voucher schools were creating and maintaining subtle barriers to avoid serving certain students.[36] One of the two named schools in the complaint, Messmer Preparatory Catholic School, was a rare school-specific beneficiary of Bradley Foundation support during that time, receiving more than $1.2 million between 2009 and 2012, while Bradley was also funding the Demonstration Project.[37] It took more than five years to eventually conclude with a finding neither admonishing nor exonerating the voucher program.[38] Years later, new investigative reporting found that the barriers alleged in that 2011 complaint did and still do exist in the voucher program, as private schools admit students with special needs to avoid oversight on the admissions process but then quietly counsel them out because retention data receives far less scrutiny.[39] But at the time, the Project's Report #35 served to help buffer the negative controversy, defending the voucher program and admonishing: "Many people are making choices in the educational environment of Milwaukee. For some parents and educators, those choices involve eschewing the formal special education label for students with disabilities. The sooner everyone accepts this important reality the sooner we can focus more effectively on unbiased evaluations and reasoned discussions of educational interventions such as parental school choice."[40]

CHOICE AND ACCOUNTABILITY

As the evaluation neared its five-year conclusion as required by Wisconsin Act 125, the voucher program came up for reauthorization and, as usual with each such milestone, possible expansion. Wisconsin Act 28 of 2009 contained no new provisions for an ongoing evaluation of the voucher program's performance, but it did construct a basic accountability and performance monitoring system similar to the No Child Left Behind requirements faced by public schools. In particular, voucher-receiving schools began mandatory testing using the same state exam (the Wisconsin Knowledge and Concepts Exam) as their public counterparts, and the results sent to the School Choice Demonstration Project per the ongoing evaluation through 2011–2012.[41] Follow-up legislation in the next two years created, first, a new voucher program modeled on Milwaukee in the nearby city of Racine, and next a statewide voucher program that led to the program in place today.[42]

Important for both the Demonstration Project's evaluation and for debates that would occur over the next decade, the fact that the 2005 law had authorized the Project to collect state exam data on a "representative sample" of voucher students implied that we could observe their outcomes both before and after the No Child Left Behind–style accountability system was put in place. Particularly important was the disclosure of private school names alongside summary test reports (a feature, recall, that was not contained in the 2005 statute). This allowed our data analysis portion of the Project's team to address a particular question of high sensitivity both then and later among school choice advocates: namely, the extent to which state oversight of private schools receiving public dollars helped or hindered their performance.[43] Our results showed, overwhelmingly, that voucher schools improved their performance once the state began requiring the results to be reported out by school name alongside the city's public schools.[44] As I noted in an article for the New Republic after the evaluation had ended, private schools with a particular evangelical bent—those teaching creationism, for example—were particularly poor performers on the state exam.[45]

The importance of accountability to voucher performance was a result that Wolf, as leader of the Demonstration Project, acknowledged both in his summary of the five-year evaluation and as coauthor on the peer-reviewed version of our final report that appeared several years later in 2014.[46] Unfortunately, this did not prevent him from taking to an unreviewed forum, Jay Greene's personal blog, to distance the Project from any implication that state oversight was a critical piece of voucher policymaking, calling our work—with his name on it—"hardly conclusive" that accountability mattered.[47] The context for Wolf's disavowal of the work is that it came in 2013, while he was just releasing preliminary results from his new evaluation of Louisiana's school voucher program, implemented by that state in the years following Hurricane Katrina. That research, a topic of later pages in this book, was beginning to make the rounds in professional research circles in unpublished form with shocking results: huge, nearly unprecedented academic loss for students who transferred to Louisiana schools using a voucher.[48] As we shall see, the shock wave of that finding, sustained over several years, was so strong that Betsy DeVos herself would have to address it as Secretary of Education.[49] As early as 2013, when Wolf pushed back against our work together in Milwaukee, showing the benefit of accountability, the explanation for what was to become a string of negative voucher results across multiple states, was government "regulation."[50]

TRAINING GROUNDS

Much, then, was to lie ahead. Just as the original Paul Peterson and Jay Greene research in Milwaukee and Cleveland begat the three-cities reports in *The Education Gap,* and both collections of that work helped make up the merits of the case in the *Zelman* decision at the Supreme Court, the subsequent new voucher program in Washington, D.C., and the major expansion of Milwaukee's voucher system at nearly the same time were to beget models for voucher systems elsewhere. Peterson's protégé Patrick Wolf, alongside Jay Greene at the Walton-seeded department at the University of Arkansas, swept up the evaluation contracts for both new programs— D.C. and Milwaukee—as well as upcoming voucher plans in states like Louisiana. The importance of the Milwaukee evaluation is that, alongside the D.C. version, it established the School Choice Demonstration Project as the key vendor for legislatures creating voucher programs to manage the initial trial process. It also brought to scale, as it were, the original model introduced by Paul Peterson for voucher advocacy-research based at a major academic institution, with all the pedigree that brings for both reporting and the broader research community.

It was also about the personal, and about personnel. For my part, the Demonstration Project came as I was building my own research career in program evaluation, in particular the evaluation of state education policy. It was also the first exposure I had to working with data on research supported by large funders in the education reform network. In the years after, I became part of a network of researchers based primarily at universities but also think tanks across the country, focusing on evidence use in policy analysis and nurturing relationships with government agencies and education stakeholders. Funding for my work reached into the millions of dollars and included support from groups like the Laura and John Arnold Foundation (now, Arnold Ventures), the Smith Richardson Foundation, and the Walton Foundation itself, as well as the US Department of Education.[51] One could credibly say I was among the researchers whose early career benefited indirectly from Bradley Foundation investments in voucher research. And although I was never a formal beneficiary, such as a Bradley Foundation Fellow, the fact that my career did begin with the School Choice Demonstration Project implies I was for a short time a part of the "counter-intelligentsia" beachhead the Foundation intended to develop.[52] My work from the Project that found mildly optimistic voucher results continues to be cited by Friedman's EdChoice as well as past Project researchers.[53] However, none of my more voluminous, skeptical scholarship, including work that began at the Project itself, has ever made it into those compendia. That omitted work includes evidence, published in the top education policy journal in the country, that Milwaukee voucher users left the program at extraordinarily high rates and improved their academic outcomes once returning to public school.[54] Also omitted from EdChoice summaries and other talking points by Bradley-funded organizations is the evidence showing the importance of government oversight of voucher programs, discussed previously.[55]

But my divergence from the Demonstration Project's ideological beachhead was an exception, not the rule. Indeed, between the Milwaukee, Washington, D.C., and Louisiana voucher evaluations and more than a dozen stand-alone efforts, the School Choice Demonstration Project and the University of Arkansas Department of Education Reform are responsible for training the bulk of researchers and fellows working on vouchers and the broader "education freedom" movement at the time of this writing.[56] One early Senior Research Fellow at the Project, Gerard Robinson, left to become president of Howard Fuller's Bradley-funded Black Alliance for Educational Options, a prominent conservative group dedicated to school choice advocacy. Robinson later served short stints as director of Departments of Education in both Florida and Virginia.[57] Other recent positions for Demonstration Project alumni are a roll call of Council of National Policy institutions introduced in chapters 1 and 2 of this book, including the Heritage Foundation, the Cato Institute, several State Policy Network affiliates, Friedman's EdChoice, and Betsy DeVos's own American Federation for Children. It is from that last group that the ongoing campaign to privatize public schools remains centered, and an Arkansas Education Reform graduate and former Project member Corey DeAngelis is primarily entrenched. As perhaps the most visible (and self-described) "school choice evangelist" in the country today, DeAngelis travels the country lobbying for vouchers and other choice policies, appearing at events organized by Moms for Liberty, the CNP affiliate Leadership Institute, and the Conservative Political Action Conference (CPAC).[58]

The crucial development then, at this point in the story, is that by the first decade of the twenty-first century the goals of the Bradley Foundation, Koch, and DeVos-affiliate groups to establish a conservative presence in the education policymaking and legal communities—and with it the broader goals of the CNP toward right-wing public policy—were at least initially achieved through and on behalf of the school vouchers movement. Whether from establishing an evidence base to motivating judicial proceedings at the highest Court in the land, or to propelling legislation at the state level—the next true frontier—the result was new arrangement of ideological advocates who by any common metric (grant-making, data collection, and institutional pedigree) were accruing the experience and expertise to continue inroads from the initial "beachhead" won in the late 1990s and early 2000s. Just as Betsy DeVos's brother and other profiteers carried wartime contracts during the same period of time of conservative presidential politics and congressional control, earning bigger jobs with higher stakes, so too did the voucher movement create its own private army—the "soldier-scholars" of chapter 2—to handle the new logistics of education reform.

What was coming, though, was not simply a fight over market principles or educational standards. Instead, as the empirical case for school vouchers on the education reform movement's preferred metric of standardized testing began to collapse in the years after the Demonstration Project completed its initial work, the conservative advocacy network around it began to retrench around more fundamental and indeed original language around parents' rights. The legislative, policy, and legal skirmishes over school vouchers were to be wrapped up as regional battles in a much larger and destructive culture war.

5

Disasters

. . . a service to the rest of the country by providing a large-scale example
of what the market can do for education when permitted to operate.

—MILTON FRIEDMAN, 2005

This is the point in the story where events took a turn, for a time, for the worse against voucher advocates. The election of Barack Obama in 2008 was seen by members of the Council for National Policy and by the adjacent Koch network as a major threat to conservative public policy, including in education, and compelled a season of retrenchment and restrategizing.[1]

Although it ushered in its own era of Democratic-led education reform on issues like charter schools and teacher evaluation, the Obama era stopped well short of vouchers at any national scope.[2] Indeed, even the D.C. Opportunity Scholarship Program, the voucher program passed in the wake of *Zelman* and a subject of chapters 3 and 4, faced constant budgetary pressure during the Obama years as the Democratic administration weighed everything from full expiration of the program to restricting funding to current voucher users only.[3] It was a reminder that even a Supreme Court blessing was only as good as the will of policy makers at the state or federal level to embrace vouchers. And that will was and remains largely consigned to conservative political priorities.

In several states—the true arena for education policy and the focus for the Council on National Policy and other right-wing organizations—a handful of voucher-like programs expanded or appeared in Wisconsin, Louisiana, Indiana, Ohio, and North Carolina as the second decade of the twenty-first century began.[4] The problem was, with these new programs came new data and evidence. A major theme of chapters 2 through 4 in this book has been the dependence of pro-voucher litigation and legislation on favorable research outcomes—up to and including the use of Paul Peterson's results in *Zelman v. Simmons-Harris*. Chapter 4 showed that post-*Zelman* voucher test score evaluations in Milwaukee and in Washington, D.C., detected no advantage for voucher users, with those findings modestly offset by favorable impacts on student attainment. But even together these were hardly the ringing endorsement or the tidal wave of evidence for which voucher advocates had hoped, planned, and funded. And, starting in the state of Louisiana, it was about to get worse.

LEARNING LOSS

When Hurricane Katrina made landfall in southeast Louisiana in August 2005, it destroyed thousands of lives and compelled a near-total rebuild of the economic and in many cases physical infrastructure in the city of New Orleans. It also destroyed the city's public school system, which had for decades existed as a tragically typical urban district wracked with systemic racism, poverty, and underinvestment in its primary population of Black and other historically marginalized students.[5] The hurricane ruined or severely damaged 110 of the city's 126 public school buildings, with the restoration or demolition process taking 18 years to complete—finishing only during the writing of this book.[6] Many surviving students were displaced with their families to other states for the upcoming school year. Many of these never returned at all. Between the 2000 and the 2010 census, New Orleans lost 43 percent of its population.[7]

With that devastation, education reformers across the political spectrum and across the United States saw opportunity. A mere two months after the hurricane, before a single school building had reopened, voucher advocates and more general school choice proponents had seized on the crisis to push options ranging from emergency vouchers for temporary private school attendance to full-scale redesign of the city's school system as a portfolio-style market of traditional public, independent charter, and publicly funded private options.[8] Writing in the *Wall Street Journal* three months after the storm and eleven months before he died, an aging Milton Friedman jumped at the chance to promote his voucher plan as a solution:

> Rather than simply rebuild the destroyed schools, Louisiana, which has taken over the New Orleans school system, should take this opportunity to empower the consumers, i.e., the students, by providing parents with vouchers of substantial size, say three-quarters of per-pupil spending in government schools, usable only for educational expenses. Parents would then be free to choose the schooling they considered best for their children . . . Parents, empowered by the voucher, would have a wide range to choose from.[9]

The result, Friedman claimed, would be "a service to the rest of the country by providing a large-scale example of what the market can do for education when permitted to operate." And although it would take a number of years to fully create, that is more or less what happened. A national cadre of privatization, charter school advocates, and a variety of philanthropic organizations descended literally and figuratively on Louisiana in a top-down, "outside-in" reconstruction run from the state capital.[10] It would be an educational recovery plan that Betsy DeVos's voucher advocacy group, the American Federation for Children, would later celebrate as an entire "restructuring of the education system and wholesale introduction of choice."[11]

That restructuring alone could occupy full volumes of research and reporting. Tulane University Professor Douglas N. Harris, with whom I have collaborated since 2015 on school choice research in New Orleans, has written what is at present the definitive treatment of the particularly prominent charter school sector, where the vast majority of the city's students now learn today.[12] With the state of Louisiana and members of both major political parties running the recovery plan under the influence of a variety of outside advocates, the new "charter school city," as Harris called it, would also eventually include a new voucher option for New Orleans students—one that would expand in the years to follow to the rest of the state.[13]

As it had for earlier voucher trials, Patrick Wolf's School Choice Demonstration Project at the Walton-created University of Arkansas Department of Education Reform, would once again secure the opportunity to evaluate the voucher portion of the post-Katrina reforms. This time, however, the right to do so was nonexclusive. Although the voucher studies were a separate entity for the purposes of data analysis, the Demonstration Project would release many of its results jointly with Harris's own center, the Education Research Alliance of New Orleans at Tulane, which was evaluating the entirety of the city's educational reconstruction.[14]

In addition, a separate team based at the Massachusetts Institute of Technology secured its own contract to study student outcomes in the voucher program. That team, a group of economists, had been studying the algorithms used to randomly assign students to overenrolled schools in New York City's school choice program.[15]

Sometime in 2013—roughly a year after the voucher program's expansion from New Orleans into a statewide system where it remains today—a conference paper version of the first-year results from the Arkansas site of voucher study began circulating in professional circles. Conference papers typically tend to include preliminary results, are usually publicly available, but do not constitute the final word on a project until the authors incorporate feedback from other researchers and their own internal quality control processes. I became aware of the Wolf team's initial Louisiana results after providing commentary for it as a discussant at the Association for Public Policy Analysis and Management in November 2013.[16] The authors themselves list a voucher advocacy conference two months later in January 2014 as the first public presentation.[17] In any case, the results were and remain shocking. Making use of the randomized nature of voucher offers of admission—the experimental design stressed years earlier by Paul Peterson and team (including Wolf) in *The Education Gap*—the Arkansas results showed that vouchers in Louisiana caused unprecedented large, negative impacts on student achievement. Martin West, a former Peterson student and now Harvard professor in his own right, described the Louisiana results to the *New York Times* as "as large as any I've seen" in the history of American education research.[18]

The M.I.T. team later released a paper showing similarly large negative impacts. The fact that two entirely separate research teams found the same result had a number of important implications. The first was that, although earlier researchers had found that voucher programs caused no increase in student achievement, no study had until that time found that vouchers actually harmed academic outcomes.[19] This raised the stakes considerably from a policy described by Kenneth Starr, Paul Peterson, and other advocates in the *Zelman* case as, at worst, a program that left academic results unchanged while making parents happier. There was now evidence that voucher interventions actually caused damage.[20] The second implication was that, because the Louisiana voucher evaluation was the first time that two teams, working independently from each other, found similar results (recall the controversies around Peterson's work in Milwaukee and then New York City outlined in chapters 2 and 3), that increased the potential of the negative outcomes to influence future voucher policymaking. Finally, the fact that Wolf's team, and its association then and now with voucher advocacy, had been one of the two teams uncovering that harmful data gave even more weight to the influence of their findings.

The story continued from there. So many outside advocacy organizations had been invested in New Orleans' and the state of Louisiana's education rebuild around school choice that there could be no simple acknowledgement that the Louisiana voucher program cast doubt on the viability of such policies for student success. There had to be a culprit. Time itself was the first potential culprit to receive blame. The gap between the Arkansas team's first distribution of its first-year negative findings in late 2013 and throughout 2014, and the M.I.T. team's release of similar results was almost two years.[21] Why the delay? In at least five separate settings, including an international conference in Spain, the Arkansas team had quietly circulated the negative results but had, at least in the presentations I attended, stressed that more time was needed—a second year, at minimum, before publicly releasing the shocking findings.[22] That restraint stands in stark contrast to the rush that Paul Peterson and Jay Greene made to release more favorable one-year results in earlier voucher evaluations, and Greene's name remained on early circulating drafts of the negative Louisiana paper withheld from a more public view.[23]

THE BLAME GAME

Vouchers needed more time to succeed; this was a position that the state superintendent for the Louisiana Department of Education also took after the M.I.T. team made the first public publication of the negative voucher results in the working paper series maintained by the prestigious National Bureau of Economic Research.[24] The state chief, a pro-voucher leader named John White, accused the authors of rushing "to meet their own publishing deadlines" without giving the Louisiana voucher system a chance to show favorable results.[25] And the *Wall Street Journal* opinion page—the same outlet that published Milton Friedman's prediction that the post-Katrina rebuild would be best served by vouchers—took the rare step of slamming the M.I.T. team on similar grounds.[26] A year later, reporting in *The 74* showed through open records requests that White and his department cancelled the M.I.T. research contract soon after the negative results were released.[27]

By then, however, there was no denying that the extraordinarily large, negative impact of the Louisiana voucher program was more than a first-year fluke. The Arkansas team under Wolf's direction finally published its own negative results in a major academic journal, finding academic losses into students' second year of voucher use as well.[28] They found no offsetting benefits to other outcomes like educational attainment, while annual student exits from the program were substantial.[29] Later results in the third and fourth years would show that students who remained in the program for years were able to recover some of the learning loss they suffered early on, but in the final, fourth-year report, Wolf's team acknowledged "the results presented here indicate large negative effects of LSP voucher usage after four years, especially in math."[30] I am among the researchers thanked by the authors of that report for early reviews of the analysis.

After that release, Patrick Wolf published a lengthy summary of the pros and cons of the Louisiana voucher program, nestling the negative results on student outcomes within other reports his team had issued on other questions, just as they had in Milwaukee and D.C.[31] These Louisiana reports included an argument for the second culprit for voucher-induced academic harm: the overregulation theory that had taken hold among conservative activists.[32] Wolf called Louisiana vouchers a "cautionary tale" but stressed their "good intentions" and paraphrased another scholar of education reform by noting "everything works at something; nothing works at everything."[33] He published that forgiving conclusion in *Education Next*, the conservative journal based at the Hoover Institute, edited by his mentor, Paul Peterson, and funded in part by the Bradley and Koch Foundations.[34] That same summer, Betsy DeVos used some of those same talking points when appearing at the Education Writers Association, arguing that program regulations "discouraged many schools from participating in it, and in fact has encouraged some schools that probably would not have been parents' first choices." That was hardly the fault of vouchers as an idea, in her explanation. Rather, DeVos insisted, the Louisiana example was just "not very well-conceived."[35]

The problem for DeVos, and for voucher research advocates like Peterson, Wolf, and their affiliates, was that Louisiana was by then no longer the only program showing substantial academic harm to voucher students. In 2017 and 2018 an independent evaluation of Washington, D.C.'s Opportunity Scholarship Program—a reauthorized version of the vouchers Wolf had studied between 2005 and 2010—published large negative student achievement results in the first two of its three years.[36] By then, the program had moved beyond the early days of its management by the voucher-advocating Washington Scholarship Fund and was being implemented by a new group called Serving Our Children.[37] The new, negative D.C. results could not be explained by either attendance at an inordinately high-performing public school for students who lost a lottery-based chance to use vouchers, or by side effects induced by the disruption of transferring schools. Rather, as the study's lead author Mark Dynarski explained in a brief for the *Brookings Institution*, students in the D.C. voucher program's religious schools were receiving fewer hours per week on core subjects. It was "plausible," therefore, "that students in private schools may have scored lower because they received less instruction in reading and math."[38]

That same summer of 2017, while the first of those new, negative impacts of D.C.'s voucher program was released and the multiple years of negative outcomes from Louisiana were becoming evident, a new evaluation of Indiana's entry into the voucher world was beginning to show dismal results of its own. Researchers led by University of Notre Dame Professor Mark Berends found that students using vouchers to attend the state's private schools had lower achievement levels, especially in mathematics. That voucher-induced academic harm was not the only thing the Indiana Choice Scholarship Program shared with their Louisiana counterpart. As in Louisiana, Indiana's pro-voucher officials were loath to permit widespread dissemination of the negative findings until either the study had undergone peer review (a standard, recall, that voucher researchers did not wait to meet before releasing favorable results earlier) or they had given enough time for voucher users to make up lost academic ground. It took an open records filing from a reporter for *Chalkbeat* to the Indiana Department of Education to pry out a draft that had been circulating offline at academic conferences and voucher advocacy meetings.[39] The large, negative results would be reported in two of the leading academic journals for education policy research.[40] The extraordinary rate of annual student exits from the Indiana program documented in Louisiana and Milwaukee as well as in Florida was apparent as well.[41]

As bitter as the negative Louisiana results were for voucher advocates going back to Milton Friedman's *Wall Street Journal* call to leverage Katrina's destruction of New Orleans schools into a post-storm voucher market, Indiana's results dealt their own specific blow to the credibility of the voucher idea. For one thing, they showed the Louisiana results were no fluke. Nor were they simply an artifact of poor program design built on overregulation, as Betsy DeVos had claimed. Louisiana and Indiana shared little with respect to their economies, demographics, or political histories. The only commonality was the voucher program itself. And moreover, at the time of the Notre Dame study, the authorized enrollment and expenditures for the Indiana voucher program had quickly grown into the nation's largest. Very particularly, voucher policy makers modeled the program closely on what Betsy DeVos herself had stressed as an ideal design for a statewide voucher system: it moved money away from the state's public schools, did not restrict participants to families near the poverty line or those enrolled in low-performing public schools, and had strong enrollment from the state's middle class.[42] Although it contained more rules and testing requirements than DeVos might have liked, they were fewer in scope and number than those in Louisiana. The poor results could not, in other words, be blamed on low-income children ill-suited for private school or for overregulation itself. The Indiana voucher program failed the proof-of-concept test for school vouchers.

SCHOOLS' CHOICE

Indiana was also the first program where widespread discrimination could be documented. In a prelude to reporting and to political culture war debates that took hold after the COVID-19 pandemic, the fiscal scope and enrollment levels in the Indiana voucher program's statewide system meant that schools with particularly extreme social or religious views were eligible to receive students. In investigative reporting, again by *Chalkbeat*, journalists tabulated totals of taxpayer funds by specific private schools and then cross-referenced those totals against language or admissions and behavioral policies targeting LGBTQ+ students and issues. All told, in the voucher program's early years, $16 million in public funds went to private schools with overtly discriminatory policies against LGBTQ+ students and their families.[43] Similar reports would surface later in Florida and Wisconsin.[44]

In the post-COVID context of attacks on LGBTQ+ issues, the rise of the Moms for Liberty extremist group, and its weaponization of so-called parents' rights around issues of gender and sexuality, these anti-LGBTQ+ restrictions in state voucher programs may be more of a feature than a bug.[45] Indeed voucher advocates like Paul Peterson's former student Jay Greene later leaned into those culture war struggles as part of the case for school vouchers, in politically tinged reports for the Council of National Policy stalwart *Heritage Foundation*.[46] In that, the use of vouchers to self-sort into schools with particularly restrictive admissions or enrollment on issues of gender and sexuality directly recalls the original argument that Milton Friedman made in the wake of *Brown v. Board of Education*, detailed in chapter 1: namely, that vouchers could provide parents of all races the ability to avoid compulsory integration and simply choose for themselves whether to enroll in racially diverse environments. The arguments made by the schools covered in *Chalkbeat's* reporting or in Greene's tracts simply restate in terms associated with LGBTQ+ issues—and in terms of values—those post-*Brown* debates as further motivation for a school choice policy environment.

But that values-based argument for discrimination, however familiar in the 1950s on the issue of race, and again today in the context of gender and culture wars, was at the time of the large, negative Louisiana and Indiana vouchers results, still outside the mainstream of political debate and reporting on the issue of vouchers and school choice. The stated purpose, dating back to the 1990s and the old controversies over Milwaukee and Cleveland results, was to beat public schools at their own academic game. The entire theory of the case that became *Zelman* rested on academic failure of Cleveland's schools—a "crisis" in Cleveland—as measured by test scores.[47] The failure of school vouchers to improve outcomes for children who transferred to private schools once the voucher idea was scaled up to

a statewide level in Louisiana or Indiana represented an existential threat
to the voucher movement.

A STORY OF SCALE

Return to the key theme in chapters 2 through 4 of this book: the extent
to which the diffusion of voucher ideology, voucher litigation, and
voucher policymaking depended, from the beginning, on the creation of
an evidence base. That was the role filled initially by Paul Peterson and
then later by his acolytes. Part of that formation of a pro-voucher research agenda includes careful interplay (see chapters 3 and 4) between
that research and litigation and the very implementation of the voucher
programs in places like Milwaukee, Cleveland, and Washington, D.C.
Recall, for example, the role played by the Washington Scholarship
Foundation and Virginia Walden Ford's D.C. Parents for School Choice
in both advocacy and school recruitment once the federal D.C. voucher
program passed. And recall the role played by groups associated with
the major Bradley Foundation beneficiary Howard Fuller in securing
the voucher program's ongoing survival in Milwaukee. Further, recall
how Paul Peterson's affidavit in *Zelman* was based on evidence in Cleveland largely from two schools set up directly by the Walton Family
Foundation.

What sets the Louisiana and Indiana voucher programs apart from
those earlier efforts—beyond their extraordinary negative impacts on student achievement, beyond their recency, and beyond their enrollment size
and scope—was that, for the most part, these programs developed outside
the careful field laboratories curated by voucher advocates. This was also
true for the second iteration of the D.C. Opportunity Scholarship Program,
which realized negative impacts on student learning comparable to those
in Louisiana and Indiana, while the program was managed away from the
politically connected Washington Scholarship Program. The same was also
true for a less-visible evaluation conducted by the economist David Figlio's
research team in a 2016 report on Ohio's voucher program expanded beyond Cleveland, which outlined the largest negative impacts on student

achievement in the research record still available, as of this writing.[48] For all of these programs, the policy design, legislative passage, and subsequent administration of daily program activities were, to be sure, the result of pro-voucher political advocacy. But the data-generating processes—school recruitment and student enrollment in particular—existed for the first time outside the ability of voucher researchers and legal defenders to directly monitor them.

WITHER EVIDENCE?

The beachhead theory of conservative policymaking prioritized by the Lynde and Harry Bradley Foundation, the Koch network, the DeVos family, and the Council for National Policy was always based largely on dogma.[49] For some it was economic self-interest combined with libertarian market ideology; for others, it was religious fundamentalism that animated their priorities. But whatever the driving force, establishing a "counter-intelligentsia" to push its policy aims at American universities, through conservative think tanks, and into legislation and litigation required more than dogma and more, even, than theory. The critical role that Paul Peterson and his acolytes served in early school voucher policymaking was to provide that apparent empirical validation of long-standing conservative principle. The weakening of the evidence-based case for school vouchers, with the dual five-year evaluations in Washington, D.C., and Milwaukee, was a warning sign. There, academic differences between public and voucher students were seemingly nonexistent in favor of or against voucher use. But, as we have seen, reports of these academic differences were actually cushioned within dozens of reports on other topics and outcomes.[50] Dating back even earlier to Kenneth Starr on the Supreme Court steps after *Zelman*, and Paul Peterson's angry letter to the *New York Times* blasting its coverage of inconclusive test score results in Milwaukee, voucher advocates have long buffered findings of "no difference in outcomes" with arguments that such results were on the whole positive because parent satisfaction broke that proverbial tie.[51] Null results, in social science, can be something of a Rorschach test. One sees what one wants to see. Especially if one is a policy maker, legislator, or judge unversed in the nuances of such matters as statistical insignificance.

But decidedly negative results are a different story. Even casual readers can intuitively understand headlines such as these:

DISMAL VOUCHER RESULTS SURPRISE RESEARCHERS AS DEVOS
ERA BEGINS

NATION'S ONLY FEDERALLY FUNDED VOUCHER PROGRAM HAS
NEGATIVE EFFECT ON STUDENT ACHIEVEMENT, STUDY FINDS

STUDY SHOWS LOUISIANA SCHOOL VOUCHER PROGRAM HURT
MATH SCORES

STUDENTS' MATH SCORES DROP FOR YEARS AFTER USING A PRIVATE
SCHOOL VOUCHER IN COUNTRY'S LARGEST PROGRAM

DO VOUCHER STUDENTS' SCORES BOUNCE BACK AFTER INITIAL
DECLINE? NEW RESEARCH SAYS NO

TRUMP ADMINISTRATION ADVANCES SCHOOL VOUCHERS DESPITE
SCANT EVIDENCE[52]

These headlines, and more like them, were published in media outlets across the country between 2016 and 2019 as the results described in this chapter unfolded on an annual basis. And, crucially, it was not simply the lopsided negative direction of this new voucher evidence that created the threat to voucher advocacy. The fact that these results came precisely when vouchers left the proverbial laboratory of Paul Peterson and the soldier-scholars introduced in chapter 2 and entered the real-life, scaled-up, statewide phase with higher-income thresholds for participation showed a fundamental weakness of the voucher idea. Ancillary studies by other researchers uncovered some of the explanations for these results: the rise of pop-up private schools rushing into the market to cash in on new government dollars, for example, and the absence of enough high-quality schools to serve at-risk students.[53] But no explanation then or now has fully explained the learning loss displayed in locations so different as Louisiana, Indiana, Washington, and Ohio as does the simplest one: that for all of Milton Friedman's purported brilliance, and for all of the millions of dollars pumped into the effort by Betsy DeVos, Charles Koch, and the Bradley

Foundation, the idea simply did not work. The bigger and more recent the voucher program is, the worse the results have been.[54]

The 2015 renewal of the federal *Elementary and Secondary Education Act (ESEA)*, known as the *Every Student Succeeds Act (ESSA)*, requires publicly funded school districts to engage in "evidence-based practices." It defines these activities along a various range from "strong," "moderate," or "promising" results from "well-designed and well-implemented" experimental, quasi-experimental, or correlational studies.[55] And one that demonstrates a rationale from "high-quality research findings or positive evaluation" supposedly ensures "that such activity, strategy, or intervention is likely to improve student outcomes or other relevant outcomes."[56]

Even before ESSA, the federal government under President George W. Bush took major steps to incentivize evidence-based use in education, under the dubious premise that research informing education policy and practice had lagged behind other social sciences.[57] My own doctoral training was funded through a federal program at the US Department of Education, established during the Bush years, to meet just such an objective among the next generation of education researchers.[58] But neither by the letter of any of the specific standards outlined in ESSA, nor in the spirit of any fundamental overhaul of the way public education is funded and delivered in this country that could be built on a base of scientific evidence, does the notion that school vouchers "work" meet a credible threshold. If other policies and practices have yet to demonstrate a totality of evidence to support their use in education, they likewise have nothing like the warning in the research record of the negative impacts of statewide vouchers in Ohio, Louisiana, Indiana, and Washington, D.C. Social science never gives answers to policy questions at a rate of 100 percent—there will always be, at minimum, a few contrary cases to any result. But the decade of voucher research that began in 2010 provided as close to a one-sided conclusion as social science gets.

If evidence meant anything to education policy, the story of school vouchers would have ended here.

6

Back to the "Beachhead"

I want to recognize the significant and influential contributions to the
advancements of school choice you've made over the years.

—BETSY DEVOS TO PAUL E. PETERSON, 2017

The election of Donald J. Trump to the US presidency, on November 8, 2016, occurred just as the policy community was becoming broadly aware of the devastating impacts of school privatization in Louisiana, Indiana, Ohio, and Washington, D.C. When Trump nominated Betsy DeVos to lead the federal Department of Education, voucher advocates heralded the pick as a sign that the Trump White House would promote school choice policy broadly, even as the decision to implement such programs remained largely a state-level concern.[1] DeVos's official stature meant that, from time to time, she would have to address the waves of negative voucher results appearing during her term—her explanation of Louisiana's voucher plan as "not very well conceived" in 2019 is a prime example of this—but it also provided a visible platform and a title that her money alone could not buy.[2]

Betsy DeVos's four-year term in government is less important for any official policymaking role she played than for its joining of the culture war and white-grievance politics that propelled Donald Trump to the White

House with the modern history of school vouchers and school privatization more broadly. Doing so at a time that evidence for voucher impacts on student outcomes was beginning to show real academic harm, the DeVos-Trump link returned the notion of "parents' rights" to the forefront of voucher advocacy.

Trump's election also recentered that notion of "parents' rights" around its original conception of the right to avoid integrating students from different family backgrounds in one public school community. That formulation, as we saw in chapter 1, began in the 1950s as segregationists looked for ostensibly race-neutral ways to avoid the orders under *Brown v. Board of Education*, settling on Milton Friedman's proposal as a viable alternative to assert parental rights on the basis of values. And although Trump did not hail from the right-wing networks that Betsy DeVos, Charles Koch, and others had developed to push Friedman's ideas and other conservative policy priorities, his presidency refueled culture wars around issues of race and gender, while the events around his defeat in 2020 fueled new distrust and, in some circles, rejection of democratic institutional norms. Events like the Charlottesville race protests, immigration controversies, Black Lives Matter, the Supreme Court nomination of Brett Kavanaugh, and Trump's personal behavior underscored deep political and cultural divisions even before COVID-19 controversies around masking, vaccines, and school closures arose.

With these events occurring at the precise moment that, in the more narrow matter of educational policymaking, negative school vouchers evidence was appearing to threaten new expansions of those programs, Trump's embrace of school choice as "the civil rights issue of our time" defined vouchers as something of a protected status category among antiestablishment followers.[3] But it would take more than Trump's mere embrace of school choice to strengthen rather than weaken its place in conservative ideology. Indeed, it would take the very establishment-oriented members of the Council for National Policy (CNP), introduced earlier in this book and from which Betsy DeVos hailed, to harness grievance politics into a new force behind their decades-long voucher agenda.

OLD NETWORKS, NEW TIMES

Much has been written about the symbiotic relationship between Donald Trump and white evangelicals—particularly evangelicals in the US South. An important feature of that mutual dependence was the role that CNP-affiliated think tanks and organizations—particularly the Heritage Foundation and the American Legislative Exchange Council (ALEC), both founded by former CNP chair Paul Weyrich—played in the courtship between Trump and politically motivated evangelicals.[4] Trump needed the electoral power of white evangelicals to win the White House, and white evangelicals were able to leverage Trump's personal brand of racial animus and strong-man politics to press a policy agenda that created new authority for religious organizations on everything from discriminatory human resource practices to new advantages in the federal tax code.[5] And above all, the offspring of this at times tempestuous courtship was a new judiciary with broad oversight on issues pertaining to race, gender, and, of course, abortion rights.[6]

School vouchers are a case in point. Betsy DeVos could do little from the offices of the Department of Education to push a voucher agenda beyond renewing the Washington, D.C., voucher program, proposing ultimately ill-fated federal legislation, or giving voice to the gaggle of private think tanks and networks of evangelical, Christian nationalism that mustered for access during the Trump years. But the renewed and growing political musculature of the CNP over the Trump years—Trump's prominent senior advisor Kellyanne Conway was once CNP treasurer—served not only to protect DeVos's voucher agenda during a perilous period in which irrefutable evidence of its academic harm spread through elite policy circles but also to embolden these groups at the state level to continue ramming voucher-related policy through state legislatures.[7] And as we will see in chapter 7, that success grew even after Trump and DeVos left office, as the Right's longstanding hostility to LGBTQ+ issues fused with a new once-in-a-generation issue of educational response to a pandemic, to further motivate the voucher agenda.

But first it is important in this chapter to revisit the contours of that CNP apparatus and to locate what became the counternarrative to widespread voucher-induced academic loss (outlined in chapter 5) among the same sources as the early period of evidence creation in the 1990s. From the early days of the modern push for vouchers beginning in Milwaukee in 1990, the express goal of CNP-aligned groups like the John B. Olin Foundation and, especially, the Lynde and Harry Bradley Foundation, was the creation of a "counter-intelligentsia" for right-wing policy formation, and a conservative "beachhead" in the elite centers of political and intellectual American power.[8] We have already seen how that network was mustered in the years leading up to the *Zelman* decision to establish vouchers in the first place. During the late Obama and early Trump years, it became critical to preserving vouchers against the wave of unprecedented negative publicity.

Weyrich's Heritage Foundation, the Cato Institute (formerly the Charles Koch Institute), and the American Enterprise Institute (AEI)—all funded by the Lynde and Harry Bradley Foundation, among others—provided new intellectual sheen for what amounted to a crisis communications strategy.[9] All three released various versions of the antiregulation explanation for harmful voucher impacts between 2016 and 2019, as well as reports and commentaries suggesting pivots to budgetary vehicles like so-called "education savings accounts," which function as direct, ATM-style payments to parents for tuition reimbursement.[10] These supplemented the volumes of reports from the School Choice Demonstration Project at the University of Arkansas on vouchers in Milwaukee, Washington, D.C., and Louisiana purporting to show favorable voucher results on measures apart from student test scores. Such reports in particular were geared toward competitive effects (the impact of voucher-induced threats of funding cuts on school districts), small gains in racial integration, and especially noncognitive outcomes like child character—defined in one study as avoiding single parenthood or substance abuse—to buffer headlines on the enormous loss to student achievement.[11] These provided counter-intelligentsia support for statements by Betsy DeVos and others like Robert Enlow from EdChoice (formerly the Milton and Rose D. Friedman Foundation) that nonacademic measures were a better way to gauge voucher success, regardless of what test scores indicated.[12]

These organizations were acting at the very heart of Washington, D.C., political and policy circles—these were not obscure outposts of conservative academic thought. The prestige associated with ivory academic towers was largely attainable for the voucher advocacy community only at a handful of redoubts like Harvard's Program on Education Policy and Governance (founded and run by Paul E. Peterson), Stanford's Hoover Institution (also a Peterson appointment), and the Arkansas Department of Education Reform (run by former Peterson students). But the gilded hallways of Heritage, AEI, and other policy conveners were well traveled not only by obscure names from the CNP's shadow network but by politicians, authors, and other influencers in conservative circles.[13] The AEI provides an especially bright example for how institutionalized voucher research, voucher politics, and broader education reform efforts were by the time the major evidence for voucher-induced learning loss became apparent. Recall from chapter 1 that it was AEI—at the time the American Enterprise Association—to which Milton Friedman introduced Virginia activist Leon Dure in the late 1950s, during Dure's effort to frame resistance to school integration as a question of individual liberty and marketplace values.[14]

"DO AEI"

The Heritage Foundation's work has been overtly political—Heritage maintains a separate Heritage Action Fund for political activity, and as a Weyrich brainchild alongside ALEC, the group is more directly devoted to specific policy and legislation. But AEI maintains a mainstream sheen of conservative policy thought that housed current and former officeholders from the Right and center-Right of American policy and politics critical to sustaining political ideology over the long term. Luminary AEI fellows include John Bolton, who served in senior national security roles under

George W. Bush and Donald Trump; author Michael Barone; former Bush White House economist Glenn Hubbard; and former Senator and US Trade Representative Rob Portman. Lecturers have included Paul Ryan, while he served as Speaker of the US House of Representatives, and former Vice President Dick Cheney.[15] Charles Murray, the infamous author of *The Bell Curve* and an original Olin/Bradley beneficiary, remains a fellow at the Institute.[16] AEI's institutional pedigree lives as the serious, sober-minded center of conservative thought across policy realms, international and domestic. In the buildup to the Iraq War, for example, then-National Security Advisor Condoleezza Rice insisted on AEI's input to provide a "facts and options" review for what would become the crucial issue of how and to what extent the United States needed to plan for postwar unrest. Rice wanted AEI specifically because it was perceived within the administration as being sufficiently supportive of the war's rationale in the first place. "Without AEI," noted one history of the period, "Rice couldn't sign on." The same history quotes Rice's own words: "This is just what we need. We'll be too busy to do it ourselves. Do AEI."[17]

Inasmuch as her family's ties are most apparent to the Heritage Foundation, with its hub of CNP activity and its centers named after her family, Betsy DeVos herself relied on AEI's particular brand of conservative prestige—she was serving on AEI's Board of Directors at the time Trump nominated her to lead the Department of Education.[18] AEI fellows wrote glowing elegies of DeVos's service when her days in the Trump cabinet came to a close (she left only after the January 6, 2021, attack on the U.S. Capitol), as well as published space for valedictory exit interviews.[19] Months after she left office, AEI published a report called, "What Conservatives Could Learn from Betsy DeVos" by former Walton Family Foundation education chief and Federalist Society contributor Jim Blew, who also served as a DeVos undersecretary.[20] And later, when DeVos launched her book, *Hostages No More*, AEI was among the first on DeVos's publicity tour, in a special session moderated by AEI Education Policy Director Frederick M. (Rick) Hess—a former student of Paul E. Peterson.[21]

From his perch at AEI, the genial Hess plays a leading role in both convening and anointing degrees of influence on federal and state education policy. Although he comes from the Peterson mentoring tree, Hess is an independent and provocative thinker, known for open-mindedness and a willingness to dialogue with multiple sides of controversial questions. His annual "Edu-Scholar Public Influence Rankings," published as part of his regular *Education Week* column, attempts to measure the impact of individual scholars, not according to their cloistered academic research but by their online and media presence—particularly around issues of policy debate.[22] The main requirement for eligibility on the list is an academic affiliation, and Hess and a group of acquaintances preselect its first 150 names based on prior year membership on the list before incorporating an ad-hoc approach for the remaining 50.[23] Hess also presides over AEI's exclusive, invitation-only biannual "K-12 Working Group," which convenes "about 70 of the nation's leading academics, state and district leaders, and education entrepreneurs to discuss new ventures and research," according to my own most recent invitation in January 2020.[24] I have attended the Working Group meeting at least six times between October 2015 and the onset of the COVID-19 pandemic in spring 2020 and, in May 2018, gave a formal presentation to the group on the topic of teacher labor markets in California, Michigan, and Washington.

Like the Hess Edu-Scholar rankings, AEI's Working Group includes some of the most prominent names and institutions in education research, leadership, and advocacy. Scholars more accustomed to the drear and drab of academic conferences—myself included, once upon a time—wait eagerly every August and January to see if they will make the exclusive invite list to the all-expense-paid visit just off DuPont Circle in Washington. The status of an AEI invitation to the sessions, which include elaborate appointments of food alongside an open bar in the evenings at a local restaurant, confers the chance for progressive education leaders to mingle with potential donors, entrepreneurs, and—crucially—stalwarts of the education reform network. The briefings are private, a designation I will broadly respect in these pages. But as the speaker, I will note that for the May 2018 briefing that I myself gave, my audience included representatives from DeVos's education department staff, the Charles Koch Foundation, EdChoice, and a variety of for-profit entrepreneurial groups alongside state and national teachers of the year, labor leaders, leading academic voices, and education reporters from major US media outlets.[25]

So I am saying nothing here that I would not say about my own profile from an earlier time. It is through gatherings like these that a policy proposal such as school vouchers—by design a radical, destabilizing plan that shifts both governance and finance away from almost a century-old framework—can persist through a decade of some of the worst evidence to accumulate against any education policy plan in the public record. The "beachhead" theory of establishing conservative policy dominance depends not merely on investing in personnel—on funding streams like the Bradley Foundation's Bradley Scholars program for doctoral students, for example— but on creating a shared stake in the outcomes of such policy among other brokers of elite opinion and influence.[26]

With that shared stake, relatively anonymous experts like me and many of my contemporaries, who by 2017 onward *all* knew about the atrocious voucher results, became almost complicit. We claimed that we cared about evidence and in many cases—including my own—actively raised money for our centers and projects on the notion that evidence should inform public policy, not least and expressly because many of us, again, myself included, *had* to raise that money.[27] Money was there and is there to be had. In late 2023 a right-wing group working to establish plans for a second Trump administration accidently posted a donor list online, and media noted the William and Flora Hewlett Foundation among its donors.[28] The Hewlett Foundation has a well-earned reputation as supporter of progressive causes, including in education, and was among the funders of work I collaborated on between 2017 and 2019. But such is the network of many mainstream or moderate influencers with conservative and increasingly right-wing organizations. When pedigreed journalists, philanthropists, investors, and insiders from across the political spectrum gather face to face with backers of an idea like vouchers and, for that matter, other education reform efforts like charter schools or reductions in teacher labor protections, an interdependence of access and advancement becomes the definition of an establishment.

"PROBABLY A JESUS SCHOOL"

In this way, the radical becomes mainstream and even elite. In the very specific case of school vouchers, organizations like AEI provide a kind of cover story for these programs, told in the language of innovation, entrepreneurialism, and the free exchange of ideas. Meanwhile more politically engaged and, in many cases, religiously oriented organizations networked through the CNP continued to build a privatization agenda despite the evidence stacking up against it. The Trump years saw not one but two Supreme Court decisions that advanced the cause further: first, *Trinity Lutheran Church of Columbia v. Comer* in 2017 and especially *Espinoza v. Montana Department of Revenue* in 2020. Both cases dealt with the use of public funding to support activity at religious institutions (in the latter case, a voucher-like program explicitly) ruling under similar logic that explicitly denying funding to organizations precisely because they are religious violated the constitutional Free Exercise provision for religious liberty.[29] For the Koch-seeded and Bradley-funded Institute for Justice, the group behind *Zelman* in 2002 and that filed the *Espinoza* case years later, "the Free Exercise Clause was an indispensable tool for achieving its distinct agenda."[30]

The *Trinity* and *Espinoza* decisions were major news at the time, but their place in the strategic agenda of religious conservatives—particularly the politically engaged Christian evangelicals in mutual dependence with Trump that formed a core of the CNP—continued to be legitimized in elite policy circles. By the time of the *Trinity* decision in mid-2017, Betsy DeVos had personally become a figure of cultural derision after her rocky confirmation hearings earlier in the year, where she had been unable to discern between basic education concepts like academic growth and proficiency measures and suggested that one reason to arm teachers in schools was in the event that grizzly bears attacked.[31] *Saturday Night Live* ran a spoof of these moments with actress Kate McKinnon as "Betsy DeVos" saying, "I don't know anything about school. But I do think there should be a school. Probably a Jesus school."[32] DeVos's final approval margin was, embarrassingly, 51–50, the closest margin for any of Trump's cabinet nominations at any time during his term.[33]

As both a balm for those personal humiliations and a beat with which to keep the privatization march moving forward in steady time, DeVos turned to collect the same bona fides that helped to create the more favorable voucher evidence base almost from nothing in the 1990s. As an example, two months after the *Trinity* decision, and as part of a broader public relations effort to repair her postconfirmation image, DeVos appeared in her role as education secretary to give a major address as the keynote for yet another "Future of School Choice" conference at Harvard University's Program on Education Policy and Governance (PEPG), hosted by Paul Peterson.[34]

Rowdy student protests greeted her in Cambridge. A few feet to her left, students hung a banner with the words "White Supremacist," while a banner in the crowd read, "Our Students are Not 4 Sale."[35] When, during her speech, in which she stressed her school choice vision—and "due process" for students with religious values—she asked rhetorically, "What do we do? What does the future hold? More funding? Does that fix the problem?" An audience member yelled "Yes!" to large applause, while DeVos meekly continued, "The data would show otherwise," citing statistics from conservative scholars.[36] After that approximately thirty-minute address, DeVos sat down for another half-hour with Peterson himself in a session titled, "A Conversation on Empowering Parents with Betsy DeVos."[37] The entire event was funded by EdChoice (the former Milton and Rose D. Friedman Foundation) and the Charles M. Koch Foundation, which by then was also providing substantial funding to Peterson's institute for general operations.[38] After a reporter flagged the Koch connection on Twitter, Peterson's institute quietly removed the Koch name from its advance materials.[39]

"A MODERN ALOYSHA"

A few months before the DeVos school choice conference, Peterson's PEPG institute had hosted another event, at that time to honor the late Supreme Justice Antonin Scalia's legal philosophy. Not one but two of the institute's

Annual Reports (2017 and 2018) devoted space to reporting on the Scalia event, complete with old photos of Peterson with Scalia himself and Scalia's son Eugene. The 2018 report included an essay entitled, "Scalia and the Secret History of School Choice."[40] The 2017 report also announced a broad investment from the Charles M. Koch Foundation in Peterson's institute to fund emerging researchers on "education entrepreneurship and school reform in the United States."[41]

A funding prospectus submitted by Peterson in 2020 to the Koch Foundation for continued annual support for the PEPG institute—and included with the final Grant Agreement between Harvard and the Koch Foundation—lists among its accomplished graduates AEI's Hess and Peterson's school choice research proteges Jay P. Greene and Patrick J. Wolf, among many others. The prospectus also celebrated the outcomes of Peterson's work as "phenomenal, beyond-our-wildest dreams successes."[42] In an illustration of the reciprocal exchange of pedigree between Harvard's Peterson and the CNP network, the Koch proposal quotes the praise for Peterson that Betsy DeVos delivered at the 2017 Harvard event: "I want to recognize the significant and influential contributions to the advancements of school choice you've [Peterson] made over the years . . . few scholars have left such indelible fingerprint on this critical conversation."[43] Later, Peterson returned the flattery in his *Education Next* journal, with a glowing review of DeVos's memoir, in which he called her a "modern Aloysha," because like that classic Dostoevsky protagonist, he gushed, DeVos "holds fast to her integrity and principles" after the best that atheists can throw at them.[44]

All of this, then, is how the voucher cause came roaring back: the energies of the conservative counter-intelligentsia, CNP-influence and dollars on both the policy side and through the ever-reliable judicial front, combined with the culture war currents exposed by Donald Trump's candidacy and election. Educational privatization—"education freedom," as it was becoming known—is at once deeply subversive and deeply established. A unifying cause for the "shadow network," as the journalist Anne Nelson calls it, and an Ivy-garnished marquee at institutions as prestigious as Harvard and the clubby D.C. think tank world.[45] The reemergence of the

Peterson-led privateers in overt defense of Betsy DeVos on a personal level is a personified version of their defense of school vouchers even as the evidence against the policy accumulated at the exact same time. Maintaining DeVos's personal viability—she lasted all four years of the Trump term—and her policy priority's viability through events like Peterson's Harvard convening and the routine publication of buffering reports noted previously was critical to the political success of the movement while the courts did their work in *Trinity* and *Espinoza*.

Failing to establish the voucher agenda alone on the terms began in the mid-1990s under Peterson's direction—not just parents' rights but academic lifelines too—the pedigree of right-wing elite intellectualism, electoral success, and even the US Supreme Court with by-then dubious reputation as an honest broker, still managed to survive and advance through the Obama and into the Trump years. And in doing so, it not only kept educational privatization alive and well but covered for its return to deeper, more sinister, and separatist roots in the post-*Brown* landscape of the 1950s. While all of this was happening, other, less-public CNP affiliates like a group called the Alliance Defending Freedom were pushing for what would become an overt common cause to the voucher movement soon enough: renewed discrimination against individual children—in this case, LGBTQ+ families—in the name of parental rights, newly protected by the judiciary on the basis of religious Free Exercise.

"BOOTS ON THE GROUND"

On culture war policy issues like gay marriage and abortion fought on religious liberty grounds, Alliance Defending Freedom (ADF) is something of a "legal boots on the ground" corollary to the Institute for Justice.[46] And both, with leaders deeply networked in the CNP and funding from various Koch groups and in ADF's case also the DeVos family, play more operation-level roles to their more famous and visible cousin, the Federalist Society—itself also partially funded by Koch and DeVos family foundations.[47] But these issue-area and organizational lines between right-wing culture war and legal and education policy are malleable. Funded in part with seed money from various DeVos family organizations and that of the Princes (Betsy DeVos's parents), the Alliance at its founding shared office space with the Family Research Council (yet another CNP stalwart), which between 2000 and 2014 received more than $10 million from the DeVos and Prince Family Foundation as well.[48] C. Boydon Gray—an advisor to Paul Peterson's Harvard PEPG institute until his death in May 2023, and the matching donor to the Bradley Foundation's private school recruitment fund for the Washington, D.C., voucher program in the mid-2000s—was one of the so-called "four horsemen" advising George W. Bush on judicial appointments.[49] The other three "horsemen" were former attorney general Ed Meese, the Republican attorney Jay Sekulow, and the infamous influential Federalist Society chief Leonard Leo.[50] Meese, himself a Heritage Foundation fellow as of this writing, endorsed a 2018 elegy volume co-edited by Paul Peterson on Scalia's legacy published after the Harvard conference, called *Scalia's Constitution: Essays on Law and Education.*[51]

During the Trump years, the Alliance's main goal shifted away from preventing gay marriage outright (it lost that fight narrowly in 2015's 5–4 *Obergefell v. Hodges* Supreme Court decision) to preventing the application of equal LGBTQ+ rights in places of business and public service.[52] This particular policy goal was the cornerstone of the Trump administration's broader "religious freedom" agenda taking shape in 2017.[53] The first Trump Attorney General, Jeff Sessions, was both the ADF and the Administration's point person on that agenda, working with ADF in both closed door and formal briefings from the perspective that civil rights laws broadly, and LGBTQ+-equality in particular, forced Christians into choosing "between living out [their] faith and complying with the law."[54]

With ADF's direction, Sessions issued guidance for all federal agencies broadly outlining a religious liberty, Free Exercise interpretation of the right for accommodation to ignore civil rights laws when they conflicted with the ideology of the Religious Right.[55] In the guidance, dated October 6, 2017—days after Betsy DeVos appeared at Peterson's Harvard summit to insist on the right of parents to win religious liberty exemptions in the education policy arena—Sessions dictated that "Americans do not give up their freedom of religion by participating in the marketplace, partaking of the public square, or interacting with the government."[56] To lead the administration's key Office of Civil Rights in the Department of Health and Human Services, Trump chose a man named Roger Severino, a lawyer who had fought against sexual orientation and gender identity protections from his perch as the director of the DeVos Center for Religion and Civil Society at the Heritage Foundation.[57] Betsy DeVos herself removed guidance established by the Obama administration directing public schools to allow transgender bathroom use by gender identity and rolled back her predecessor's initiatives on racial disparities in school discipline.[58]

Up and down the Trump administration, key appointments in Justice, the Department of Education, and the Department of Health and Human Services were filled from the ranks of far-right religious ideological think tanks and activist organizations.[59] If neither DeVos within government, nor ADF, Heritage, or other CNP allies remaining nominally on the outside were able to use the federal apparatus to push large-scale funding streams for vouchers per se, they nevertheless laid the regulatory groundwork to promote Free Exercise exemptions to a variety of civil rights protections in and around tax-supported education as part of the broader push for "religious liberty" in government oversight.

"WHAT WE PLAN TO DO"

All of this was occurring, recall, exactly at the same time—within a matter of weeks, in some cases—that the academic results for DeVos's more narrow policy goal of school vouchers in the states were coming in publicly, and to devastating effect against that agenda. The religious freedom element of the CNP policy agenda—particularly its use to resist civil rights laws from racial to gender-related practices—well predated the voucher push. But by the time Trump and DeVos took office, they began to work not just in parallel but in sync.

Somewhere, then, between the halls of Harvard's PEPG and Stanford's Hoover Institution, the corridors of D.C. think tanks, and the nondescript offices of politically oriented Religious Right activism, the "values"-based push for vouchers that was always the underlying goal replaced academic success as the overt objective as well. Applied to publicly funded education, ADF's successful push to win legal guidance from the Trump administration holding that broad elements of civil rights protections in government entities could be ignored when in conflict with religious values, settled naturally within the modern voucher movement. Just as "the right of parents" during massive resistance to *Brown* appealed to segregationist legislators and activists as a potentially race-neutral pathway to avoid integration, so too does a Free Exercise vision of vouchers that parents not only may but—if taken radically—have the express *right to use* public dollars to self-segregate.

The temptation is to see all of this as a metaphor. It is instead a literal plan. A key tenet of ADF's religious liberty agenda was and remains a judicial ruling that states not only could offer taxpayer support for religious education (i.e., *Zelman's* ruling) but in fact must do so, if they used public funds for schooling purposes at all. They have said as much, as has Betsy DeVos. The ADF's Trump-era president, Michael Farris (a CNP member), worked for years across the country on a number of "parental rights" activities that included both lawsuits and legislative lobbying. On private donor calls held for wealthy conservative activists after Trump left office and unearthed by investigative reporting later, Farris pitched a legal strategy in which ADF filed lawsuits in lower courts that would end with the US Supreme Court declaring a constitutional right to school vouchers— nullifying Blaine Amendment prohibitions in individual states.[60] Betsy DeVos previewed the same strategy in an opinion piece for *USA Today* before leaving office. Under a subheader "What We Plan To Do Going Forward," she wrote, "We are especially eager for the Supreme Court to put an end to the 'last acceptable prejudice' made manifest in bigoted Blaine Amendments to thirty-seven constitutions that deny students the freedom to pursue faith-based education."[61] For both DeVos and the ADF, to which she and her family had given material and financial support, the animating force in this context was a put-upon sense of religious persecution for their vehement opposition to LGBTQ+ rights.[62]

IDEOLOGY OVER EVIDENCE

The Trump presidency breathed new life into the school vouchers movement. Just a few years earlier, even so prominent an advocate as Milwaukee's Howard Fuller, the "godfather of the school choice movement" had noted "any honest assessment would have to say that there hasn't been the deep, wholesale improvement in" academic results for his city. And no less than Paul Peterson, so prominent in these pages, had admitted that the push for vouchers had "stalled," in part because vouchers had failed, on the whole, to live up to the academic promise held by adherents to the market model for education. This was a problem driven, Peterson admitted, by "new voucher schools [that] were badly run, both fiscally and educationally."[63] And that was even before the truly negative voucher-induced results had come in.

Before that catastrophic evidence on voucher programs began to appear routinely in the second decade of the twenty-first century, state legislatures controlled largely but not entirely by Republicans were quietly building collections of voucher programs through vehicles such as tuition tax credits, special education vouchers, and eventually education savings accounts (ESAs) as well as traditional public appropriations for private school tuition.[64] These appeared at a regular clip of one or two a year, beginning with Milwaukee's in 1990, with Arizona and especially Florida maintaining long-standing and multiple iterations.[65] The Louisiana and Indiana programs that would show such devastating harm to student achievement—up to twice the size of COVID-19-induced test score drops years later—began in 2009 and 2010, respectively. Between the time Trump took office and the time he left, however, only a handful of states actively passed or expanded programs.

What Trump did was put the politics of exclusion and resentment back into the voucher movement. He did this through both his personal brand of calling white, Christian, and often male grievance into an overt political force, and through his appointment of leaders like Jeff Sessions, Betsy DeVos, and lesser-known figures like Roger Severino to head the Office of Civil Rights at HHS. The issue of "parental rights" had been a latent political force for years, rising with the Religious Right in the 1980s—and recall, from chapter 1, Betsy DeVos's own rise on the issue in the early 1990s—but it was during the Trump years that the right to essentially opt out of participating in any number of basic civil rights requirements became central to Republican ideology. Also during this time was the move from a libertarian fringe to right-wing, conservative orthodoxy. As a matter of education policy, this meant shifting the key rationale for vouchers away from academic improvements and to a means to avoid adhering to civil rights guidance. In that, vouchers returned ideologically and politically to their appeal when Milton Friedman first proposed them in the late 1950s, in the wake of *Brown v. Board of Education*.

Many of the foot soldiers in that march toward new ideological ground were the same members of the CNP that had developed a conservative "counter-intelligentsia" in the 1980s and early 1990s. Alongside the same individual research-advocates who, by creating a supposed evidence base for vouchers, had done so much to propel vouchers forward toward the *Zelman* decision in 2002. During the lean years of evidence—the disastrous voucher results coming in waves after 2012—this effort was sustained in no small part by the sheer prestige of outlets like Harvard's Program on Education Policy and Governance and Stanford's Hoover Institution, which nourished the policy agenda while Trump officials and the Supreme Court, in *Trinity* and *Espinoza*, respectively, created regulatory and judicial scaffolding for the Free Exercise, religious liberty school choice push that was to come.

MOVING PICTURES

Absent the kind of evidence they had once been able to assemble in the run up to *Zelman*, voucher pushers turned not only to the buffering and bundling method of distributing reports on obscure measures of voucher success described previously and in chapter 4 but to stories and pictures.[66] They turned to marketing. Nothing illustrates the interplay between large-dollar, CNP voucher activism, research, and messaging like the 2019 film *Miss Virginia*. Recall from chapter 3, the Washington, D.C., voucher activist

Virginia Walden Ford, whose story of a desperate search for a high-quality education for her children became the backstory for the movie, as did the villainous liberals in D.C. dramatically cast to stop her ability to choose. The film was produced by The Moving Picture Institute, a State Policy Network affiliate with financial backing from other CNP member groups, including the Bradley Foundation, DonorsTrust, the Mercer family, and foundations backed by the Scaife and Koch organizations.[67] Marketing for *Miss Virginia* included special screenings by EdChoice, on whose board Virginia Walden Ford sat and, as of this writing, remains.[68] None too subtle, the Institute for Justice—the voucher movement's legal defense group, seeded with personal donations from Charles Koch—itself held such screenings as well.[69]

As if that origin story were not enough, the Heritage Foundation hosted an event prior to the film's distribution, which served nominally for Virginia Walden Ford to receive an advocacy award. The ceremony served also for Betsy DeVos to give another friendly keynote on perils of resisting the voucher movement and to assuage any fears about the academic harm voucher research was at that moment uncovering.[70] Shrugging off negative impacts released by the US Department of Education's independent evaluation of D.C.'s voucher program in 2018, while she was secretary, DeVos noted, "Anytime we change anything, it takes awhile to get up to speed" (the program was created in 2004).[71] As if to provide the assurance of intellectual pedigree, DeVos's fellow panelist Patrick Wolf—the former Peterson student and the evaluator of Milwaukee, Louisiana, and the first iteration of D.C. vouchers—implied the negative results were a wash: "In some of the studies, [students] end up ahead. In some of them, they've just recovered the lost ground on the test score side." But "the real clear advantage for the choice kids" was to be found later, Wolf insisted, on non-academic outcomes.[72] On that Heritage panel, then, with Ford, DeVos, and Wolf each playing their respective role as mother, champion of parents, and certified expert, the full-scale preservation strategy for the voucher movement was on display. Nowhere in *Miss Virginia*, nor on the Heritage panel, was the political craft behind Ford's group, D.C. Parents for School Choice, ever mentioned. None of these encomia included the television ads that Ford's

"D.C. Parents" ran during the legislative fight over the original D.C. voucher program, targeting key votes like those of Senator Edward Kennedy by accusing him of betraying his brothers' legacy on civil rights by opposing vouchers. Nowhere was included the group's campaign that flipped the historical script and compared Kennedy and other voucher opponents to the segregationist Bull Conner with his Birmingham firehoses.[73]

The cruel irony of such efforts to preserve, protect, and defend school vouchers during a period of disintegrating evidence-based rationale for their expansion is that, as the Trump-era wound down, the legal and administrative groundwork laid for a religious liberty motivation became an engine of aggression and attack. On the eve of the COVID-19 pandemic, the last word on voucher academic outcomes was test score losses for voucher participants that rivaled what the pandemic would do to test scores over the next three years. Forces unleashed by Trump officials in the effort dictated by so-called religious liberty groups like the Alliance Defending Freedom and perhaps—though less quantifiable—through events like the Charlottesville white supremacy marches, the Brett Kavanaugh hearings, the *Access Hollywood* tapes, and the Black Lives Matter protests would lean the voucher movement fully into the sway of overwhelmingly white religious nationalism.

7

Values

*To get universal school choice, you really need to operate
from a premise of universal public school distrust.*

—CHRISTOPHER F. RUFO, 2022

In March of 2022, I took a call from NBC News asking for comment on a
new school voucher push in my home state of Michigan, largely underwritten by Betsy DeVos. The plan, known officially as "Let MI Kids Learn,"
intended to exploit a constitutional loophole in the state's law-making
process that allowed the legislature to create a law without the governor's
signature if it was submitted to the chamber by direct voter petition.[1] The
petition, structured as a tax credit system, would create a voucher program
covering private tuition and additional allowable expenses like tutoring and
textbooks. It essentially mirrored the bill that the Republican legislature
had passed in late 2021 before it was vetoed by the Democratic governor
Gretchen Whitmer. Under the new pivot, Whitmer's signature would no
longer be necessary.

My comments to NBC reflected some incredulity that the policy push
was continuing both in Michigan and beyond. I noted the recent devastating effects that voucher plans had on student outcomes (detailed in this
book in chapter 5), with those studies linked to in the report. And I said

DeVos's plan was about "creating a narrative that public schools are teaching our children things that we—whatever 'we' means—collectively disagree with or are skeptical about."[2] I was beginning my eighteenth year in the professional evaluation community working on voucher programs and broader school choice studies. Little did I know, however, what was about to come.

WHAT'S LOCAL IS NATIONAL

Between March 2022 and March 2023, more than one hundred bills related to school vouchers appeared in forty states, with seven new states creating new voucher programs and nine more expanding existing efforts. The actual passage rate was largely a red state phenomenon—all but two were won by Donald Trump in 2020—but that did not stop EdChoice (the former Milton and Rose D. Friedman Foundation) from declaring 2023 the "Year of Universal Choice" for its unprecedented number of programs operating without income limits on participation.[3] There is no question that, for the sheer volume of bills sponsored and passed, more state legislatures adopted new or expanded voucher plans between the 2022 and 2023 sessions than any previous to date.[4]

Republican lawmakers packaged most of these new bills as "education savings accounts": programs that, like DeVos's effort in Michigan, were a voucher-plus design that included the private school tuition component like those discussed in this book, plus additional expenses related to private school attendance or homeschool education.[5] The technical distinction is minor—simply reflecting what, apart from private tuition, is covered as a nonpublic expense—but the politics of the name mattered. Pollsters have found that voters are more sympathetic to voucher schemes when surveys frame the question as a matter of simply allowing parents to send their children to the school of their choice (public or private). But voters are deeply skeptical when the word "voucher" is used, or the question notes that the plans send public dollars to private or religious schools.[6]

In Michigan, the same right-wing consultants hired by the DeVos operation to push her voucher proposal were at the same time also running opposition to a ballot proposal to enshrine reproductive freedom into the state's constitution in the wake of the *Dobbs v. Jackson Women's Health Organization*.[7] This was no mere reflection of scarce personnel able and willing to work on statewide ballot drives. The lead consultant, a man named Fred Wszolek, was also the director of a DeVos-backed Super PAC called Michigan Strong, which was working on behalf of the DeVos-endorsed gubernatorial candidate Tudor Dixon.[8] In addition to strong opposition to abortion rights—she told an interviewer during the campaign that she opposed abortion in even cases of rape or incest of a minor child because there could be "healing through that baby"—Dixon's campaign's education platform was built not only on the DeVos voucher plan but the broader notion of "parents' rights" beginning to re-form in conservative politics.[9] At one point, Dixon called a press conference outside the Michigan Department of Education to demand the agency take down training videos purporting to show "grooming" on LGBTQ+ issues, and offered to send a young reporter examples of what she deemed to be pornography in schools.[10]

The DeVos-Dixon political campaign in Michigan during the fall of 2022 then, with its focus on vouchers, opposition to reproductive rights, and a broad push to ban books with so-called pornographic content (namely, books with LGBTQ+ issues featured), perfectly encapsulated the "education freedom" push that DeVos and the larger Council for National Policy network were backing at the same time.[11] The Michigan education training videos to which Dixon objected had been unearthed from an obscure link on the department's website by the conservative provocateur Christopher F. Rufo—the filmmaker whose career had been launched by the Koch-funded, State Policy Network affiliate Moving Pictures Institute, which also produced the Virginia Walden Ford film *Miss Virginia*.[12] It was Rufo who, in a 2020 appearance on Fox News's *Tucker Carlson Tonight* program, almost single-handedly ignited the right-wing outrage over the notion of *critical race theory* instruction in American public schools.[13] Carlson booked Rufo on the show after a series of articles the latter had produced for the Manhattan Institute—the conservative think tank funded by the Lynde and Harry Bradley Foundation, among many others.[14] Betsy DeVos pointed to one of those articles, called "Woke Elementary," in her 2022 book. There, DeVos devoted eight of the thirty pages in her penultimate chapter, ostensibly on COVID-19 school policy, to what she called the "racialized, divisive ideas" and the "racist ideology" behind critical race theory.[15]

Rufo's focus on issues of race and gender in public school classrooms was not only part of a larger right-wing strategy in a broad struggle within American politics but very specifically part of the effort to undermine confidence in American public schools. He has made no secret of that effort. In a 2022 speech entitled, "Laying Siege to the Institutions," Rufo declared, "To get universal school choice, you really need to operate from a premise of universal public school distrust."[16] He made that speech at Hillsdale College, the far-Right Michigan college at the center of most of the K–12 culture war debates in American education, whose president, at the time of this writing, is also a member of the Council for National Policy (CNP).[17]

WHAT ABOUT "WOKE"?

If Christopher Rufo has a benefactor in elected office, it is Florida governor Ron DeSantis—a former candidate in the 2024 presidential election. Although attacks on the so-called "woke" agenda on issues of racial and gender diversity are staples of Republican public postering, no other Republican official has leaned into attacks on the "woke agenda" like DeSantis, who has gone so far as to appoint Rufo to prominent advisory positions in his state.[18] DeSantis pushed a *Stop the W.O.K.E. Act* to "give businesses, employees, children and families tools to fight back against woke indoctrination" specifically on the front opened by Rufo on critical race theory.[19] In a much-mocked speech, the governor cribbed from Winston Churchill's famous "We Shall Fight on the Beaches" speech, declaring, "We will fight the woke in the schools. We will fight the woke in the legislature. We will fight the woke in the corporations," among a number of other supposed battlefields.[20]

As if to prove Rufo's broader point, the key policy victory for Ron DeSantis during the 2023 session was precisely his expansion of Florida's voucher program to universal status and the largest in the nation.[21] The program soon began to fund primarily existing private school students and approve expenditures on questionable items such as big-screen televisions, kayaks, and Disney World field trips through its structure as an education savings account.[22] Prior to that expansion, Florida's voucher program made national news for open hostility among many of its recipient schools to LGBTQ+ students, families, and teachers.[23]

Thus the "escape velocity" of school vouchers legislation making 2023 the "year of universal choice," celebrated by Friedman's acolytes at Ed-Choice, must then be considered exactly alongside book bans, salvos on issues of race and diversity, gender identity, and sexuality. Betsy DeVos's voucher plan, and her hand-picked candidate, Tudor Dixon, lost in Michigan in 2022 on these issues. But in Ron DeSantis's Florida, and in other red states, the package of voucher bills and culture war struggles has succeeded mightily. In Arkansas and Iowa, for example, where (respectively) Republican governors Sarah Huckabee Sanders and Kim Reynolds pushed new voucher bills through hesitant state legislatures in early 2023, both laws either contained (in the former case) or were soon followed by (in the latter) new restrictions on the teaching of race, on issues related to gender identity, and on certain books in public schools and spaces.[24] In Texas, where rural Republicans in the House of Representatives blocked the bill for reasons of their own, the key voucher legislation included detailed prohibitions on issues related to race and gender in the state's traditional public schools.[25]

In all three states, a very public presence for Betsy DeVos's American Federation for Children, with vast new spending on legislative races (including Republican primaries) was the subject of national reporting.[26] Her chief lobbyist, a thirtysomething man named Corey DeAngelis—an advisee of Paul Peterson's former students Jay Greene and Patrick Wolf, and graduate of the University of Arkansas Department of Education Reform, set up by the Walton family—had personal meetings with the governors in Arkansas, Iowa, Texas, Oklahoma, and elsewhere and then posted selfies with each of those leaders on social media.[27] DeVos's organization spent more than $9 million—$2.5 million from DeVos and her husband, Dick, alone—on political organizing leading up to the 2023 session.[28] These efforts included ousting the anti-voucher Education Committee chair of the Iowa House of Representatives in the state's *Republican* primary.[29]

All told, in addition to the one-hundred-plus voucher proposals between the 2022 and 2023 legislative sessions, more than 140 pieces of so-called "parental rights" legislation on topics like race and gender identity, and more than eighty pieces of book ban legislation for content on similar topics, also appeared in state legislatures.[30] And the Council for National Policy's network, notably rooted at the Heritage Foundation on the issue, ran substantial interference on all of these topics. At Heritage, Jay Greene (alongside a roster of assistants and coauthors), churned out a veritable mass production of self-proclaimed studies and reports that functioned as something of a political campaign style war room on issues of "educational freedom" ranging from vouchers to gender identity to book bans—many targeted specifically to arm Republican backers with new talking points. In 2022 and 2023 Greene's Heritage publications included titles such as the following:

EMPOWERING PARENTS WITH SCHOOL CHOICE REDUCES "WOKE-ISM"
   IN EDUCATION
AUTHORITARIANS SLANDER PARENT GROUPS AS BOOK BANNERS
ARE SCHOOL LIBRARIES BANNING THOUSANDS OF BOOKS? HERE'S WHY
   YOU SHOULDN'T TRUST THE LEFT'S NARRATIVE
SCHOOL CHOICE PRIMARILY BENEFITS STUDENTS WHO WEREN'T
   ALREADY IN PUBLIC SCHOOLS
DOES SCHOOL CHOICE AFFECT PRIVATE SCHOOL TUITION?
DOES "GENDER-AFFIRMING CARE" FOR TRANS KIDS ACTUALLY REDUCE
   SUICIDE? HERE'S WHAT THE DATA SAY

In addition to the reports noted previously that specifically pushed back against the narrative of book bans, two of the reports addressed real-time criticisms of voucher legislation in the states. The report on school choice beneficiaries singled out criticism from me specifically, after I pointed out in media interviews that data on voucher programs indicate an overwhelming majority of new users in expanded programs had already been in private school (in Florida, for example, after DeSantis's expansion, 69 percent of users had already been in private school prior to receiving a voucher), and after reporters in Texas noted that the issue of prior private enrollment was a potential stumbling block to passing the bill.[31] The report on private school tuition was pushback to a series of data released on social media by Princeton professor Jennifer Jennings, who had tracked tuition increases reported by journalists covering the aftermath of voucher bill passage.[32] In the run-up to the 2023 legislative push, Greene's Heritage operation released an "Education Freedom Report Card," ranking each state on school choice policy along a dimension aligning with what its summary called "Milton Friedman's vision." The top state on the *Heritage* index was Florida, and model legislation suggested by the report sent readers to sample bills from the Independent Women's Forum (an organization funded by the Koch network), the Goldwater Institute (Arizona's contribution to the State Policy Network), the Heritage Foundation itself, and the ever-present Institute for Justice.[33]

THE LINKS TO DOBBS

It is important to pause in the middle of this litany of new voucher plans, and of the larger education freedom agenda, to mark the destruction of the federal right to reproductive autonomy. The Supreme Court ruling in *Dobbs v. Jackson Women's Health Organization* occurred precisely at the same time, and through the same energy and much of the same financial backing as the "year of universal choice" in education. Michigan's ballot initiatives for so-called education freedom and against reproductive freedom were run by the same person, in the same office, at the same time; this is only one embodiment of that shared reality.

In the most proximate sense, the *Dobbs* decision was handed down the same week in June 2022, by the same six justices, as another decision: *Carson v. Makin*, which extended the Free Exercise rulings (see chapter 6) in *Trinity v. Lutheran Church of Columbia, Inc. v. Comer* (2017), and *Espinoza v. Montana Department of Revenue* (2020). Under *Carson*, states with private school tuition assistance programs cannot exclude schools either for their religious status or, extending earlier rulings, for their use of taxpayer funds for religious purposes. In essence, *Carson* requires states with voucher programs to now permit payments for religious education, not just payments to religious schools per se.[34] It had been filed initially by a right-wing religious group called the Free Liberty Institute, along with the Institute for Justice.[35]

Throughout the fall of 2022 and spring of 2023, armed with *Dobbs* as well as *Carson*, legislators in many of the same states expanding so-called education freedom began to restrict reproductive freedom with the same pens. In Florida, for example, Ron DeSantis signed a six-week ban on abortions less than two weeks after signing his massive voucher expansion.[36] In Iowa, Kim Reynolds signed a similar six-week ban a few months after she signed the state's new voucher program into law.[37] In Arkansas, a near-total ban on abortions previously passed by the legislature went into effect the day the Supreme Court announced *Dobbs*. Six months later, and three weeks after Sarah Huckabee Sanders signed her voucher bill, the state's legislature voted down proposed incest and medical exemptions to its newly effective ban. That vote occurred ten days after Sanders signed a bill creating a state monument near the capitol to the number of abortions performed in the state prior to the *Dobbs* decision.[38] In all, twenty-four states moved to fully ban or severely restrict abortion in the year following *Dobbs*—the same year dubbed by voucher advocates as the "year of universal choice."[39]

ROLLING BACK LGBTQ+ RIGHTS

Deep and longstanding cleavages on the issues of race, gender, and sexuality in American political life became reflected in both law and public policy at precisely the same moments as new expansions in educational privatization. Those developments are anything but historical accidents. Recall from chapter 6 the Alliance Defending Freedom, which, alongside the Institute for Justice on school choice matters, functions as something of a boots-on-the-ground platoon of lawyers providing the tactical support for larger strategic objectives laid out by the more prominent Federalist Society. The history of Supreme Court jurisprudence since the 1990s alone reflects all three organizations in active advocacy and coordination over each of the major litigations of the time on issues pertaining to education, gender, and the priorities of the Religious Right that connect them.[40]

Funded with seed money from multiple DeVos family foundations, the Alliance Defending Freedom's particular brand of political self-pity—that requirements for the equal treatment of LGBTQ+ citizens are an onerous burden on Free Exercise—is an especially salient theme in the school voucher movement.[41] The same is true for the Trump presidency, which provided the majority for *Dobbs* at the Supreme Court while the Alliance Defending Freedom was also changing the regulatory structure of US Department of Education and other agencies to reflect what amounted to a religious right to discriminate.[42] Before and after her term as Trump's education secretary, Betsy DeVos made the rollback of LGBTQ+ protections in schools and in higher education—in the name of religious freedom—a corresponding priority for both federal policy and federal dollars. She made national news early in her tenure for refusing to commit to LGBTQ+ protections in any new federal school choice push she planned to back, coyly relying on opaque statutory language where enforcement and interpretation lay at the discretion of the very regulatory framework the ADF was working at the same time to change.[43]

While DeVos was in federal office, that legal-policy campaign against LGTBQ+ equality in the states in spaces of education shifted to physical contexts that evoked safety, comfort, and above all the ever-present and ever-charged call of parental rights. School bathrooms, school locker rooms, and athletic playing fields became the battlegrounds. With model legislation it called the "Student Physical Privacy Act," the Alliance Defending Freedom ghost-wrote bills introduced in fifteen states during the first year of the Trump administration that intended to force transgender people to use bathrooms consistent with their birth gender.[44] For the ADF, the focus on schools is strategic: "ADF has long viewed public schools as an ideal testing ground for their ideas," wrote the legal reporter Mark Joseph Stern. "ADF has a clear vision of how these students should act, and how their bodies should look, and it tried to conscript schools to enforce that vision."[45] Representative Mike Johnson, elected as Speaker of the US House of

Representatives in October 2023, was until 2010 a staff attorney for ADF. His case work in that role included partnership with a firm called *Exodus*, which specialized in "conversion therapy" for LGBTQ+ people.[46]

The ADF's public presence is equally focused. During the drafting of this chapter, for example, on a representative day the Alliance's X (formerly Twitter) account blared, "Fully two thirds of American voters oppose biological males who identify as women competing in women's athletics."[47] The same day as the ADF's posts, the account attributed to Betsy DeVos exhorted: "We can, we must, we will save women's sports!"[48] Also that day, ADF's feed celebrated its involvement in a case that would prevent access to the abortion pill mifepristone, and its role in a case against what it called "un-American" school district rule forcing "students to view everyone and everything through the lens of race."[49] Two weeks earlier, the *Washington Post* broke the story of ADF's long-term plan to litigate an interpretation of the Free Exercise clause that would extend *Espinoza* and *Carson* into mandatory school vouchers in states that fund (as all do) public school systems. That is the same plan previewed by Betsy DeVos in an opinion column before she left office.[50]

MOMS FOR LIBERTY

The freshest face for this dark money movement to wrap school vouchers and culture war issues into one political operation is an organization known as Moms for Liberty. The group formed in 2021 ostensibly as an outfit of suburban mothers and school board members in Florida concerned over the direction of public schools on issues related to pandemic-era policies like masking, vaccines, and school shutdowns. Within two years it grew to include nearly 300 local chapters with more than 120,000 members nationwide. A particularly aggressive force in local school board and—following the Council for National Policy playbook—state legislative elections, Moms for Liberty succeeded throughout the 2022 campaign cycle and the 2023 legislative sessions by focusing on ADF-style topics like LGTBQ+ content in school library books and classroom instruction, the teaching of critical race theory topics, bathroom access for transgender children, and other issues it calls determinative of "parent power."[51] Its local success on these issues made it the parents' rights version of the Obama-era Tea Party organizations that won major local statehouse victories and heavily influenced the 2010 federal midterms.

Whatever its publicly postured origin story as a group of moms raising money through T-shirt sales and small dollar donations, Moms for Liberty is a 501(c)(4) organization with deep ties to right-wing donors, the Ron DeSantis political operation in Florida, and an attentive conservative media following.[52] As early in its history as June 2021, the group hosted a fundraiser featuring the former Fox News personality Megyn Kelly, with tickets ranging from $50 entry to $20,000 packages.[53] Its first annual summit in the summer of 2022 featured Governor DeSantis, former Trump Health and Human Services and conservative political figure Ben Carson, Florida Senator and head of the National Republican Senate Campaign Committee Rick Scott, and Betsy DeVos, whose speech was titled "End the [U.S.] Education Department" she once led.[54]

The financial backer of the 2022 summit at the "Presenting" level was the CNP's Leadership Institute, led by CNP founding member Morton Blackwell, which trains young conservative activists. The "Bronze" level funder was none other than the Heritage Foundation, which had recently sponsored the CNP's own summit earlier in the year.[55] Cosponsoring the summit with Heritage at the "Bronze" level was a group called Parents Defending Education. That group, focusing on book bans and other activities related to educational content, and which also hosts links to Moms for Liberty local chapters on its website, joined Moms for Liberty on activities like lobbying the US Department of Education to end a grant program funding instructional materials on the horrors of slavery.[56] The Parents Defending Education founder and, as of this writing, director, is Nicole Neilly, who in the revolving door world of Koch-network and CNP staffing was previously the director of the Koch organization Independent Women's Forum, and prior to that was on the staff at the Cato Institute.[57]

By its 2023 summit, which it called its "Joyful Warriors" summit, Moms for Liberty was so prominent in Republican Party politics that it was a veritable must-attend for all of the major presidential candidates, including

DeSantis, former South Carolina Governor Nikki Haley, and Donald Trump.[58] Also giving speeches were Heritage Foundation president and CNP board governor Kevin Roberts, and the superintendents of Florida, Arkansas, and Oklahoma state departments of education: Manny Diaz, Jacob Oliva, and Ryan Walters, respectively.[59] In their joint appearance, the superintendents stressed school vouchers and other school choice initiatives in their home states, with Diaz quoting the group's slogan, "We don't co-parent with the government" to describe Florida's school choice policy agenda.[60] As *Chalkbeat* summarized the three-day event: "Republican politicians, far-right activists, and aspiring local school board members are focused on opposing comprehensive sex education and inclusive gender identity policies in schools as they work to expand school-choice programs that will allow families to opt out of their public education systems."[61] DeSantis's speech was representative, tying public school curricular content on issues he called "that type of garbage in our schools" like drag queens, "pedophilia," and "hard core pornography," as one motivation for his voucher program: "Parents have a fundamental right to direct the education and upbringing of their children. And that means being involved in what is being taught in their school. And it also means that every parent in this country should have the wherewithal to be able to send their kids to the school of their choice. We've made that a reality in Florida. We signed universal education savings account legislation so the money will follow the student and the parent."[62]

A few months later, Moms for Liberty became entangled in its own sex scandal. Christian Ziegler, Florida GOP state chairperson and husband of Moms for Liberty cofounder Bridget Ziegler, fell under criminal investigation in that state for allegedly sexually assaulting a woman with whom the couple had engaged in three-way sexual activity. The apparent hypocrisy of politically targeting LGBTQ issues while engaging in (consensual) bisexual behavior created substantial outcry in the fall of 2023 and may have ended the political careers of both Zieglers—one-time allies of Governor DeSantis as well.[63] Future election cycles will determine the long-term influence of Moms for Liberty as a player in right-wing politics, but history will record that the group reached its national notoriety at the very same moment that school vouchers reached new legislative heights in red states across the country.

EDUCATION FREEDOM TODAY

This then, is the education freedom agenda in its entirety: increasingly overt conflict on issues of race, gender, and sexuality with the express intent of devaluing public schools as a civic institution and reorienting the notion of education from a public good to a private enterprise. The "year of universal choice" expansion of school voucher programs in state legislatures culminated a thirty-month period from the spring of 2021 through fall of 2023 that also saw an explosion of legislation and policy decision-making of overt hostility to LGBTQ+ families, to curricular focuses on the issue of race, and to transgender identity broadly. And with these changes in governance across the states rose the political force of Moms for Liberty and its affiliates. The Council for National Policy efforts—most visibly the Heritage Foundation, the Koch network, and Betsy DeVos—marks the through-line to it all and to the national-historic moment that saw at the same time the end to a federal, constitutional right to reproductive freedom.

The school voucher movement is the parents' rights movement, and the parents' rights movement is religious nationalism.[64]

With these big, momentous political currents, a final glance backward at the role of specialists and of the meaning of facts and of evidence may seem overly technical or perhaps a question of an author's self-indulgence. But the fundamental message of this book is the absolute dependence of thirty years of right-wing policymaking in education on a small, narrow band of soldier-scholars forming the "counter-intelligentsia" intended by conservative donors so many years ago. From the authors of influential books funded by some of the most prominent players in conservative American politics, to researchers ensconced in otherwise obscure academic departments quietly endowed with millions of dollars from agenda-oriented philanthropists, to the gilded halls of Stanford, Harvard, and other pillars of the nation's university infrastructure, to the new breed of lobbyists with words like "research" or "fellow" in their official job titles at advocacy organizations disguised as think tanks: whether readers of this book or even I myself claim that the creation of a supposed evidence base to motivate *education freedom* is key to its success, the point is that its dearest ideologues believe that it is.

That belief is why Clint Bolick, working from Koch-seed funding, arranged for Harvard's Paul Peterson to testify during Wisconsin's voucher expansion.[65] It is why Ken Starr and Bolick's Institute for Justice, working on the Bradley Foundation's dime, led their Supreme Court brief with a "crisis in Cleveland" narrative based on public school data. It is why voucher advocates cited Peterson before the hallowed Supreme Court in *Zelman*, and why Justice Sandra Day O'Connor quoted Peterson in her concurrence. It is why a School Choice Demonstration Project exists at the University of Arkansas, and why that Demonstration Project led three politically significant multiyear evaluations of Milwaukee, Washington, D.C., and Louisiana vouchers. It is why Betsy DeVos cited eleven different studies from Peterson or researchers directly connected to him in her 2022 book, *Hostages No More*. It is why the main character in the Koch-funded *Miss Virginia* film, screened at right-wing outlets across the country, without mentioning Paul Peterson by name referred nevertheless to miracle results from his studies in Cleveland and Milwaukee. And it is why the last line of the film isn't a Milton Friedman quote or the words of a philosopher, but a data point from advocacy research on the Washington, D.C., voucher program.

The mere creation of a right-wing political agenda itself hardly depends on concepts like evidence or data. But its implementation does. I began this book by noting that the rush to war in Iraq in late 2002 and early 2003 was based not only on abstract concepts like freedom and liberty for the Iraqi people but on a steady stream of purported evidence about Saddam Hussein's possession of weapons of mass destruction. The march to privatize education shares more in common with the run-up to war in Iraq than just the think tanks like the American Enterprise Institute or conservative intellectuals pushing both.[66] The common themes are the appearance of expertise, the value of pedigree and prestige among those making the case, the use of quick, unvetted data points culled from intelligence chatter (in the Iraq case) or preliminary reports (in the case of vouchers) at key decision-points ranging from legislative resolutions to judicial rulings. And above all, what Operation Iraqi Freedom shared with the longer march toward so-called education freedom is the direct and deliberate creation of a base of dubious facts to support a predetermined ideological objective.

A second contemporary parallel is the opioid crisis. As with the Iraq War, whole volumes of journalism, history, and first-hand testimony now detail the ravages that an industry-sponsored campaign to pharmaceutically eliminate pain brought to communities across the country. And with those accounts comes the unmistakable conclusion that to do so required a fundamental altering of established medical practice and the clinical use of opiates in everyday life. It was "imperative," as one consultant wrote in a memo to the infamous Sackler family behind Purdue Pharma's Oxycontin brand, "that we establish a literature," to upend perceived conventional wisdom and push opiates not just for palliative care but toward "the broadest range of use," making pain the "5th vital sign" for patient care.[67] One might call that plan, in a word, *universal*.

All of that despite, in all three instances, the extraordinary caution urged by other career specialists. That the creation of an evidence base to support an ideological push for school vouchers is directly and inextricably tied to the effort to end reproductive rights, to anti-LGBTQ+ policies and book bans, to efforts to mute a race-conscious telling of American history, and to a final goal of undermining public education is a warning sign that something truly radical is taking place. One need not be fluent in every study of the harm vouchers have done thus far, as surveyed in the Introduction to this book, to hear the storm sirens. Ideological data collection and industry-backed research can collect a few facts that are in isolation right but taken together wrong. Evidence is not the same thing as truth. The very word "freedom," so invoked across the political spectrum, should bring, if not doubt, a healthy degree of skepticism.

What kind of freedom makes the use of tax dollars to attend religious school sacred over the right of half the population to control the destiny of their own bodies? To marry whom they wish? To read what they will? What standard of evidence is sufficient to alter the educational histories of millions of children, when the chief bearers of that standard are propelled by ideology and righteous sense of moral valor? If school choice is indeed "the civil rights issue of our time," as the right-wing saying goes, whose rights and even whose history is that declaration about to supplant? When have answers to the basic problems of equity, governance, and human rights ever been solved with a single panacea, as two famous scholars backed by the Bradley Foundation once declared school choice policy to be?[68] One need not have definitive answers to these questions, nor defend every element of public education, to be nevertheless aghast at the empty works and promises of school voucher advocacy. Whether in a "Mission Accomplished" banner hung from an aircraft carrier, or in a prescription pad scribble promising a quick fix to chronic pain, or in the bumper sticker jingo "fund students not systems" to avoid the tough questions of tolerance and community, the first response is the same: if it sounds too good to be true, it probably is.

Epilogue

Enabling

If you're a candidate or lawmaker who opposes school choice
and freedom in education—you're a target.

—AMERICAN FEDERATION FOR CHILDREN PRESS RELEASE
ON THE FORMATION OF A NEW SUPER PAC, 2023

In the spring of 2023, at a Nashville retreat for conservative donors assembled by the Republican National Committee, an activist lawyer named Cleta Mitchell gave a fifty-slide presentation called "A Level Playing Field for 2024." The presentation, obtained by the *Washington Post*, stressed an issue raised by right-wing activists for several recent cycles, and spearheaded by Mitchell herself across the country: namely, the issue of "election integrity." The presentation focused on voter-prevention strategies like opposition to same-day registration and automatic ballot mailing, as well as the prohibition of voting on college campuses.[1] These were tactics Mitchell had pushed before, in trainings prior to the 2022 midterms, where she also advocated for rigorous poll watching operations.[2] Such stoking "stop the steal" outrage was otherwise nothing new: Mitchell had joined Donald Trump on his infamous phone call to Georgia officials, whom the president was pressuring to "find" enough votes to alter the 2020 election, and her name appeared throughout the January 6th congressional investigation report.[3] Both then, and still now as of this writing, Cleta Mitchell is also an officer on the board of directors for the Lynde and Harry Bradley Foundation.[4]

A 2021 investigative report by the *New Yorker* on "the big money behind the Big Lie" of Trump's 2020 victory named the Bradley Foundation as "the extraordinary force" convening multiple actors we have encountered in this book, including the American Legislative Exchange Council (ALEC) and Heritage Action, the political arm of the Heritage Foundation.[5] Cleta Mitchell herself is reportedly a member of the Council for National Policy, along with the Bradley Foundation's president, Richard Graber.[6] Dating back to Horace Mann, advocates for public schooling have long philosophically argued that a robust democracy relies on a well-educated citizenry and that public schooling plays a critical role in meeting that need.[7] But here, that theoretical proposition becomes literal.

Mitchell's work on poll watching and voter restriction activity, and that of the Bradley Foundation and Heritage Action, are overt and illustrative examples of the way that the privatization of American schooling and restrictions basic democratic processes are mutually dependent outcomes. But they are hardly unique. From ending reproductive rights to restricting LGBTQ+ rights, to litigating voucher cases themselves—efforts outlined in chapters 6 and 7 of this book—the Alliance Defending Freedom, the Federalist Society, and the Institute for Justice all at various times relied heavily on what amounts to political capture of the judiciary, the federal regulatory apparatus, and state lawmaking processes.

VOTING AND ELECTIONS

If the dominant theme of this book is the utter inseparability of right-wing politics and conservative policy formation in the education arena, then the last message of these pages will be: it is now all the more so. There would and will be no more success for the so-called parents' rights agenda—whether for school vouchers, for book bans in school libraries, for aggressively conservative school bathroom policies or restrictions on classroom curricula—without the intellectual aid and comfort provided by the soldier-scholar experts in and around the Council for National Policy (CNP) and its vast, aligned network of libertarians and religious nationalists. The policy depends on the politics, and the politics depend on the policy.

Although erstwhile Trump allies like Betsy DeVos and the Koch organization Americans for Prosperity publicly distanced themselves from election denial causes, the broader strategic interest remains in achieving right-wing policy objectives through influencing democratic processes ranging from voting guidelines to state and federal legislative redistricting.[8] The Koch network in particular, and the CNP in general, has long prioritized state elections, and substantial reporting documents the particular interest that conservative activists have in state legislatures as a means to push right-wing policy.[9] As the 2023 legislative session wrapped up, Betsy DeVos's American Federation for Children announced the formation of a Super PAC to influence state legislative races across the country in the 2024 election cycle. "If you're a candidate or lawmaker" opposing vouchers, announced the group's executive director, "you're a target."[10] The group also circulated an investor slide deck, noting that it had mustered $250 million between 2010 and 2023—the "most deployed resources"—to score "200+" legislative victories in 26 states and 1,828 electoral victories in 19 states to bolster its school choice agenda.[11] This is a scope and bankroll beyond anything a genuine grassroots organization could ever dream.

More examples abound, like local theaters of combat that follow a universal declaration of war. Witness the Heritage Foundation's president Kevin Roberts, ahead of the 2024 election, dispensing with any pretense to an organizational wall and taking on the additional duties as director of the political side at Heritage Action.[12] Recall that it was Heritage that helped launch Moms for Liberty, and Roberts himself who presided over a CNP gathering months earlier.[13] It is Heritage whose Center for Education Policy, with Paul Peterson's protégé Jay Greene its most visible figure, that is operating the campaign-style war room pushing back on media reporting ranging from school voucher–induced tuition hikes to the widespread book banning initiatives in Florida and elsewhere (see chapter 7).

Meanwhile, Heritage Action itself has spent millions in what *The Guardian* reported as a previously undisclosed effort to "block federal voting rights legislation and advance an ambitious plan to spread its far-right agenda calling for aggressive voter suppression measures in battleground states." The new reporting highlighted the "pivotal role that Heritage Action is increasingly playing in shaping the rules that govern US democracy."[14]

IMPLEMENTATION, PART II

Chapter 3 of this book was titled "Implementation." We now return to a new iteration of that theme. The Heritage Foundation quite openly launched a project to completely alter the structure of the federal government, from its health care agencies to the US Department of Education, upon restoration of a Donald Trump presidency.[15] In an extraordinary strategy based on a series of proposed enabling acts to gut the federal regulatory state upon a new Trump term, Heritage has created Project 2025 outlining these plans. On the health care side, the policy lead is Roger Severino—the vehement anti-LGBTQ+ opponent introduced in chapter 6. On education, it is Lindsey Burke, director of Heritage's Center for Education Policy.[16] The education schematic begins—as most of the leading GOP presidential candidates during the 2024 primary cycle did with a call to end the US Department of Education.[17] After quoting Milton Friedman, the remainder of the plan details where to place elements of the department that remain—absent an organizing authority to monitor and enforce basic student protections provided under statute like Title IX of the federal code. The breadth and depth of these proposals are truly radical—but they are sophisticated in their radicalism. These policy advocates know what they are doing. In these schematics, they are only extending the playbook introduced by groups like the Alliance Defending Freedom during the first Trump term: a stripping-bare of the ability of the US government to monitor and enforce basic commitments to human rights and equality that run counter to the moral framework advanced by the Religious Right.[18]

At the state level, see institutional members of the CNP's State Policy Network following Heritage's national example. In 2023 alone, the Badger

Institute (Wisconsin), the Buckeye Institute (Ohio), the Commonwealth Institute (Pennsylvania), the Cardinal Institute (West Virginia), the Goldwater Institute (Arizona), and the Texas Public Policy Foundation—a sponsoring member of Heritage's Project 2025—all created local scaffolding for new or expanded school voucher bills and the push for educational privatization through policy analysis and media outreach.[19] Every single one of those organizations received funding from the Lynde and Harry Bradley Foundation within the last three tax years of this book's writing.[20] Those recipients were only part of a larger array of the Bradley Foundation— more than $86 million in just 2022, for example—to right-wing policy networks, media outlets, and litigation groups. The largest single Bradley donation that year, $27.1 million, was to something called America First Legal, a new right-wing litigation outfit founded by former Trump aide Stephen Miller.[21]

Much of the education-specific effort concerned the question of school voucher "implementation," following the banner year of legislative success in the 2023 session. Recall (from chapter 3) that implementation has been a watchword for the policy-oriented voucher advocacy community since at least the first iteration of the Washington, D.C., voucher program in 2004. And recall that the Bradley Foundation contributed up to $400,000 in 2005 and 2006 for school recruitment—a sum matched by the GOP lawyer C. Boydon Gray, one of the "four watchmen" influencing conservative judicial nominations through the Federalist Society, and until his death a board member of Peterson's institute at Harvard.[22] Further, as if on a shadow panel of erudite thinkers offering comments on a great question of the day, at least five different advocates between March and August 2023—including those from EdChoice, the State Policy Network, and the Koch network's Stand Together group published articles on "implementation" in *Education Next*, the journal founded by Paul Peterson, housed at the Hoover Institute, and supported by both the Bradley and Charles Koch Foundations.[23]

In its 2023 iteration, the implementation push was not only articulated by local directors of state policy think tanks but centralized at the Manhattan Institute, where a former Arkansas doctoral student named Michael

McShane (the national research director at Milton Friedman's EdChoice) and a Notre Dame law professor named Nicole Garnett published a detailed canonical rendering that reads like a best-practices plan to avoid oversight, accountability, and therefore a repeat of the horrific voucher-induced academic outcomes from the previous decade (see chapter 5).[24] Shortly after, the Heritage Foundation announced the hire of a man named Matthew Ladner to head its "school choice implementation" portfolio. Ladner's previous positions included writing for ALEC and a stint at the Charles Koch Institute.[25]

Law professor Garnett leads down other pathways. She is a former clerk to Supreme Court Justice Clarence Thomas and staffer, before taking her faculty position, at the Institute for Justice, the Koch-seeded group appearing throughout this book, whose own founder, Clint Bolick, was a former Thomas aide in the 1980s. At the Institute, Garnett was among the group of staff attorneys assisting the defense for both the Milwaukee and Cleveland voucher programs in the late 1990s.[26] As of this writing, she is also the lead outside lawyer assisting the controversial effort to authorize a Catholic charter school in Oklahoma.[27] She was a colleague and friend of Supreme Court Justice Amy Coney Barrett while Barrett taught at Notre Dame (Barrett is godmother to one of Garnett's daughters).[28] Throughout the spring of 2023, when investigative reporting detailed long-standing ties between Justice Thomas and right-wing billionaire donors, including Charles and David Koch, Garnett's social media feed was a testimonial to Thomas's courage and character: "I've known Justice Thomas for 25 years," one post reads, "He is the rare person whose goodness matches his greatness. It breaks my heart that so many are willing to go so far to attack a good, and great, man for political gain."[29] While not defending her former boss, Garnett took time to applaud the work of her former student, Joseph Connor, the founder and CEO of an education vendor called Odyssey. That vendor has the third-party contract for administering the new school voucher program in Iowa (see chapter 7) as well as accounts running vouchers in Missouri and Idaho.[30] The link between profiteering and proselytizing in the voucher movement runs through groups like Odyssey.

NO MORE "STATISTICAL ARGUMENTS"

A young man named Corey DeAngelis in many ways embodies today's education freedom campaign: white, male, aggressive, and well financed. Officially a "senior research fellow" at Betsy DeVos's American Federation for Children, DeAngelis is a 2015 college graduate from the University of Texas-San Antonio and a 2018 doctoral graduate from the University of Arkansas Department of Education Reform. At Arkansas, he worked at the School Choice Demonstration Project under Paul Peterson protégés Jay Greene and Patrick Wolf, while also working at the Koch- and Bradley-backed Reason Foundation.[31] During that time, DeAngelis published an article for the Foundation for Economic Education called "Legalizing Discrimination Would Improve the Education System."[32] As the DeVos-fueled legislative push across individual states ramped up in late 2022 and throughout 2023, DeAngelis became "the public face of the effort, traveling from state to state, holding rallies, making media appearances, and tweeting constantly," including photos of one-on-one meetings with multiple voucher-backing state governors.[33] DeAngelis has also appeared at the Conservative Political Action Conference and events held by Moms for Liberty and the Leadership Institute, as well as with Christopher Rufo—Rufo calls him a "friend and colleague"—with the message that the voucher push "started winning when it stopped making statistical arguments about performance metrics and started making moral arguments about parental rights and the content of the curriculum."[34]

Those supposedly moral arguments increasingly turn back to a full embrace of discrimination. Corey DeAngelis's state tour on behalf of Betsy DeVos's group included a return to Arkansas to promote that state's new voucher bill, branded as the "LEARNS" law for short.[35] As the first months of the voucher law rolled out, the Arkansas Department of Education began promoting it heavily, and the state's politically appointed superintendent Jacob Oliva spoke that summer at the Moms for Liberty convention.[36] Local reporting showed that 95 percent of initial voucher recipients had never been in Arkansas public schools.[37] Part of the state's marketing campaign for those vouchers, officially called "education freedom accounts" in the LEARNS bill, included the creation of new promotional videos for select private schools. The state agency distributed those videos on its website. One such video promoted a private school that refused admission to students from LGBTQ+ families and required applicants to sign sexual morality pledges to attend.[38]

My old friend and coauthor (see chapter 4), Patrick Wolf, remains a professor, and head of the School Choice Demonstration Project at the University of Arkansas. But despite being the lead investigator for the Louisiana voucher evaluation that showed some of the largest academic losses on record in education research, Wolf remains an ardent voucher supporter. It was he who appeared with Betsy DeVos and Virginia Walden Ford at the Heritage event honoring Ford in 2019, defending voucher schemes as needing a wait-and-see approach to outcomes.[39] Wolf has argued forcefully for voucher expansion and appeared at venues like the Independent Women's Forum (a Koch-funded organization and member of the CNP) to make the case for a "school choice journey."[40] I am grateful to Patrick Wolf for the opportunity to work on voucher evaluations early in my career. He even wrote me a reference letter for the faculty job I now occupy at Michigan State University. Once, in 2015, and after I became a senior member of the field, he and Jay Greene even asked me to serve on the independent audit team for their university department's five-year review as required by state law. We never worked together after 2013, but we were always cordial. It was not until I began publicly commenting on the by-then well-documented evidence against school vouchers that we became truly estranged. I believed Patrick Wolf in 2008—and I looked up to him—when he introduced our Milwaukee work together by writing, "Our shared commitment is to faithfully and carefully follow the evidence, wherever it may lead."[41]

More than fifteen years later, the evidence has led strongly away from school vouchers as a solution to educational inequity. There have been some favorable outcomes from time to time—notably on graduation rates and the ever-present metric of parental satisfaction—but even these are based largely on students who remain in voucher programs over long periods of time. The vast majority, as the Introduction to this book describes, return to public schools. Most of these are more academically or financially at-risk than their peers who stay. And in recent years, even the educational attainment advantage for children who remain in voucher programs has disappeared.[42] What is left—or rather, where the debate over vouchers has returned—is to the ill-defined notion of parental rights. With that return has come the full enveloping of the school privatization movement into the putsch of religious nationalism.

THERE IS A VAST RIGHT-WING CONSPIRACY

Nothing like this vast, overlapping network of donors, advocates, and soldier-scholars I describe in these pages exists in the advocacy community for public education. There are, of course, the teachers' unions—that permanent *bete noire* for Betsy DeVos and the apparatus of right-wing education reformers. These organizations have succeeded from time to time in using both political clout and dollars to block major reform initiatives, including school vouchers.[43] And at both the state and the local level, stakeholder groups representing the professional interests of district superintendents, principals, and school board members join the teachers' unions on some parts of a public education policy agenda, but at other times they diverge. As an example in my own state, these organizations have come together and drifted apart across multiple coalitions they have formed over time, often with state business leaders included. The current version, called Launch Michigan, has sought to "transform public education," and draws contributions from multiple foundations in our state, with nominal bipartisan support.[44] But despite the backing of the state's largest teachers' union and key business groups, most of the education stakeholder groups have left that "supergroup" coalition—mostly over differences over which reforms to support.[45]

I see similar examples as I speak, testify, and travel across the country, warning about the impacts of educational privatization. Although groups like multiple state affiliates of the American Association of School Administrators and the National School Boards Association, as well as of the

National Education Association and the American Federation of Teachers have lined up squarely against school vouchers, there are few agreements about even how to counter the privatization push—much less about alternatives. When it comes to overlapping priorities, funding streams, and key personnel, there is no progressive or public school-based equivalent of the network I describe in this book: the Heritage Foundation, the Cato Institute, or the American Federation for Children. There is no liberal Charles Koch, and no billionaire heiress investing in public schools to counter Betsy DeVos. There is no left-wing Council for National Policy.

Perhaps the single leading voice in that space is that of Randi Weingarten, longtime head of the American Federation of Teachers. Or perhaps Dr. Jill Biden, the First Lady of the United States as of this writing, and a former educator. Both of these women have access to substantial political networks, to be sure, but both serve different constituencies, and both are largely bound by the financial, legal, and political realities of the roles they inhabit. I have met Weingarten on multiple occasions since developing a public voice in the voucher space. I have found her to be warm, genuine, forceful, and dedicated. But like Dr. Biden in the White House, Randi Weingarten has many policy areas she must speak to, and she also represents the professional interests of more than one hundred thousand educators. Both women have, literally, another day job. Employing dozens of operatives and financially seeding countless more, Betsy DeVos has no one but herself and her family and, if you take her at her word, her God to whom she answers.

LOOKING AHEAD

While receiving feedback on early proposals for this book, I received one important response across multiple readers: a request to close with a series of policy recommendations. The idea is to both leave readers with a sense of optimism and to offer—especially to policy makers and practitioners who have turned these pages—a concrete suggestion for next, tractable steps. Let my observations in the brief paragraphs earlier, about advocacy coalitions and networks, represent the first of such recommendations.

Opposition to school vouchers, to education privatization more generally, and to radical, religious nationalism above all needs a shared set of explicit priorities. This opposition also needs a shared commitment to put aside secondary principles in conflict with one another toward a greater and more unified—and more unifying—sense of educational and indeed democratic purpose.

But what about first principles? What would it mean to offer an evidence-based but also equity-based and ethical representation of an alternative to the deceptive simplicity of parents' rights and private school choice as a cure-all? The field of education is replete with curricular fixes, expert takes, innovations, scale-ups and scale-backs, and long lists of "what works"—there's even a clearinghouse managed by the US Department of Education.[46] But *practice guides, intervention reports, reviews of educational individual studies,* and *data from study reviews*—all sections of that clearinghouse's public-facing portal—don't exactly have the same riotous ring as "education freedom"! And as a policy matter, what would it mean to get behind a plan to meet that first principle in the same way that the Right has organized and financed on behalf of school vouchers? Any suggestion I have would draw from the old adage, "You get what you pay for" and from a more spiritual level—for those more inclined to seek such truths in the first place—to call on the Gospel of Matthew, read to me by my own parents when I was a child: *where our treasure is, there our hearts will be also.*

Fund public schools. It really is that simple. Voucher advocates know that—it's why from Christopher Rufo on down, there requires a deeply rooted skepticism of public education to pass universal choice. There are only so many dollars to pay for it all. And in as much as the last decade of rigorous evidence on school vouchers has identified some of the largest academic losses in the research record, the last decade has also solidified a growing consensus among experts that the more money we spend on schools, the better off children are, not simply academically, but in later-life outcomes like higher wages and fewer encounters with the criminal justice system. Even expert proponents of old narratives still pushed by DeVos and others—that "throwing money at the problem" doesn't work—have distanced themselves from those claims in recent years.[47]

Because now the evidence abounds that school spending matters. In just the five years leading up to the writing of this book alone, study after study takes that conclusion new steps further. Academic outcomes improve dramatically.[48] Educational attainment levels rise.[49] Later-in-life incomes grow for workers who were children when policy makers decided to spend new dollars on their public schools.[50] Poverty levels fall, and the chances that those children will commit future crimes and become incarcerated fall with them.[51] When states take on the task of spending equalization across local districts, intergenerational economic mobility improves.[52] And we know that when school spending declines—as research showing what happens in an economic recession has confirmed—the results are equally apparent in the opposite direction: cuts to public school funding stalls academic progress.[53] That means that even the best case scenario for school voucher impacts—evidence that vouchers will spur improvement when public and private schools compete for scarce financial resources—is in the long run a failed strategy for educational opportunity.[54] And not all dollars are created equal: the evidence on intergenerational mobility is clear that those results depend on states leveling the playing field for districts with different access to resources.[55] That means that voucher plans that move state funds into private schools and leave public districts with only a local funding base—even if that base is secure in the short run—are setting those communities up for disaster when inevitable economic downturns come.

As a result of all this, any policy recommendation or key takeaway from a book like this must begin with a vigorous commitment to make direct and sustained investments in public education—every other initiative depends on that. Of course, how we spend that money still matters, both in terms of the specific funding sources and in the programs and services that money supports. Other books can and do detail evidence-based spending targets.[56] But my view is from a big picture perspective, and from the standpoint of motivating renewed investments not only in the operation of public education but for its *purpose*. And from that vantage point answers must form around whole-child approaches, the idea of schools as communities, and the idea of learning as a lifelong endeavor. Ideas include universal school meals that nourish kids throughout the day and alleviate the stigma of poverty; school-based health clinics not simply for children but for the adults who serve them; weighted-funding formulas that reflect the true cost of educating diverse learners; grow-your-own teacher training programs drawing on local talent; early childhood investments alongside after-school and summer school programs that recognize education is no longer just 8 A.M. to 3 P.M., Monday through Friday, 180 days a year. Each of these have a stronger base of evidence to support them than school vouchers. And each in its own way provides a rationale for public education that affects daily life.

Then, because of who and what religious nationalists are attacking both implicitly and increasingly explicitly when they speak about "education freedom," there does require a direct defense of public education as a matter of human rights. The marginalization of LGBTQ+ families, reproductive rights, environmental justice, and histories of underserved communities in the United States not only coincides with but are weapons in the attack on public schools. They are potent because they measure commitments to future generations of Americans who will define their *own* identities and their own destinies rather than having their parents and grandparents define their futures for them. Our children are not ourselves. They are with us, the poet cautions, but do not belong to us.[57]

What the rapid erosion of key American institutions, legal precedents, and even the commitment to international peacemaking over the last twenty years have in common are many of the same organizational forces— huge dollar and dark money financial backing and increasingly radical disengagement from shared civic responsibility. American public schools reflect our social strengths but also our weaknesses. Issues of racial and economic segregation, the inability to fully meet the needs of students with exceptional needs, and the challenges of embracing student populations that enter the building every morning from vastly different home experiences will remain problems in public education so long as they remain problems in American life. The fundamental threat to democracy posed by religious nationalism—whether in our schools or in our communities writ large—is not religious, per se. It is what comes from that form of religious radicalism: in the case of US education a dangerous, domestic form of isolationism oriented toward a notion of every child and family outside of a church sanctuary left to fend for themselves.

That is the policy reality of fully realized Friedmanism, at its core. And those are the parental values stressed in the modern school voucher movement. Betsy DeVos is on record lamenting that public schools "displaced" churches as centers of community, and for her belief that school choice will reverse that trend.[58] Any recommendation away from that view in the language of policy analysis, or any tenet in the language of civic values, would start with an unconditional rejection of the reckless disregard held by Christian nationalists for children who do not look, love, or pray the way they do. It would be based on the reality that rigorous evidence from political science, economics, sociology, and educational thought strongly points away from school vouchers entirely—and from much of school choice policymaking more broadly—as anything resembling a comprehensive solution to the problems still entrenched in American education.

Such a recommendation would itself become a moral statement. One that acknowledges the sins of our parents, reckons with the limits of our own mercy today, and demands a future of grace for all children.

Notes

Preface

1. George Packer, *The Assassins' Gate: America in Iraq* (New York: Farrar, Straus and Giroux, 2005), 219.
2. Adam Wren, "How Amy Coney Barrett's Religious Group Helped Shape a City," *Politico*, September 27, 2020.
3. Alexander Smith, "Pope Francis Signals Openness to Blessings for Same-Sex Couples," NBC News, October 3, 2023, https://www.nbcnews.com/news/world/pope-francis -signals-open-blessing-same-sex-unions-catholic-priests-rcna118525.
4. "Pope Says Some Conservatives in US Catholic Church Have Replaced Faith with Ideology," Associated Press, August 23, 2023, https://apnews.com/article/pope-francis -vatican-conservatives-abortion-us-bbfc346c117bd9ae68a1963478bea6b3.

Introduction

1. I have found these works especially useful: Nancy MacLean, *Democracy in Chains: The Deep History of the Radical Right's Stealth Plan for America* (New York: Penguin, 2017); Jane Mayer, *Dark Money: The Hidden History of the Billionaires Behind the Rise of the Radical Right* (New York: Doubleday, 2016); Anne Nelson, *Shadow Network: Media, Money and the Secret Hub of the Radical Right* (New York: Bloomsbury, 2019); Sarah Posner, *Unholy: Why White Evangelicals Worship at the Alter of Donald Trump* (New York: Random House, 2020); Katherine Stewart, *The Power Worshippers: Inside the Dangerous Rise of Religious Nationalism* (New York: Bloomsbury, 2019).
2. See Mark Lieberman, "Most Students Getting School Choice Funds Aren't Ditching Public Schools," *Education Week*, October 4, 2023, https://www.edweek.org/policy -politics/most-students-getting-new-school-choice-funds-arent-ditching-public-schools /2023/10; Gloria Rebecca Gomez, "Private School Students Flock to Expanded School Voucher Program," *Arizona Mirror*, September 1, 2022, https://www.azmirror.com /2022/09/01/private-school-students-flock-to-expanded-school-voucher-program; Danielle Prieur, "Florida Policy Institute Asked for School Voucher Data, Here's What Step Up for Students Provided," WMFE NPR, September 14, 2023, https://www.wmfe .org/education/2023-09-14/florida-policy-institute-school-voucher-data-step-up-for

-students; Talia Richman and Allie Morris, "Who Would Texas' ESAs Benefit? Tension Emerges Over Who Would Get Money for Private School," *Dallas Morning News*, March 24, 2023, https://www.dallasnews.com/news/education/2023/03/24/who-would -texas-education-savings-accounts-be-for-a-divide-over-homeschoolers-emerges/ ?outputType=amp; Robin Opsahl, "More Than 29,000 Apply for Iowa Private School Funds in First Year," *Iowa Capital Dispatch*, July 6, 2023, https://iowacapitaldispatch .com/2023/07/06/more-than-29000-apply-for-iowa-private-school-funds-in-first-year; Blythe Bernhard, "Missouri Lawmakers Look to Expand Tax-Credit Voucher Program Serving Mostly Religious Schools," *St. Louis Post-Dispatch*, January 15, 2023, https:// www.stltoday.com/news/local/education/missouri-lawmakers-look-to-expand-tax -credit-voucher-program-mostly-serving-religious-schools/article_ef0b7afb-6805-586b -a668-67b2d10ecd64.html; Ethan Dewitt, "Most Education Freedom Account Recipi- ents Not Leaving Public Schools, Department Says," *New Hampshire Bulletin*, March 28, 2022, https://newhampshirebulletin.com/briefs/most-education-freedom-account -recipients-not-leaving-public-schools-department-says/; Sarah Budusen and Mark Ackerman, "The Cost of Choice: Most Students Who Benefit from Ohio EdChoice Vouchers Have Always Attended Private School," ABC News 5 Cleveland, January 30, 2020, https://www.news5cleveland.com/news/local-news/investigations/the-cost-of -choice-most-students-who-benefit-from-ohio-edchoice-vouchers-have-always -attended-private-school; Edgar Mendez, "75 Percent of State Voucher Applicants Already in Private School," *Milwaukee Journal Sentinel*, May 24, 2014, https://archive .jsonline.com/news/education/75-of-state-voucher-program-applicants-already-attend -private-school-b99274333z1-259980701.html/.

3. Ty Rushing, "Kim Reynolds' Private School Voucher Plan Led to Tuition Hikes," Iowa Starting Line, May 12, 2023, https://iowastartingline.com/2023/05/12/kim-reynolds -private-school-voucher-plan-led-to-tuition-hikes/; "Florida's New Voucher Law Allows Private Schools to Boost Revenue," *Tampa Bay Times*, June 2, 2023, https://www .tampabay.com/news/education/2023/05/30/floridas-new-voucher-law-allows-private -schools-boost-revenue/.

4. See Atila Abdulkadiroğlu, Parag A. Pathak, and Christopher R. Walters, "Free to Choose: Can School Choice Reduce Student Achievement?" *American Economic Journal: Applied Economics* 10, no. 1 (2018): 175–206; Jonathan N. Mills and Patrick J. Wolf, "Vouchers in the Bayou: The Effects of the Louisiana Scholarship Program on Student Achievement After 2 Years," *Educational Evaluation and Policy Analysis* 39, no. 3 (2017): 464–84.

5. Mark Dynarski, Ning Rui, Ann Webber, and Babette Gutmann, *Evaluation of the DC Opportunity Scholarship Program: Impacts After One Year* (NCEE 2017–4022), Washington, DC: National Center for Education Evaluation and Regional Assistance, Institute of Education Sciences, U.S. Department of Education, 2017, https://ies.ed.gov /ncee/pubs/20174022/pdf/20174022.pdf; Mark Dynarski and Austin Nichols, "More Findings on School Vouchers and Test Scores, and They Are Still Negative," Brookings Institution, July 13, 2017, https://www.brookings.edu/articles/more-findings-about -school-vouchers-and-test-scores-and-they-are-still-negative/; R. Joseph Waddington and Mark Berends, "Impact of the Indiana Choice Scholarship Program: Achievement Effects for Students in Upper Elementary and Middle School," *Journal of Policy Analysis and Management* 37, no. 4 (2018): 783–808; Mark Berends and R. Joseph Waddington,

"School Choice in Indianapolis: Effects of Charter, Magnet, Private, and Traditional Public Schools," *Education Finance and Policy* 13, no. 2 (2018): 227–55.

6. David Figlio and Krzysztof Karbownik, "Evaluation of Ohio's EdChoice Scholarship Program: Selection, Competition and Performance Effects," Thomas B. Fordham Institute, July 7, 2016, https://fordhaminstitute.org/ohio/research/evaluation-ohios -edchoice-scholarship-program-selection-competition-and-performance.

7. Megan Kohfield, Jim Soland, Karyn Lewis, and Emily Morton, "The Pandemic Has Had Devastating Impacts on Learning, What Will It Take to Help Catch Up?" Brookings Institution, March 3, 2022, https://www.brookings.edu/articles/the-pandemic-has-had -devastating-impacts-on-learning-what-will-it-take-to-help-students-catch-up/.

8. Joshua M. Cowen, David J. Fleming, John F. Witte, Patrick J. Wolf, and Brian Kisida, "School Vouchers and Student Attainment: Evidence from a State-Mandated Study of Milwaukee's Parental Choice Program," *Policy Studies Journal* 41, no. 1 (2013): 147–68; Patrick J. Wolf, Brian Kisida, Babette Gutmann, Michael Puma, Nada Eissa, and Lou Rizzo, "School Vouchers and Student Outcomes: Experimental Evidence from Washington, DC," *Journal of Policy Analysis and Management* 32, no. 2 (2013): 246–70; Matthew M. Chingos and Brian Kisida, "School Vouchers and College Enrollment: Experimental Evidence From Washington, DC," *Educational Evaluation and Policy Analysis* 45, no. 3 (2023): 422–36; Heidi H. Erickson, Jonathan N. Mills, and Patrick J. Wolf, "The Effects of the Louisiana Scholarship Program on Student Achievement and College Entrance," *Journal of Research on Educational Effectiveness* 14, no. 4 (2021): 861–99.

9. Joshua Cowen, "Apples to Outcomes? Revisiting the Achievement v. Attainment Differences in School Vouchers Studies," Brookings Institution, September 1, 2022, https://www.brookings.edu/articles/apples-to-outcomes-revisiting-the-achievement-v -attainment-differences-in-school-voucher-studies/.

10. Michael R. Ford and Fredrik O. Andersson, "Determinants of Organizational Failure in the Milwaukee School Voucher Program," *Policy Studies Journal* 47, no. 4 (2019): 1048–68.

11. Yujie Sude, Corey A. DeAngelis, and Patrick J. Wolf, "Supplying Choice: An Analysis of School Participation Decisions in D.C., Indiana, and Louisiana," *Education Research Alliance of New Orleans*, June 26, 2017, https://educationresearchalliancenola.org/files /publications/Sude-DeAngelis-Wolf-Supplying-Choice.pdf.

12. Michael R. Ford, "Funding Impermanence: Quantifying the Public Funds Sent to Closed Schools in the Nation's First Urban School Voucher Program," *Public Administration Quarterly* (2016): 882–912; Ford and Andersson, "Determinants of Organizational Failure," 1048–68.

13. Daniel M. Hungerman and Kevin Rinz, "Where Does Voucher Funding Go? How Large-Scale Subsidy Programs Affect Private-School Revenue, Enrollment, and Prices," *Journal of Public Economics* 136 (2016): 62–85; Neil Morton, "Arizona Gave Families Money for Private Schools. Then Private Schools Raised Tuition," Hechinger Report, November 27, 2023, https://hechingerreport.org/arizona-gave-families-public-money -for-private-schools-then-private-schools-raised-tuition/.

14. R. Joseph Waddington, Ron Zimmer, and Mark Berends, "Cream Skimming and Pushout of Students Participating in a Statewide Private School Voucher Program," *Educational Evaluation and Policy Analysis* (2023): 01623737231183397.

15. Joshua M. Cowen, David J. Fleming, John F. Witte, and Patrick J. Wolf, "Going Public: Who Leaves a Large, Longstanding, and Widely Available Urban Voucher Program?" *American Educational Research Journal* 49, no. 2 (2012): 231–56; Deven Carlson, Joshua M. Cowen, and David J. Fleming, "Life After Vouchers: What Happens to Students Who Leave Private Schools for the Traditional Public Sector?" *Educational Evaluation and Policy Analysis* 35, no. 2 (2013): 179–99.

16. Erickson, Mills, and Wolf, "Effects of the Louisiana Scholarship"; Waddington, Zimmer, and Berends, "Cream Skimming and Pushout"; Daniel Kuehn, Matthew Chingos, and Alexandra Tinsley, "Most Students Receive a Florida Private School Choice Scholarship for Two Years or Fewer: What Does That Mean?" Urban Institute, March 6, 2020, https://www.urban.org/urban-wire/most-students-receive-florida-private-school-choice -scholarship-two-years-or-fewer-what-does-mean.

17. Erickson, Mills, and Wolf, "Effects of the Louisiana Scholarship"; Kuehn, Chingos, and Tinsley, "Most Students Receive a Florida Private School Choice Scholarship for Two Years or Fewer."

18. Phoebe Petrovic, "False Choice: Wisconsin Taxpayers Support Schools That Can Discriminate," *Wisconsin Watch*, May 5, 2023, https://wisconsinwatch.org/2023/05 /wisconsin-voucher-schools-discrimination-lgbtq-disabilities/; Julia Donheiser, "Choice for Most: In Nation's Largest Voucher Program, $16 million Went to Schools with Anti-LGBT Policies," Chalkbeat, August 10, 2017, https://www.chalkbeat.org/2017/8/10 /21107318/choice-for-most-in-nation-s-largest-voucher-program-16-million-went-to -schools-with-anti-lgbt-polici.

19. Jason Bedrick, "The Folly of Overregulating School Choice," *Education Next*, January 5, 2016, https://www.educationnext.org/the-folly-of-overregulating-school-choice/.

20. John F. Witte, Patrick J. Wolf, Joshua M. Cowen, Deven E. Carlson, and David J. Fleming, "High-Stakes Choice: Achievement and Accountability in the Nation's Oldest Urban Voucher Program," *Educational Evaluation and Policy Analysis* 36, no. 4 (2014): 437–56.

21. Joshua Cowen, "How Taxpayer-Funded Schools Teach Creationism—And Get Away with It," *New Republic*, January 30, 2014, https://newrepublic.com/article/116410/school -choice-tax-funded-private-schools-should-be-accountable-test.

22. National Center for Research on Educational Access and Choice, Tulane University, https://reachcentered.org/about.

23. Jane A. Lincove, Joshua M. Cowen, and Jason P. Imbrogno, "What's in Your Portfolio? How Parents Rank Traditional Public, Private, and Charter Schools in Post-Katrina New Orleans' Citywide System of School Choice," *Education Finance and Policy* 13, no. 2 (2018): 194–226; Douglas N. Harris and Matthew F. Larsen, "What Schools Do Families Want (and Why)? Evidence on Revealed Preferences from New Orleans," *Educational Evaluation and Policy Analysis* 45, no. 3 (2023): 496–519.

24. Steven Glazerman and Dallas Dotter, "Market Signals: Evidence on the Determinants and Consequences of School Choice from a Citywide Lottery," *Educational Evaluation and Policy Analysis* 39, no. 4 (2017): 593–619.

25. Jane Arnold Lincove, Jon Valant, and Joshua M. Cowen, "You Can't Always Get What You Want: Capacity Constraints in a Choice-Based School System," *Economics of Education Review* 67 (2018): 94–109.

26. Anna J. Egalite and Jonathan N. Mills, "Competitive Impacts of Means-Tested Vouchers on Public School Performance: Evidence from Louisiana," *Education Finance and Policy* 16, no. 1 (2021): 66–91; David Figlio and Cassandra M. D. Hart, "Competitive Effects of Means-Tested School Vouchers," *American Economic Journal: Applied Economics* 6, no. 1 (2014): 133–56; Cecilia Elena Rouse, Jane Hannaway, Dan Goldhaber, and David Figlio, "Feeling the Florida Heat? How Low-Performing Schools Respond to Voucher and Accountability Pressure," *American Economic Journal: Economic Policy* 5, no. 2 (2013): 251–81.
27. C. Kirabo Jackson and Claire L. Mackevicius, "What Impacts Can We Expect from School Spending Policy? Evidence from Evaluations in the US," *American Economic Journal: Applied Economics* (2023); Matt Barnum, "4 New Studies Bolster the Case: More Money for Schools Helps Low-Income Students," Chalkbeat, August 13, 2019, https://www.chalkbeat.org/2019/8/13/21055545/4-new-studies-bolster-the-case-more-money-for-schools-helps-low-income-students.
28. Joshua Cowen, "After Two Decades Studying Voucher Programs, I'm Now Firmly Opposed to Them," Hechinger Report, July 20, 2022, https://hechingerreport.org/opinion-after-two-decades-of-studying-voucher-programs-im-now-firmly-opposed-to-them/.
29. Joshua Cowen, "How School Voucher Programs Hurt Students," *Time*, April 19, 2023, https://time.com/6272666/school-voucher-programs-hurt-students/.
30. See National Center for Research on Education Access and Choice, Tulane University, https://reachcentered.org/team.
31. Brett Samuels, "Trump Calls School Choice the Civil Rights Issue of the Decade," The Hill, June 16, 2020, https://thehill.com/homenews/administration/502961-trump-calls-school-choice-the-civil-rights-issue-of-the-decade/.

Chapter 1

1. Andrew Coulson, "Giving School Choice the Milton Friedman Test," Cato Institute, August 12, 2013, https://www.cato.org/commentary/giving-school-choice-milton-friedman-test#.
2. Nancy MacLean, "How Milton Friedman Exploited White Supremacy to Privatize Education" (working paper series no. 161, Institute for New Economic Thinking, September 2021), https://papers.ssrn.com/sol3/papers.cfm?abstract_id=3932454.
3. Milton Friedman, "The Role of Government in Education," in *Economics and the Public Interest*, edited by Robert A. Solo (New Brunswick, NJ: Rutgers University Press, 1955), 123–44, footnote 2.
4. Friedman, "Role of Government in Education," footnote 2.
5. "Inaugural Address of Governor George C. Wallace," Alabama Department of Archives and History, https://digital.archives.alabama.gov/digital/collection/voices/id/2952/.
6. "American Experience: Lynching In America: The Murder of Emmett Till," PBS, April 23, 2023, https://www.pbs.org/wgbh/americanexperience/features/emmett-lynching-america/.
7. MacLean, "How Milton Friedman Exploited."
8. MacLean, 8.
9. MacLean, 9.
10. MacLean, 10.
11. MacLean, 11.

12. MacLean, 12.

13. Steve Suitts, *Overturning Brown: The Segregationist Legacy of the Modern School Choice Movement* (Montgomery, AL: NewSouth Books, 2020); Cara Fitzpatrick, *The Death of Public School: How Conservatives Won the War Over Education in America* (New York: Basic Books, 2023).

14. MacLean, "How Milton Friedman Exploited," 13.

15. MacLean, 14.

16. MacLean, 14.

17. MacLean, 17.

18. *Report of the Legal and Legislative Subcommittee of the Texas Advisory Committee on Segregation*, Legislative Reference Library of Texas, 54th R.S. Library Call Number G1073.3 R299L, 1955, Updated September 1, 1956, https://lrl.texas.gov/committees /reportDisplay.cfm?cmteID=9434.

19. *Report of the Legal*, 2.

20. *Report of the Legal*, 29.

21. Mike Hixenbaugh, "Inside the Rural Texas Resistance to the GOP's Private School Choice Plan," NBC News, March 21, 2023, https://www.nbcnews.com/news/us-news /rural-texas-resistance-gop-private-school-choice-voucher-rcna75775.

22. Fitzpatrick, *Death of Public School*, 46.

23. Robert Solow, "Why Is There No Milton Friedman Today?" *Econ Journal Watch* 10, no. 2 (2013):214–6.

24. Dan Voorhis, "What It's Like to Grow up a Koch," *Wichita Eagle*, November 7, 2016, https://www.kansas.com/news/business/article113168633.html.

25. Cato Institute, "Milton Friedman and Cato," https://www.cato.org/milton-friedman; Laurie Bennett, "The Kochs Aren't the Only Funders of Cato," *Forbes*, March 3, 2012, https://www.forbes.com/sites/lauriebennett/2012/03/13/the-kochs-arent-the-only -funders-of-cato/?sh=70977bcc2096.

26. Cato Institute, "The Milton Friedman Prize for Advancing Liberty," https://www.cato .org/friedman-prize-2023.

27. Anne Nelson, *Shadow Network: Media, Money and the Secret Hub of the Radical Right* (New York: Bloomsbury Publishing, 2019), 118.

28. Jane Mayer, *Dark Money: The Hidden History of the Billionaires Behind the Rise of the Radical Right*, chapters 1, 4–5 (New York: Doubleday, 2016).

29. David D. Kirkpatrick, "The 2004 Campaign: The Conservatives; Club of the Most Powerful Gathers in Strictest Privacy," *New York Times*, August 28, 2004, https://www .nytimes.com/2004/08/28/us/2004-campaign-conservatives-club-most-powerful -gathers-strictest-privacy.html.

30. Nelson, *Shadow Network*, chapters 5, 6, 8.

31. Nelson, 110.

32. Clare Hendrickson, "Pence Visits Michigan to Tout DeVos-Backed Scholarship Opponents Deride as Voucher Scheme," *Detroit Free Press*, May 17, 2022, https://www .freep.com/story/news/politics/2022/05/17/mike-pence-visits-michigan-let-mi-kids -learn/9800129002/.

33. Nelson, *Shadow Network*, 127.

34. Nelson, 127.

35. Mayer, *Dark Money*, 233.

36. Theda Skocpol and Alexander Hertel-Fernandez, "The Koch Network and Republican Party Extremism," *Perspectives on Politics* 14, no. 3 (September 2016): 681–99.

37. Nancy MacLean, *Democracy in Chains: The Deep History of the Radical Right's Stealth Plan for America* (New York: Viking, 2017).

38. Nelson, *Shadow Network*, 34. Nelson reports that the Council for National Policy meets two to three times a year in "opulent" hotel surroundings, which it justifies to the Internal Revenue Service to keep its 501(c)(3) status because its members are accustomed to luxury.

39. Friedman, "Role of Government in Education," footnote 2.

40. Personal website of Betsy DeVos, https://betsydevos.com/issues/school-choice/.

41. Lisa Miller, "Who Is Betsy DeVos and How Did She Get to Be Head of Our Schools?" *New York Magazine*, July 24, 2017, https://nymag.com/intelligencer/2017/07/betsy-devos -secretary-of-education.html.

42. Katherine Stewart, *The Power Worshippers: Inside the Dangerous Rise of Religious Nationalism* (New York: Bloomsbury, 2019), 187.

43. Nelson, *Shadow Network*, chapter 3.

44. Evan Thomas, "Profile: Blackwater's Erik Prince," *Newsweek*, October 13, 2007, https://www.newsweek.com/profile-blackwaters-erik-prince-103877.

45. American Federation for Children Slide Deck, "AFC Is The Most Successful Force for Education Freedom in America," obtained by author, December 2023.

46. Miller, "Who Is Betsy DeVos?"; Kate Zernike, "How Trump's Education Nominee Bent Detroit to Her Will on Charter Schools," *New York Times*, December 12, 2016, https://www.nytimes.com/2016/12/12/us/politics/betsy-devos-how-trumps-education -nominee-bent-detroit-to-her-will-on-charter-schools.html.

47. Casandra Ulbrich, "Michigan Charters Run by For-Profits, Bringing Mediocrity, Secrecy," Bridge Michigan, February 13, 2013, https://www.bridgemi.com/guest -commentary/opinion-michigan-charters-run-profits-bring-mediocrity-secrecy.

48. Zernike, "How Trump's Education Nominee."

49. Miller, "Who Is Betsy DeVos?"

50. Steven Harmon, "DeVos: Michigan Workers Paid Too Much," *Grand Rapids Press*, April 28, 2004, reprinted in *Free Beacon*, https://freerepublic.com/focus/f-news/1126279 /posts.

51. Miller, "Who Is Betsy DeVos?"

52. Janet Reitman, "Betsy DeVos's Holy War," *Rolling Stone*, March 8, 2017, https://www .rollingstone.com/politics/politics-features/betsy-devos-holy-war-126026/.

53. Reitman, "Betsy DeVos's Holy War."

54. Max Weber, *The Protestant Ethic and the Spirit of Capitalism: And Other Writings* (New York: Penguin, 2002).

55. Miller, "Who Is Betsy DeVos?"

56. Miller.

57. Skocpol and Hertel-Fernandez, "Koch Network."

58. Nelson, *Shadow Network*.

59. Miller, "Who Is Betsy DeVos?"

60. MacLean, "How Milton Friedman Exploited," 18.

61. MacLean, 18.

62. See Suitt, *Overturning Brown*, in particular, 54–60.

Chapter 2

1. Anne Nelson, *Shadow Network: Media, Money and the Secret Hub of the Radical Right* (New York: Bloomsbury Publishing, 2019), 124.
2. For an extensive discussion of these developments during the 1970s and 1980s, see Nelson, *Shadow Network*; Jane Mayer, *Dark Money: The Hidden History of the Billionaires Behind the Rise of the Radical Right* (New York: Doubleday, 2016).
3. Mayer, *Dark Money*, chapter 3.
4. Anne Nelson, "The 10 People You've Never Heard of Who Are Destroying Democracy," *New Republic*, April 18, 2022, https://newrepublic.com/article/165984/10-people -destroying-democracy.
5. Mayer, *Dark Money*, 112.
6. Jim Carl, *Freedom of Choice: Vouchers in American Education* (Santa Barbara, CA: Praeger, 2011), 120.
7. Katherine Stewart, *The Power Worshippers: Inside the Dangerous Rise of Religious Nationalism* (New York: Bloomsbury, 2019), 71.
8. Mayer, *Dark Money*, 102.
9. Mayer, 113.
10. Mayer, 113.
11. Carl, *Freedom of Choice*, 120.
12. Carl, 121.
13. "Badger Institute," State Policy Network, https://spn.org/organization/badger-institute/; Nelson, *Shadow Network*, 59.
14. Mayer, *Dark Money*, 102.
15. John E. Chubb and Terry M. Moe, *Politics, Markets and America's Schools* (Washington, DC: Brookings Institution Press, 1990).
16. Mayer, *Dark Money*, 100; see also the Center for Media and Democracy's SourceWatch project: "Contributions of the Bradley Foundation," a compilation of annual IRS 990 forms from 1998–2021, https://www.sourcewatch.org/index.php/Contributions_of_the _Bradley_Foundation.
17. Terry Moe would go on to release a follow-up volume a decade later, also funded by the Olin and Bradley Foundations as well as the pro-voucher Walton Family Foundation and others. See Terry M. Moe, *Schools, Vouchers and the American Public* (Washington, DC: Brookings Institution Press, 2001); on the other Olin/Bradley names: see Mayer, *Dark Money*, 105–106. David Brock later recanted and disowned the book.
18. Carl, *Freedom of Choice*, 129.
19. John F. Witte, *The Market Approach to Education: An Analysis of America's First Voucher Program* (Princeton, NJ: Princeton University Press, 2000), 55.
20. Witte, *Market Approach to Education*, viii–viv.
21. For a review, see, for example, Cynthia E. Coburn and William R. Penuel, "Research–Practice Partnerships in Education: Outcomes, Dynamics, and Open Questions," *Educational Researcher* 45, no. 1 (2016): 48–54.
22. John F. Witte, "First-Year Report: Milwaukee Parental Choice Program" (report, University of Wisconsin-Madison Lafollette School of Public Affairs Data and Information Services Center Archive, 1991), https://www.disc.wisc.edu/archive/choice /FirstYear.pdf; the book is Witte, *Market Approach to Education*.

23. Kimberly J. McLarin, "In Test of School-Voucher Idea: The Sky's Not Falling, but Neither Is Manna," *New York Times*, April 19, 1995.

24. McLarin, "In Test of School-Voucher."

25. Paul E. Peterson, "Milwaukee Parents Like Choice," letter to the editor, *New York Times*, April 27, 1995.

26. Paul E. Peterson and Mark C. Rom, *Welfare Magnets: The Case for a National Standard* (Washington, DC: Brookings Institution Press, 1990).

27. Paul E. Peterson, curriculum vitae, March 2021, http://paulepeterson.org/sites/default /files/Peterson_Long_CV_2021Mar.pdf.

28. See Peterson, curriculum vitae, March 2021, "A Study of the Milwaukee Choice Plan," funded by the Anne Casey and John Olin Foundations 1994–1995. The Annie E. Casey Foundation is a politically moderate grant-making organization with focus on children, community development and cost-effectiveness. http://paulepeterson.org/sites/default /files/Peterson_Long_CV_2021Mar.pdf.

29. Paul E. Peterson, "A Critique of the Witte Evaluation of Milwaukee's School Choice Plan" (occasional paper no. 95-2, Center for American Political Studies, February 1995); Jay P. Greene, Paul E. Peterson, and Jiangtao Du, with Leesa Boeger and Curtis L Frazier, "The Effectiveness of School Choice in Milwaukee: A Secondary Analysis of Data from the Program's Evaluation" (paper prepared for presentation before the Panel on the Political Analysis of Urban School Systems at the August–September 1996 meetings of the American Political Science Association, San Francisco, CA, August 30, 1996), https://files.eric.ed.gov/fulltext/ED401597.pdf.

30. Greene et al., "Effectiveness of School Choice in Milwaukee," 22, 34.

31. Greene et al., 33.

32. Jay P. Greene, Paul E. Peterson, and Jiangtao Du, "Effectiveness of School Choice: The Milwaukee Experiment," *Education and Urban Society* 31, no. 2 (1999): 190–213 (quote on page 194).

33. Greene, Peterson, and Du, "Effectiveness of School Choice: Milwaukee."

34. Witte, *Market Approach to Education*.

35. A third-party, Cecelia E. Rouse—then an early-career economist at Princeton—weighed in with a paper ultimately published in the most prestigious outlet attained by the three research teams, the *Quarterly Journal of Economics*. Rouse's results essentially split the difference between the Witte and Peterson teams, finding more favorable results than Witte, but less favorable than what was reported by Peterson and Greene. See Cecilia Elena Rouse, "Private School Vouchers and Student Achievement: An Evaluation of the Milwaukee Parental Choice Program," *Quarterly Journal of Economics* 113, no. 2 (1998): 553–602.

36. Mayer, *Dark Money*, 103.

37. Daniel McGroarty, "School Choice Slandered," *The Public Interest*, Fall 1994, 97.

38. Debra Viadero, "Researcher at Center of Storm Over Vouchers," *Education Week*, August 5, 1998.

39. See Paul E. Peterson, curriculum vitae, March 2021, "A Study of the Milwaukee Choice Plan," funded by the Anne Casey and John Olin Foundations 1994–1995.

40. Witte, *Market Approach to Education*, chapter 7, and Carl, *Freedom of Choice*, chapter 4, for extensive review of the Bradley Foundation's efforts during this time.

41. Greene, Peterson, and Du, "Effectiveness of School Choice in Milwaukee."

42. Witte, *Market Approach to Education*, chapter 7.

43. Witte, *Market Approach to Education*, 178; Brian Dotts, "*Lochner's* Redeemers: How the Federalist Society and the Institute for Justice Impact the School Privatization Movement," edited by Kathleen deMarrais, Brigette A. Herron, and Janie Copple, *Conservative Philanthropies and Organizations Shaping U.S. Educational Policy and Practice* (Gorham, ME: Myers Education Press, LLC) 2020.

44. Mayer, *Dark Money*, 146.

45. See Witte, *Market Approach to Education*, 176, and Carl, *Freedom of Choice*, 182, for notes on Starr's involvement.

46. Witte, *Market Approach to Education*, 179.

47. Carl, *Freedom of Choice*, chapter 5.

48. Carl, 156.

49. Quoted in Carl, *Freedom of Choice*, 172.

50. Carl, 173.

51. For a summary of yearly reports see Kim K. Metcalf, Stephen D. West, Natalie Legan, Kelli Paul, and William J. Boone, "Evaluation of the Cleveland Scholarship and Tutoring Program, 1998–2001. Summary and Technical Report," Indiana Center for Evaluation (Bloomington: Indiana University, 2002), https://files.eric.ed.gov/fulltext/ED479162.pdf.

52. Jay P. Greene, William G. Howell, and Paul E. Peterson, "Lessons from the Cleveland Scholarship Program," in *Learning from School Choice*, edited by Paul E. Peterson and Bryan C. Hassel (Washington, DC: Brookings Institution Press, 1998), 357–92; Paul E. Peterson, William G. Howell, and Jay P. Greene, "An Evaluation of the Cleveland Voucher Program After Two Years Prepared by the Program on Education Policy and Governance," Harvard University, June 1999, 10, https://files.eric.ed.gov/fulltext/ED451260.pdf.

53. Jay P. Greene, William G. Howell, and Paul E. Peterson, "Lessons from the Cleveland Scholarship Program," Program on Education Policy and Governance; jointly sponsored by the Taubman Center on State and Local Government and the Center for American Political Studies (paper presented at the Annual Meeting of the Association of Public Policy and Management, Washington, DC, November 1997), 3. https://files.eric.ed.gov/fulltext/ED453569.pdf.

54. Greene, Howell, and Peterson, "Lessons from the Cleveland Scholarship Program," (1998 version), 380.

55. Peterson, "Evaluation of the Cleveland Voucher Program," 3.

56. Quotation taken from title of Greene, Howell, and Peterson, "Lessons from the Cleveland Scholarship Program" (1998 version).

57. Viadero, "Researcher at Center of Storm."

58. Viadero.

59. Chieh-Chen Bowen, "Two Sides of One Story," in *Evaluation in Practice: A Methodological Approach*, edited by Richard D. Bingham and Claire L. Felbinger (New York: Seven Bridges Press), 349.

60. Viadero, "Researcher at Center of Storm."

61. Paul E. Peterson and Bryan C. Hassel, *Learning from School Choice* (Washington, DC: Brookings Institution Press, 1998).

62. Zelman v. Simmons-Harris 234 F. 3d 945, (2002); US Supreme Court, Oral Argument in Zelman v. Simmons-Harris, February 20, 2002, 12. https://www.supremecourt.gov/oral_arguments/argument_transcripts/2001/00-1751.pdf.

63. Greene, Peterson and Du, "Effectiveness of School Choice in Milwaukee," 33.

64. William G. Howell and Paul E. Peterson, *The Education Gap: Vouchers and Urban Schools* (Washington, DC: Brookings Institution Press, 2002), xi.

65. Howell and Peterson, *Education Gap.*

66. Paul E. Peterson, David Myers, and William G. Howell, *An Evaluation of the New York City School Choice Scholarships Program: The First Year* (Cambridge: Harvard University Program on Education Policy and Governance, 1998), https://files.eric.ed.gov/fulltext/ED453307.pdf.

67. Peters, Myers, and Howell, *Evaluation of the New York City,* 29.

68. William G. Howell, Patrick J. Wolf, Paul E. Peterson, and David E. Campbell, "Test-Score Effects of School Vouchers in Dayton, Ohio, New York City, and Washington, D.C.: Evidence from Randomized Field Trials" (paper presented at the Annual Meeting of the American Political Science Association, Washington, DC, September 2000), https://eric.ed.gov/?id=ED445147.

69. Edward Wyatt, "Study Finds Higher Test Scores Among Blacks with Vouchers," *New York Times,* August 29, 2000, https://www.nytimes.com/2000/08/29/us/study-finds-higher-test-scores-among-blacks-with-vouchers.html.

70. Kate Zernike, "New Doubt Is Cast on Study That Backs Voucher Efforts," *New York Times,* September 15, 2000, https://www.nytimes.com/2000/09/15/us/new-doubt-is-cast-on-study-that-backs-voucher-efforts.html.

71. Zernike, "New Doubt."

72. Zernike.

73. Viadero, "Researcher at Center of Storm."

74. Zernike, "New Doubt."

75. See Nancy MacLean, "How Milton Friedman Exploited White Supremacy to Privatize Education" (working paper series no. 161, Institute for New Economic Thinking, September 2021), https://papers.ssrn.com/sol3/papers.cfm?abstract_id=3932454; Robert Solow, "Why Is There No Milton Friedman Today?" *Econ Journal Watch,* 10, no. 2 (May 2013): 214–16.

76. Mayer, *Dark Money,* 102.

77. Nelson, "10 People."

78. Mayer, *Dark Money,* 113.

79. Witte, *Market Approach to Education,* 176.

80. Children's Scholarship Fund: https://scholarshipfund.org/about/history/.

81. Pam Vogel, "Here Are the Corporations and Right-Wing Funders Backing the Education Reform Movement: A Guide to the Funders Behind a Tangled Network of Advocacy, Research, Media, and Profiteering That's Taking Over Public Education," Media Matters, April 26, 2016, https://www.mediamatters.org/daily-caller/here-are-corporations-and-right-wing-funders-backing-education-reform-movement.

82. Bruce Murphy, "When We Were Soldier-Scholars," *Milwaukee Magazine,* March 9, 2006. Quoted in Mayer, *Dark Money,* 113.

83. Mayer, *Dark Money,* 113.

Chapter 3

1. Jay P. Greene, William G. Howell, and Paul E. Peterson, "Lessons from the Cleveland Scholarship Program," in *Learning from School Choice*, edited by Paul E. Peterson and Bryan C. Hassel (Washington, DC: Brookings Institution Press, 1998), 357–92.
2. William G. Howell and Paul E. Peterson, *The Education Gap: Vouchers and Urban Schools* (Washington, DC: Brookings Institution Press, 2002).
3. Debra Viadero, "Researcher at Center of Storm Over Vouchers," *Education Week*, August 5, 1998.
4. Zelman v. Simmons-Harris 234 F. 3d 945 (2002).
5. Starr was the lead outside counsel, but the case was argued by Ohio Assistant Attorney General Judith L. French. See also *Zelman v. Simmons-Harris* nos. 00–1751, 00–1777, 00–1779, Brief of State Petitioners on Writ of Certiorari to the United States Court of Appeals for the Sixth Circuit.
6. Jane Mayer, *Dark Money: The Hidden History of the Billionaires Behind the Rise of the Radical Right* (New York: Doubleday, 2016), 147.
7. Brian Dotts, "*Lochner's* Redeemers: How the Federalist Society and the Institute for Justice Impact the School Privatization Movement," in *Conservative Philanthropies and Organizations Shaping U.S. Educational Policy and Practice*, edited by Kathleen deMarrais, Brigette A. Herron, and Janie Copple (Gorham, ME: Myers Education Press, LLC, 2020), 67.
8. The Center for Media and Democracy's SourceWatch project: "Contributions of the Bradley Foundation," a compilation of annual IRS 990 forms from 1998–2021, https://www.sourcewatch.org/index.php/Lynde_and_Harry_Bradley_Foundation.
9. Bradley Foundation Prize Award 2012 Winner: William H. Mellor, https://www.bradleyfdn.org/prizes/winners/william-h.-mellor.
10. See Paul E. Peterson, William G. Howell, and Jay P. Greene, "An Evaluation of the Cleveland Voucher Program After Two Years Prepared by the Program on Education Policy and Governance," Harvard University, June 1999, 10, https://files.eric.ed.gov/fulltext/ED451260.pdf.
11. Oral Argument in *Zelman v. Simmons-Harris* February 20, 2002, 12, https://www.supremecourt.gov/oral_arguments/argument_transcripts/2001/00-1751.pdf.
12. Zelman v. Simmons-Harris 2001 WL 34093993 (US) (Joint Appendix) Appendix P: Affidavit of Paul E. Peterson.
13. Dale Mezzacappa, "Market Forces: Professor Paul Peterson's Influential Protégés," *Connecting the Dots* (Washington, DC: Education Sector) 2006.
14. Zelman v. Simmons-Harris 2001 WL 34093993 (US) (Joint Appendix) Appendix II: The Racial, Economic, and Religious Context of Parental Choice in Cleveland).
15. State Policy Network: The Buckeye Institute https://spn.org/organization/the-buckeye-institute/; see also SourceWatch, "Contributions of the Bradley Foundation."
16. "25 Years and Counting: EdChoice Celebrates a Quarter Century of Expanding Education Opportunities for American Families," State Policy Network, https://spn.org/articles/edchoice-25-year-anniversary/.
17. Howell and Peterson, *Education Gap*, xix.
18. *Zelman* Brief of State Petitioners, 3–7.
19. Oral Argument in *Zelman v. Simmons-Harris* February 20, 2002, 12; *Zelman v. Simmons-Harris 234 F. 3d 945* (2002).

20. Paul E. Peterson, "Milwaukee Parents Like Choice," letter to the editor, *New York Times*, April 27, 1995.
21. Comments of Judith French, Counsel of Record, "Supreme Court News Conference," C-SPAN, February 20, 2002, https://www.c-span.org/video/?168764-1/supreme-court -news-conference.
22. Comments of Kenneth Starr, Outside Counsel, "Supreme Court News Conference," C-SPAN, February 20, 2002, https://www.c-span.org/video/?168764-1/supreme-court -news-conference.
23. Howell and Peterson, *Education Gap*.
24. Howell and Peterson, 146–47.
25. Howell and Peterson, xii.
26. Spencer S. Hse, "How Vouchers Came to D.C.," *Education Next*, June 30, 2006, https://www.educationnext.org/howvoucherscametodc/
27. Howell and Peterson, *Education Gap*, xii.
28. Paul E. Peterson, ed. *The Future of School Choice* (Stanford, CA: Hoover Institute Press, 2003).
29. Paul E. Peterson, "Introduction," in *The Future of School Choice*, edited by Paul E. Peterson (Stanford, CA: Hoover Institute Press, 2003), 2, 6.
30. Kenneth W. Starr, "The Equality Principle," in *The Future of School Choice*, edited by Paul E. Peterson (Stanford, CA: Hoover Institute Press, 2003), 25–34.
31. The Lynde and Harry Bradley Foundation, The Bradley Prizes, https://www.bradleyfdn .org/prizes/winners/peter-berkowitz; Committee for Justice, "CFJ Mourns the Passing of Its Founder Boyden Gray," https://www.committeeforjustice.org/single-post/cfj -mourns-the-death-of-its-founder-boyden-gray; Clint Bolick, "Sunshine Replaces the Cloud," in *The Future of School Choice*, edited by Paul E. Peterson (Stanford, CA: Hoover Institute Press, 2003), 77–79.
32. Paul E. Peterson, "Preface," in *The Future of School Choice*, edited by Paul E. Peterson (Stanford, CA: Hoover Institute Press, 2003), x.
33. Alan B. Krueger and Pei Zhu, "Another Look at the New York City School Voucher Experiment," *American Behavioral Scientist* 47, no. 5 (2004): 658–98. As of the writing of this chapter, in July 2023, the three-cities trials still represent the foundational evidence around which advocacy publications such as EdChoice's annual 123's of School Choice, are presented. See EdChoice, *The 123s of School Choice: What Research Says About Private School Choice in America*, 2023, https://www.edchoice.org/wp-content /uploads/2023/07/123s-of-School-Choice-WEB-07-10-23.pdf.
34. US National Archives, "President Discusses Education Reform," Kipp D.C. Key Academy, https://georgewbush-whitehouse.archives.gov/news/releases/2003/07/20030701-3.html.
35. Hse, "How Vouchers Came to D.C."; George W. Bush Institute, "A Lifetime of Fighting for Education for All," https://www.bushcenter.org/catalyst/still-leaving-them-behind /virginia-walden-ford-a-lifetime-fighting-for-education.
36. Hse, "How Vouchers Came to D.C."
37. Hse.
38. Patrick J. Wolf, Babette Gutmann, Nada Eissa, Michael Puma, and Marsha Silverberg, "Evaluation of the DC Opportunity Scholarship Program: First Year Report on Participation," US Department of Education, National Center for Education Evaluation and Regional Assistance (Washington, DC: US Government Printing Office, 2005).

39. Kate Zernike, "New Doubt Is Cast on Study That Backs Voucher Efforts," *New York Times*, September 15, 2000, https://www.nytimes.com/2000/09/15/us/new-doubt-is-cast-on-study-that-backs-voucher-efforts.html; Krueger and Zhu, "Another Look."

40. Wolf et al., "Evaluation of the DC Opportunity," x.

41. Patrick J. Wolf, Babette Gutmann, Michael Puma, and Marsha Silverberg, "Evaluation of the DC Opportunity Scholarship Program: Second Year Report on Participation," US Department of Education, Institute of Education Sciences (Washington, DC: US Government Printing Office, 2006), 2.

42. The Center for Media and Democracy's SourceWatch project: "Contributions of the Bradley Foundation," a compilation of annual IRS 990 forms from 1998–2021.

43. US Government Accountability Office, "District of Columbia Opportunity Scholarship Program: Additional Policies and Procedures Would Improve Internal Controls and Program Operations," November 2007, 3. https://www.gao.gov/assets/gao-08-9.pdf.

44. US Government Accountability Office, "District of Columbia Opportunity Scholarship Program: Additional Policies and Procedures," 3.

45. US Government Accountability Office, "District of Columbia Opportunity Scholarship Program: Additional Policies and Procedures," 17.

46. US Government Accountability Office, "District of Columbia Opportunity Scholarship Program: Additional Policies and Procedures," 4.

47. The Center for Media and Democracy's SourceWatch project: "Contributions of the Bradley Foundation," a compilation of annual IRS 990 forms from 1998–2021.

48. Patrick J. Wolf, "School Vouchers in Washington, DC: Achievement Impacts and Their Implications for Social Justice," *Educational Research and Evaluation* 16, no. 2 (2010): 131–50.

49. US Government Accountability Office, "District of Columbia Opportunity Scholarship Program: Additional Policies and Procedures," 6.

50. US Government Accountability Office "District of Columbia Opportunity Scholarship Program: Actions Needed to Address Administration and Oversight," September 2013, 19.

51. Hse, "How Vouchers Came to D.C."; Wolf et al., "Evaluation of the DC Opportunity: Second Year," 2.

52. US National Archives, "President Discusses Education Reform."

53. The Center for Media and Democracy's SourceWatch project, "Moving Picture Institute," https://www.sourcewatch.org/index.php/Moving_Picture_Institute; Anne Nelson, *Shadow Network: Media, Money and the Secret Hub of the Radical Right* (New York: Bloomsbury Publishing, 2019).

54. Philanthropy Roundtable, "A Big Close-up for Educational Opportunities," https://www.philanthropyroundtable.org/magazine/a-big-close-up-for-educational-opportunities/.

55. EdChoice, "Who We Are," https://www.edchoice.org/who-we-are/our-team/; EdChoice 2021 Annual Report, 9, https://www.edchoice.org/wp-content/uploads/2022/05/EdChoice-Annual-Report-041222.pdf; Philanthropy Roundtable, "A Big Close-up for Educational Opportunities."

56. Frank E. Lockwood, "Backer of School Choice Saluted: Arkansan Helped Start D.C. Awards," *Northwest Arkansas Times*, January 27, 2019, https://www.nwaonline.com/news/2019/jan/27/backer-of-school-choice-saluted-2019012/.

57. Pro-Publica, "Non-Profit Explorer," IRS Form 990, Moving Picture Institute, https://projects.propublica.org/nonprofits/organizations/203237801.

58. John F. Witte, *The Market Approach to Education: An Analysis of America's First Voucher Program* (Princeton, NJ: Princeton University Press, 2000).

59. Jim Carl, *Freedom of Choice: Vouchers in American Education* (Santa Barbara, CA: Praeger, 2011); Howard Fuller, *No Struggle, No Progress: A Warrior's Life from Black Power to Education Reform* (Milwaukee, WI: Marquette University Press, 2014).

60. School Choice Wisconsin, https://schoolchoicewi.org/.

61. Carl, *Freedom of Choice*, 156.

62. See Howard L. Fuller and George A. Mitchell, *The Impact of School Choice on Integration in Milwaukee Private Schools* (Report No. AS-CEI-2000-02). Milwaukee, WI: Marquette University, Milwaukee College of Arts and Sciences, 2000, https://eric.ed.gov/?id=ED443939; Howard L. Fuller and George A. Mitchell, *Selective Admission Practices? Comparing the Milwaukee Public Schools and the Milwaukee Parental Choice Program*, Milwaukee, WI: Marquette University Institute for the Transformation of Learning, 2000, https://eric.ed.gov/?id=ED441904; Howard L. Fuller and George A. Mitchell, *The Impact of School Choice on Racial and Ethnic Enrollment in Milwaukee Private Schools*, Milwaukee, WI: Marquette University Institute for the Transformation of Learning, 2000, https://eric.ed.gov/?id=ED441903.

63. Oral Argument in *Zelman v. Simmons-Harris*, February 20, 2002, 30.

64. *Zelman v. Simmons-Harris* 2001 WL 34093993 (US) (Joint Appendix) Appendix LL: Declaration of Dr. Howard L. Fuller.

65. See John F. Witte, *The Market Approach to Education*, page 169, for background on Fuller's occupation of the Bradley-endowed Marquette chair; The Center for Media and Democracy's SourceWatch project: "Contributions of the Bradley Foundation," a compilation of annual IRS 990 forms from 1998–2021.

66. The Center for Media and Democracy's SourceWatch project: "Black Alliance for Educational Options," https://www.sourcewatch.org/index.php/Black_Alliance_for_Educational_Options.

67. Daniel P. Schmidt and Michael E. Hartmann, "A Conversation with Howard Fuller," *Philanthropy Daily*, https://philanthropydaily.com/a-conversation-with-howard-fuller-part-2-of-2/.

68. Mario Koran, "Longtime Civil Rights Activist Howard Fuller on Trump, DeVos, and What It's Like to Advocate for School Choice in an Age of 'Hypocrisy," *The 74*, July 15, 2018, https://www.the74million.org/article/74-interview-longtime-civil-rights-activist-howard-fuller-on-trump-devos-and-what-its-like-to-advocate-for-school-choice-in-an-age-of-hypocrisy/.

69. Freedom Coalition for Charter Schools, "Dr. Howard Fuller's 60 Years of Service Celebration The Team. . . . Fighting for the DREAM!" Twitter, June 23, 2023, https://twitter.com/FreedmCoalition/status/1672319199686070272; Freedom Coalition for Charter Schools, "Dr. Howard Fuller's 60 Years of Service Celebration," Twitter, June 23, 2023, https://twitter.com/FreedmCoalition/status/1672316208300044288; "Celebrate Howard Fuller" Event Registration, https://www.celebratehowardfuller.com/.

Chapter 4

1. Corey Flintoff, "Timeline: Blackwater and Security Regulations," NPR, December 14, 2007, https://www.npr.org/2007/12/14/17269881/timeline-blackwater-and-security-regulations.

2. See Peter Singer, "The Dark Truth About Blackwater," *Brookings Institution Commentary*, October 2, 2007, https://www.brookings.edu/articles/the-dark-truth-about-blackwater/; Corey Flintoff, "Blackwater's Prince has GOP, Christian Group Ties," NPR, September 25, 2007, https://www.npr.org/templates/story/story.php?storyId =14659780; Evan Thomas, "Profile: Blackwater's Erik Prince," *Newsweek*, October 13, 2007, https://www.newsweek.com/profile-blackwaters-erik-prince-103877.

3. Dan Roberts, "U.S. Jury Convicts Blackwater Guards in 2007 Killing of Iraqi Civilians," *The Guardian*, October 14, 2014, https://www.theguardian.com/us-news/2014/oct/22/us -jury-convicts-blackwater-security-guards-iraq.

4. David E. Rosenbaum, "A Closer Look at Cheney and Halliburton," *New York Times*, September 28, 2004, https://www.nytimes.com/2004/09/28/us/a-closer-look-at-cheney -and-halliburton.html.

5. Jane Mayer, *Dark Money: The Hidden History of the Billionaires Behind the Rise of the Radical Right* (New York: Doubleday, 2016), 103.

6. 2005 Wisconsin Act 125, Section 228.119.23(7), https://docs.legis.wisconsin.gov/2005 /related/acts/125.pdf.

7. 1989 Wisconsin Act 336, Section 228.119.23(5), https://docs.legis.wisconsin.gov/1989 /related/acts/336.pdf.

8. See Daniel McGroarty, "School Choice Slandered," *The Public Interest*, Fall 1994; Paul E. Peterson, "A Critique of the Witte Evaluation of Milwaukee's School Choice Plan" (occasional paper no. 95-2, Center for American Political Studies, Department of Government, Harvard University, 1995).

9. 2005 Wisconsin Act 125.

10. Kathleen deMarrais, Brigette A. Herron, and Janie Copple, "The Walton Family Foundation: Key Players, Initiatives, and Its Growing Influence on Colleges and Universities," in *Conservative Philanthropies and Organizations Shaping U.S. Educational Policy and Practice*, edited by Kathleen deMarrais, Brigette A. Herron, and Janie Copple (Gorham, ME: Myers Education Press, LLC) 2020, 153–84.

11. Although my graduate funding came from the US Department of Education Institute for Education Sciences, Witte served as my primary academic advisor in the University of Wisconsin-Madison Department of Political Science.

12. Patrick J. Wolf, *The Comprehensive Longitudinal Evaluation of Milwaukee Parental Choice Program: Summary of Baseline Reports* (report #1, Fayetteville: University of Arkansas, Department of Education Reform, 2008), 2, https://scdp.uark.edu/the -comprehensive-longitudinal-evaluation-of-the-milwaukee-parental-choice-program -summary-of-baseline-reports/.

13. John F. Witte, Patrick J. Wolf, Joshua M. Cowen, David J. Fleming, and Juanita M. Lucas-McLean, *MPCP Longitudinal Educational Growth Study Baseline Report* (report #5, Fayetteville: University of Arkansas, Department of Education Reform, 2008), 3, https://bpb-us-e1.wpmucdn.com/wordpressua.uark.edu/dist/9/544/files/2018/10/report -5-mpcp-longitudinal-educational-growth-study-baseline-report-23l4k92.pdf.

14. 2005 Wisconsin Act 125.

15. Jay P. Greene, Paul E. Peterson, Jiangtao Du, Leesa Boeger, and Curtis L Frazier, "The Effectiveness of School Choice in Milwaukee: A Secondary Analysis of Data from the Program's Evaluation" (paper prepared for presentation before the Panel on the Political

Analysis of Urban School Systems at the August–September 1996 meetings of the American Political Science Association, San Francisco, CA, Friday, August 30, 1996), https://files.eric.ed.gov/fulltext/ED401597.pdf.

16. Corey A. DeAngelis, "The Evidence on School Choice Is Far from 'Mixed,'" Commentary, The Cato Institute, January 30, 2018, https://www.cato.org/commentary/evidence -school-choice-far-mixed#.

17. See, for example, Cynthia E. Coburn, and William R. Penuel, "Research–Practice Partnerships in Education: Outcomes, Dynamics, and Open Questions," *Educational Researcher* 45, no. 1 (2016): 48–54.

18. Wolf, *Comprehensive Longitudinal Evaluation of the Milwaukee*, report #1.

19. The difference between a nationally norm-referenced exam, which allows practitioners to assess student outcomes relative to a national percentile of test-takers, and a criterion referenced exam, which assesses knowledge of specific content against a predetermined standard, is largely incidental to the story here. The point is that voucher schools could select their own exam for general testing purposes but had to use a separate, state-mandated exam, for the subset of voucher pupils under study by the School Choice Demonstration Project.

20. See John F. Witte, *The Market Approach to Education: An Analysis of America's First Voucher Program* (Princeton, NJ: Princeton University Press, 2000), page 167, for discussion of the Mitchells, and page 169 for that of Fuller and his Bradley-endowed chair. See also The Center for Media and Democracy's SourceWatch project: "Contributions of the Bradley Foundation," a compilation of annual IRS 990 forms from 1998–2021, https://www.sourcewatch.org/index.php/Contributions_of_the_Bradley_Foundation.

21. George Mitchell, email to author, September 27, 2023. Mitchell was angry because I drew on my time on the Demonstration Project evaluation, the experience described in these pages to make those comments critical of School Choice Wisconsin's report. For those comments, see Ruth Coniff, "How Anti-Government Ideologues Targeted Wisconsin Public Schools," *Wisconsin Examiner*, September 5, 2023, https:// wisconsinexaminer.com/2023/09/05/how-anti-government-ideologues-targeted -wisconsin-public-schools/; Josh Cowen, "The Truth About Vouchers in Milwaukee," September 22, 2023, https://dianeravitch.net/2023/09/22/josh-cowen-the-truth-about -vouchers-in-milwaukee/.

22. See Wolf, *Comprehensive Longitudinal Evaluation of the Milwaukee*, 2, and footnote 11, for similar acknowledgments.

23. 2005 Wisconsin Act 125.

24. See Wisconsin Legislative Audit Bureau, *Letter Report*, "Test Score Data for Pupils in the Milwaukee Parental Choice Program" (September 2008), https://legis.wisconsin.gov /lab/reports/08-SchoolChoice_ltr.pdf. The decision to remove school names is a common one among education researchers. Although advocates in the voucher community were especially concerned about specific school performance being reported out by school name for reasons of their own, the Project's decision to keep those school names confidential falls well within norms and practices common especially for qualitative, but also quantitative, inquiry. Many published peer review papers might refer, for example, to evidence from "a large urban school district" rather than naming the location directly.

25. School Choice Demonstration Project, "Milwaukee Parental Choice Program Evaluation," University of Arkansas Department of Education Reform, https://scdp.uark.edu/milwaukee-parental-choice-program-evaluation/.
26. See School Choice Demonstration Project, "Milwaukee Parental Choice Program Evaluation" for full list. See also Oral Argument in Zelman v. Simmons-Harris, February 20, 2002, 12 https://www.supremecourt.gov/oral_arguments/argument_transcripts/2001/00-1751.pdf, and Zelman v. Simmons-Harris 2001 WL 34093993 (US) (Joint Appendix) Appendix P: Affidavit of Paul E. Peterson, for questions raised on school integration, fiscal and academic impacts of voucher competition on public schools, and parent satisfaction in the judicial proceedings.
27. School Choice Demonstration Project, "D.C. Opportunity Scholarship Program Evaluation," University of Arkansas Department of Education Reform, https://scdp.uark.edu/dc-opportunity-scholarship-program-evaluation/.
28. See Heritage Foundation, "Experts on Education," https://www.heritage.org/education; and EdChoice, "Who We Are: Our Team," https://www.edchoice.org/who-we-are/our-team/.
29. 2005 Wisconsin Act 125.
30. Debra Viadero, "Researcher at Center of Storm Over Vouchers," *Education Week*, August 5, 1998.
31. Mayer, *Dark Money*, 103.
32. Patrick J. Wolf, John F. Witte, and David J. Fleming, *Special Education and the Milwaukee Parental Choice Program* (report #35, Fayetteville, University of Arkansas, Department of Education Reform, 2012), https://scdp.uark.edu/special-education-and-the-milwaukee-parental-choice-program/.
33. Wolf, Witte, and Fleming, *Special Education and the Milwaukee*, i.
34. Wolf, Witte, and Fleming, 17.
35. Wolf, Witte, and Fleming, 17.
36. American Civil Liberties Union, "Complaint Under § 504 of the Rehabilitation Act of 1973 and Title II of the Americans with Disabilities Act," https://www.aclu.org/sites/default/files/field_document/complaint_to_doj_re_milwaukee_voucher_program_final.pdf; Tom Held, "School Choice Program Shuts Out Disabled, Federal Complaint Says," *Milwaukee Journal Sentinel*, June 7, 2011, https://archive.jsonline.com/news/education/123374903.html.
37. The Center for Media and Democracy's SourceWatch project, "Contributions of the Bradley Foundation."
38. Erin Richards, "Feds Quietly Close Long-Running Probe of Milwaukee Voucher Program," *Milwaukee Journal Sentinel*, January 4, 2016, https://archive.jsonline.com/news/education/feds-quietly-close-long-running-probe-of-milwaukee-voucher-program-b99644914z1-364068331.html/.
39. Phoebe Petrovic, "False Choice: Wisconsin Taxpayers Support Schools That Can Discriminate," *Wisconsin Watch*, May 5, 2023, https://wisconsinwatch.org/2023/05/wisconsin-voucher-schools-discrimination-lgbtq-disabilities/.
40. Wolf, Witte, and Fleming, *Special Education and the Milwaukee*, 17.
41. 2009 Wisconsin Act 28, https://dpi.wi.gov/parental-education-options/choice-programs/statutes.

42. Wisconsin Department of Public Instruction, "Private School Choice Programs: Statutes and Rules," https://dpi.wi.gov/parental-education-options/choice-programs/.

43. Joshua Cowen, "Oversight or Overregulation: Debating School Choice Accountability," Brookings Institution Commentary, January 12, 2017, https://www.brookings.edu /articles/oversight-or-overregulation-debating-school-choice-accountability/.

44. John F. Witte, Patrick J. Wolf, Joshua M. Cowen, Deven E. Carlson, and David J. Fleming, "High-Stakes Choice: Achievement and Accountability in the Nation's Oldest Urban Voucher Program," *Educational Evaluation and Policy Analysis* 36, no. 4 (2014): 437–56.

45. Joshua Cowen, "How Taxpayer-Funded Schools Teach Creationism—And Get Away With It," *New Republic*, January 30, 2014, https://newrepublic.com/article/116410/school -choice-tax-funded-private-schools-should-be-accountable-test.

46. Witte, Wolf, Cowen, Carlson, and Fleming, "High-Stakes Choice"; see also: Patrick J. Wolf, *The Comprehensive Longitudinal Evaluation of the Milwaukee Parental Choice Program: Summary of Final Reports* (report #36, Fayetteville: University of Arkansas, Department of Education Reform, 2012), https://scdp.uark.edu/the-comprehensive -longitudinal-evaluation-of-the-milwaukee-parental-choice-program-summary-of -final-reports/.

47. Patrick J. Wolf, "This Time It Counts," *Jay P. Greene* (blog), July 19, 2013, https:// jaypgreene.com/2013/07/19/this-time-it-counts/.

48. For example, see Jonathan Mills, Patrick J. Wolf, Anna Egalite, and Jay P. Greene, "Participant and Competitive Effects of the Louisiana Student Scholarships for Educational Excellence Program, First Year Impacts" (paper presented at the Association for Public Policy Analysis and Management, Washington, D.C, Friday, November 8, 2013). https://appam.confex.com/appam/2013/webprogram/Paper7776.html. I was a discussant on this paper: a public commentor assigned by the conference to discuss preliminary results and findings. This is to my knowledge the first public appearance of these negative results, which were eventually published by the School Choice Demonstration Project as *The Effects of the Louisiana Scholarship Program on Student Achievement After Two Years* (joint report 1, New Orleans, LA: Tulane University, Education Research Alliance for New Orleans, and Fayetteville: University of Arkansas, Department of Education Reform, 2016), https://scdp.uark.edu/the-effects -of-the-louisiana-scholarship-program-on-student-achievement-after-two-years/. The findings also in multiple outlets over subsequent years (see chapter 5).

49. Matt Barnum, "Betsy DeVos's Explanation for Negative Voucher Results: Program 'Not Very Well Conceived,'" Chalkbeat, May 6, 2019, https://www.chalkbeat.org/2019/5/6 /21108070/betsy-devos-s-explanation-for-negative-voucher-results-program-was-not -very-well-conceived.

50. Corey DeAngelis, "When It Comes to School Choice, Government-Regulated Managed Competition Is Bad in Theory and in Practice," The 74, March 7, 2018, https://www .the74million.org/article/deangelis-when-it-comes-to-school-choice-government -regulated-managed-competition-is-bad-in-theory-and-in-practice/; Jason Bedrick, "The Follow of Over-Regulating School Choice" *Education Next*, January 5, 2016, https://www.educationnext.org/the-folly-of-overregulating-school-choice/.

51. See Note on Sources and Funding at the beginning of this book.

52. Lynde and Harry Bradley Foundation, "Bradley Fellows," https://www.bradleyfdn.org /bradley-fellows.

53. EdChoice, *The 123s of School Choice: What Research Says About Private School Choice in America*, 2023, https://www.edchoice.org/wp-content/uploads/2023/07/123s-of-School -Choice-WEB-07-10-23.pdf.

54. Deven Carlson, Joshua M. Cowen, and David J. Fleming, "Life After Vouchers: What Happens to Students Who Leave Private Schools for the Traditional Public Sector?" *Educational Evaluation and Policy Analysis* 35, no. 2 (2013): 179–99.

55. Witte et al., "High-Stakes Choice."

56. See School Choice Demonstration Project bibliography of reports and authors https:// scdp.uark.edu/.

57. Wolf, *Comprehensive Longitudinal Evaluation of the Milwaukee*, report #2; Center for Media and Democracy SourceWatch, "Black Alliance for Educational Options," https://www.sourcewatch.org/index.php/Black_Alliance_for_Educational_Options; Institute for Advanced Studies in Culture, Biography of Gerard Robinson, https:// iasculture.org/scholars/profiles/gerard-robinson.

58. Tyler Kingkade, "A Betsy DeVos-Backed Group Helps Fuel a Rapid Expansion of Public Money for Private School," NBC News, March 30, 2023, https://www.nbcnews.com /politics/politics-news/betsy-devos-american-federation-children-private-school -rcna76307; Rekha Basu, "Your Tax Dollars for Their Private School? More and More States are Saying Yes," *Los Angeles Times*, February 12, 2023, https://www.latimes.com /opinion/story/2023-02-12/school-vouchers-private-public-school-iowa-kim-reynolds -lgbtq-parental-rights; Camille Camdessus and AFP, "At US Con-Fab, Republicans Embrace 45 Commandments for Victory," Digital Journal, March 3, 2023, https://www .digitaljournal.com/world/at-us-confab-republicans-embrace-45-commandments-for -victory/article.

Chapter 5

1. Jane Mayer, *Dark Money: The Hidden History of the Billionaires Behind the Rise of the Radical Right* (New York: Doubleday, 2016); Anne Nelson, *Shadow Network: Media, Money and the Secret Hub of the Radical Right* (New York: Bloomsbury Publishing, 2019).

2. Matt Barnum, "Obama's Education Legacy Mirrors the Rest of His Presidency— Accomplished, but Polarizing," The 74, January 17, 2017, https://www.the74million.org /article/barnum-obamas-education-legacy-mirrors-the-rest-of-his-presidency -accomplished-but-polarizing/.

3. Arianna Prothero, "D.C. School Vouchers Once Again Caught Up in Federal Fiscal Fight," Education Week, March 3, 2015, https://www.edweek.org/policy-politics/d-c -school-vouchers-once-again-caught-up-in-federal-fiscal-fight/2015/03.

4. Bella DiMarco and Liz Cohen, *The New Wave of Public Funding of Private Schooling, Explained*, FutureEd, March 9, 2023, https://www.future-ed.org/the-new-wave-of -public-funding-of-private-schools-explained/.

5. See Gary Rivlin, *Katrina: After the Flood* (New York: Simon and Schuster, 2016); Douglas N. Harris, *Charter School City: What the End of Traditional Public Schools in New Orleans Means for American Education* (Chicago: University of Chicago Press, 2020).

6. Carlie Kollath Wells, "New Orleans Finally Completes Post-Katrina School Restoration Project," *Axios*, May 14, 2023, https://www.axios.com/local/new-orleans/2023/05/14/new-orleans-hurricane-katrina-schools-rebuild.

7. Katy Reckdahl, "The Lost Children of Katrina," *The Atlantic*, April 2, 2015, https://www.theatlantic.com/education/archive/2015/04/the-lost-children-of-katrina/389345/.

8. Robert Tomsho, "After Katrina, School Choice Gains New Fans," *Wall Street Journal*, November 16, 2005, https://www.wsj.com/articles/SB113210963943298571.

9. Milton Friedman, "The Promise of Vouchers," *Wall Street Journal*, December 5, 2005, https://www.wsj.com/articles/SB113374845791113764.

10. Harris, *Charter School City*, 70.

11. Paul Dauphin, "10 Years After Katrina: Louisiana's Landscape of School Choice," American Federation for Children, Updated July 19, 2022, https://www.federationforchildren.org/10-years-katrina-louisianas-landscape-school-choice/.

12. Harris, *Charter School City*.

13. See Kim Chatalein, "The Cost of Choice: How Louisiana Steered Families into D and F Private Schools," WWNO, May 7, 2019, https://www.wwno.org/education/2019-05-07/the-cost-of-choice-how-louisianas-voucher-program-steered-families-into-d-and-f-private-schools.

14. Jonathan N. Mills and Patrick J. Wolf, *The Effects of the Louisiana Scholarship Program on Student Achievement After Two Years* (Louisiana Scholarship Program Evaluation Report #1, School Choice Demonstration Project, Fayetteville: University of Arkansas, and Education Research Alliance, New Orleans, LA: Tulane University, 2016), https://educationresearchalliancenola.org/files/publications/Report-1-LSP-Y2-Achievement.pdf.

15. Matt Barnum, "Who Gets Access to School Data? A Case Study on How Privacy, Politics and Budget Research Can Affect Education Research," The 74, August 2, 2017, https://www.the74million.org/article/who-gets-access-to-school-data-a-case-study-in-how-privacy-politics-budget-pressures-can-affect-education-research/.

16. Jonathan Mills, Patrick J. Wolf, Anna Egalite, and Jay P. Greene, "Participant and Competitive Effects of the Louisiana Student Scholarships for Educational Excellence Program, First Year Impacts" (paper presented at the Association for Public Policy Analysis and Management, Friday November 8, 2013), https://appam.confex.com/appam/2013/webprogram/Paper7776.html. This is, to my knowledge, the first public appearance of the results.

17. Mills and Wolf, "Effects of the Louisiana Scholarship Program," 8.

18. Kevin Carey, "Dismal Voucher Results Surprise Researchers as DeVos Era Begins," *New York Times*, February 23, 2017, https://www.nytimes.com/2017/02/23/upshot/dismal-results-from-vouchers-surprise-researchers-as-devos-era-begins.html.

19. See, for example, John F. Witte, *The Market Approach to Education: An Analysis of America's First Voucher Program* (Princeton, NJ: Princeton University Press, 2000); Patrick J. Wolf, *The Comprehensive Longitudinal Evaluation of the Milwaukee Parental Choice Program: Summary of Final Reports* (report #36, Fayetteville: University of Arkansas, Department of Education Reform, 2012), https://scdp.uark.edu/the-comprehensive-longitudinal-evaluation-of-the-milwaukee-parental-choice-program-summary-of-final-reports/; Patrick J. Wolf, Brian Kisida, Babette Gutmann, Michael Puma, Nada Eissa, and Lou Rizzo, "School Vouchers and Student Outcomes:

Experimental Evidence from Washington, DC," *Journal of Policy Analysis and Management* 32, no. 2 (2013): 246–70.

20. Comments of Kenneth Starr, Outside Counsel, "Supreme Court News Conference," C-SPAN, February 20, 2002, https://www.c-span.org/video/?168764-1/supreme-court -news-conference; Zelman v. Simmons-Harris 2001 WL 34093993 (US) (Joint Appendix) Appendix P: Affidavit of Paul E. Peterson.

21. Atila Abdulkadiroğlu, Parag A. Pathak, and Christopher R. Walters, *School Vouchers and Student Achievement: Evidence from the Louisiana Scholarship Program* (Cambridge, MA: National Bureau of Economic Research, 2015), https://www.nber.org /system/files/working_papers/w21839/revisions/w21839.rev1.pdf?sy=839. The paper would eventually be published as Atila Abdulkadiroğlu, Parag A. Pathak, and Christopher R. Walters, "Free to Choose: Can School Choice Reduce Student Achievement?" *American Economic Journal: Applied Economics* 10, no. 1 (2018): 175–206.

22. For a list of academic appearances of the Arkansas team's negative voucher results, see Mills and Wolf, "Effects of the Louisiana Scholarship Program," 8.

23. On Peterson and Greene's historical release of first year, favorable results, see Debra Viadero, "Researcher at Center of Storm Over Vouchers," *Education Week*, August 5, 1998, and Kate Zernike, "New Doubt is Cast on Study That Backs Voucher Efforts," *New York Times*, September 15, 2000, https://www.nytimes.com/2000/09/15/us/new-doubt-is -cast-on-study-that-backs-voucher-efforts.html. For a list of academic appearances of the Arkansas team's negative voucher results see Mills and Wolf, "Effects of the Louisiana Scholarship Program," 8; Mills et al., "Participant and Competitive Effects of the Louisiana Student."

24. Barnum, "Who Gets Access?"

25. John C. White, "Give Vouchers Time: Low Income Families Need as Many Quality School Options as Possible" Brookings Institution, June 23, 2016, https://www .brookings.edu/articles/give-vouchers-time-low-income-families-need-as-many-quality -school-options-as-possible/.

26. "Bad to Bad Schools in the Bayou," *Wall Street Journal,* editorial, March 18, 2016, https://www.wsj.com/articles/back-to-bad-schools-in-the-bayou-1458342194.

27. Barnum, "Who Gets Access?"

28. Jonathan N. Mills and Patrick J. Wolf, "Vouchers in the Bayou: The Effects of the Louisiana Scholarship Program on Student Achievement After 2 Years," *Educational Evaluation and Policy Analysis* 39, no. 3 (2017): 464–84.

29. Heidi H. Erickson, Jonathan N. Mills, and Patrick J. Wolf, "The Effects of the Louisiana Scholarship Program on Student Achievement and College Entrance," *Journal of Research on Educational Effectiveness* 14, no. 4 (2021): 861–99.

30. Jonathan N. Mills and Patrick J. Wolf, *The Effects of the Louisiana Scholarship Program on Student Achievement After Four Years* (EDRE working paper 2019–10, Fayetteville: University of Arkansas, Department of Education Reform), 2. https://bpb-us-e1 .wpmucdn.com/wordpressua.uark.edu/dist/9/544/files/2019/04/Mills-Wolf-LSP -Achievement-After-4-Years-final-ut3mor.pdf.

31. Patrick J. Wolf, "What Happened in the Bayou? Examining the Effects of the Louisiana Scholarship Program," *Education Next* 19 no. 4 (2019): 48–56.

32. Corey DeAngelis, Lindsey Burke, and Patrick J. Wolf, "Do Voucher Regulations Reduce Anticipated Program Participation and School Quality?" Cato Institute, October 29,

2018, https://www.cato.org/commentary/do-voucher-regulations-reduce-anticipated-voucher-program-participation-school-quality#.

33. Wolf, "What Happened?"

34. The Center for Media and Democracy's SourceWatch Project: "Contributions of the Bradley Foundation," a compilation of annual IRS 990 forms from 1998–2021 https://www.sourcewatch.org/index.php/Lynde_and_Harry_Bradley_Foundation; Charles M. Koch Foundation, "Grant Agreement," July 1, 2020, https://charleskochfoundation.org/app/uploads/2021/12/Harvard-University-Grant-Agreement-2020.pdf.

35. Matt Barnum, "Betsy DeVos's Explanation for Negative Voucher Results: Program Was 'Not Very Well-Conceived,'" Chalkbeat, May 6, 2019, https://www.chalkbeat.org/2019/5/6/21108070/betsy-devos-s-explanation-for-negative-voucher-results-program-was-not-very-well-conceived.

36. Mark Dynarski, Ning Rui, Ann Webber, and Babette Gutmann, *Evaluation of the DC Opportunity Scholarship Program: Impacts Two Years After Students Applied* (NCEE 2018–4010, Washington, DC: National Center for Education Evaluation and Regional Assistance, Institute of Education Sciences, US Department of Education, 2018), https://ies.ed.gov/ncee/pubs/20184010/pdf/20184010.pdf.

37. Mark Dynarski, Ning Rui, Ann Webber and Babette Gutmann, *Evaluation of the DC Opportunity Scholarship Program: Impacts After One Year* (NCEE 2017–4022, Washington, DC: National Center for Education Evaluation and Regional Assistance, Institute of Education Sciences, US Department of Education, 2017), https://ies.ed.gov/ncee/pubs/20174022/pdf/20174022.pdf.

38. Mark Dynarski and Austin Nichols, "More Findings on School Vouchers and Test Scores, and They Are Still Negative," Brookings Institution, July 13, 2017, https://www.brookings.edu/articles/more-findings-about-school-vouchers-and-test-scores-and-they-are-still-negative/.

39. Matt Barnum, "First Study of Indiana's Voucher Program—The Country's Largest—Finds It Hurts Kids' Math Skills at First, but Not Over Time," Chalkbeat, June 26, 2017, https://www.chalkbeat.org/2017/6/26/21107284/first-study-of-indiana-s-voucher-program-the-country-s-largest-finds-it-hurts-kids-math-skills-at-fi.

40. R. Joseph Waddington and Mark Berends, "Impact of the Indiana Choice Scholarship Program: Achievement Effects for Students in Upper Elementary and Middle School," *Journal of Policy Analysis and Management* 37, no. 4 (2018): 783–808; Mark Berends and R. Joseph Waddington, "School Choice in Indianapolis: Effects of Charter, Magnet, Private, and Traditional Public Schools," *Education Finance and Policy* 13, no. 2 (2018): 227–55.

41. Erickson, Mills, and Wolf, "Effects of the Louisiana Scholarship Program"; R. Joseph Waddington, Ron Zimmer, and Mark Berends, "Cream Skimming and Pushout of Students Participating in a Statewide Private School Voucher Program," *Educational Evaluation and Policy Analysis* (2023): 01623737231183397; Joshua M. Cowen., David J. Fleming, John F. Witte, and Patrick J. Wolf, "Going Public: Who Leaves a Large, Longstanding, and Widely Available Urban Voucher Program?" *American Educational Research Journal* 49, no. 2 (2012): 231–56; Daniel Kuehn, Matthew Chingos, and Alexandra Tinsley, "Most Students Receive a Florida Private School Choice Scholarship for Two Years or Fewer: What Does That Mean?" Urban Institute, March 6, 2020, https://www.urban.org/urban-wire/most-students-receive-florida-private-school-choice-scholarship-two-years-or-fewer-what-does-mean.

42. Shaina Cavazos, "Six Things to Know About Indiana's State Voucher Program: A Model Betsy DeVos Could Support," Chalkbeat, November 30, 2016, https://in.chalkbeat.org/2016/11/30/21099520/six-things-to-know-about-indiana-s-school-voucher-program-a-model-betsy-devos-could-support.
43. Julia Donheiser, "Choice for Most: In Nation's Largest Voucher Program, $16 Million Went to Schools with Anti-LGBT Policies," Chalkbeat, August 10, 2017, https://www.chalkbeat.org/2017/8/10/21107318/choice-for-most-in-nation-s-largest-voucher-program-16-million-went-to-schools-with-anti-lgbt-polici.
44. Annie Martin, "Florida Private School That Bans LGBTQ Students Gets $1.6 Million in Tax Dollars" *Orlando Sentinel*, August 25, 2022, https://www.orlandosentinel.com/2022/08/25/private-florida-school-that-bans-lgbtq-students-gets-16-million-in-tax-dollars/; Phoebe Petrovic, "False Choice: Wisconsin Taxpayers Support Schools That Can Discriminate," *Wisconsin Watch,* May 5, 2023, https://wisconsinwatch.org/2023/05/wisconsin-voucher-schools-discrimination-lgbtq-disabilities/.
45. "Profile: Moms for Liberty," Southern Poverty Law Center, https://www.splcenter.org/fighting-hate/extremist-files/group/moms-liberty.
46. Jay P. Greene, "It's Time for the School Choice Movement to Embrace the Culture War," Heritage Foundation, February 9, 2022, https://www.heritage.org/education/report/time-the-school-choice-movement-embrace-the-culture-war.
47. Zelman v. Simmons-Harris, Nos. 00–1751, 00–1777, 00–1779, Brief of State Petitioners on Writ of Certiorari to the United States Court of Appeals for the Sixth Circuit.
48. David Figlio and Krzysztof Karbownik, "Evaluation of Ohio's EdChoice Scholarship Program: Selection, Competition and Performance Effects," Thomas B. Fordham Institute, July 7, 2016, https://fordhaminstitute.org/ohio/research/evaluation-ohios-edchoice-scholarship-program-selection-competition-and-performance.
49. Mayer, *Dark Money*, 102–13.
50. See School Choice Demonstration Project, "D.C. Opportunity Scholarship Program Evaluation," University of Arkansas Department of Education Reform, https://scdp.uark.edu/dc-opportunity-scholarship-program-evaluation/; School Choice Demonstration Project, "Milwaukee Parental Choice Program Evaluation," University of Arkansas Department of Education Reform, https://scdp.uark.edu/milwaukee-parental-choice-program-evaluation/.
51. See Comments of Kenneth Starr, Outside Counsel, "Supreme Court News Conference," C-SPAN, February 20, 2002, https://www.c-span.org/video/?168764-1/supreme-court-news-conference; Paul E. Peterson, "Milwaukee Parents Like Choice," letter to the editor, *New York Times*, April 27, 1995.
52. Kevin Carey, "Dismal Voucher Results Surprise Researchers as DeVos Era Begins," *New York Times*, February 23, 2017, https://www.nytimes.com/2017/02/23/upshot/dismal-results-from-vouchers-surprise-researchers-as-devos-era-begins.html; Emma Brown and Mandy McLaren, "Nation's Only Federally Funded Voucher Program Has Negative Effect on Student Achievement, Study Finds," *Washington Post*, April 27, 2017, https://www.washingtonpost.com/local/education/federal-study-of-dc-voucher-program-finds-negative-impact-on-student-achievement/2017/04/27/e545ef28-2536-11e7-bb9d-8cd6118e1409_story.html; "Study Shows Louisiana School Voucher Program Hurt Math Scores," WWNO New Orleans Public Radio, April 23, 2019, https://www.wwno.org/education/2019-04-23/study-shows-louisiana-school-voucher-program-hurt

-math-scores; Matt Barnum, "Students' Math Scores Drop for Years After Using a Private School Voucher in Country's Largest Program," Chalkbeat, August 9, 2018, https://www.chalkbeat.org/2018/8/9/21107311/students-math-scores-drop-for-years -after-using-a-private-school-voucher-in-country-s-largest-progra; Matt Barnum, "Do Voucher Students' Scores Bounce Back After Initial Decline? New Research Says No," Chalkbeat, April 23, 2019, https://www.chalkbeat.org/2019/4/23/21055489/do-voucher -students-scores-bounce-back-after-initial-declines-new-research-says-no; Peg Tyre, "Trump Administration Advances School Vouchers Despite Scant Evidence," *Scientific American*, August 1, 2017, https://www.scientificamerican.com/article/trump -administration-advances-school-vouchers-despite-scant-evidence/.

53. Michael R. Ford and Fredrik O. Andersson, "Determinants of Organizational Failure in the Milwaukee School Voucher Program," *Policy Studies Journal* 47, no. 4 (2019): 1048–68; Jane Arnold Lincove, Jon Valant, and Joshua M. Cowen, "You Can't Always Get What You Want: Capacity Constraints in a Choice-Based School System," *Economics of Education Review* 67 (2018): 94–109.

54. Christopher Lubienski and Yusaf Canbolet, *Evolving Evidence on School Vouchers*, (Bloomington: Indiana University, Center for Evaluation and Education Policy, November 2022), https://ceep.indiana.edu/education-policy/policy-briefs/2022/evolving -evidence-on-school-voucher-effects.pdf.

55. US Department of Education, Institute for Education Sciences, "What Is Evidence-Based Practice?" https://ies.ed.gov/EvidenceBased/dataliteracy/ds-ebp.asp.

56. US Department of Education, "What Is Evidence-Based Practice."

57. Grover J. Whitehurst, "Making Education Evidence-Based: Premises, Practices, Pragmatics and Politics," IPR Distinguished Public Policy Lecture Series 2003–2004, Northwestern University, April 26, 2004, https://ies.ed.gov/director/pdf/2004_04_26 .pdf.

58. US Department of Education Institute for Education Sciences, "Predoctoral Interdisciplinary Research Training Programs in the Education Sciences," https://ies.ed.gov/ncer /projects/program.asp?ProgID=16.

Chapter 6

1. Emma Brown, "School Choice Advocates Divided Over Trump and His Education Pick, Betsy DeVos," *Washington Post*, December 12, 2016, https://www.washingtonpost.com /local/education/school-choice-advocates-divide-over-trump-and-his-education-pick -betsy-devos/2016/12/09/6c377824-b806-11e6-b8df-600bd9d38a02_story.html.

2. Matt Barnum, "Betsy DeVos's Explanation for Negative Voucher Results: Program Was 'Not Very Well-Conceived,'" Chalkbeat, May 6, 2019, https://www.chalkbeat.org/2019/5 /6/21108070/betsy-devos-s-explanation-for-negative-voucher-results-program-was-not -very-well-conceived.

3. Alyson Klein and Andrew Ujifusa, "Trump Calls Education the 'Civil Rights Issue of Our Time,' Pushes Choice," Education Week, February 28, 2017, https://www.edweek .org/policy-politics/trump-calls-education-civil-rights-issue-of-our-time-pushes-choice /2017/02.

4. Sarah Posner, *Unholy: Why White Evangelicals Worship at the Altar of Donald Trump* (New York: Random House, 2020).

5. Posner, *Unholy*, chapters 2, 6, 7.

6. See Posner, *Unholy*, and Katherine Stewart, *The Power Worshippers: Inside the Dangerous Rise of Religious Nationalism* (New York: Bloomsbury Publishing, 2019).

7. On Conway: see Anne Nelson, *Shadow Network: Media, Money and the Secret Hub of the Radical Right* (New York: Bloomsbury Publishing, 2019).

8. Jane Mayer, *Dark Money: The Hidden History of the Billionaires Behind the Rise of the Radical Right* (New York: Doubleday, 2016).

9. The Center for Media and Democracy's SourceWatch project: "Contributions of the Bradley Foundation," a compilation of annual IRS 990 forms from 1998–2021, https://www.sourcewatch.org/index.php/Lynde_and_Harry_Bradley_Foundation.

10. Lindsay Burke, "Regulations Threaten to Limit Best Schooling Options for Children," Heritage Foundation, November 9, 2018, https://www.heritage.org/education/commentary/regulations-threaten-limit-best-schooling-options-children; Lindsay Burke and Jason Bedrick, "Recalibrating Accountability: Education Savings Accounts as Vehicles for Choice and Innovation," Heritage Foundation, December 12, 2016, https://www.heritage.org/education/report/recalibrating-accountability-education-savings-accounts-vehicles-choice-and; Jason Bedrick, "The Folly of Over-Regulating School Choice," Cato Institute, January 5, 2016, https://www.cato.org/commentary/folly-overregulating-school-choice#; Frederick M. Hess, "Making Sense of the Lousy Louisiana Voucher Results," American Enterprise Institute and Education Week, https://www.aei.org/articles/making-sense-of-the-lousy-test-results-in-louisianas-voucher-program/; Frederick M. Hess, "School Choice Research Is Not a Weapon," American Enterprise Institute, May 2, 2017, https://www.aei.org/articles/school-choice-research-is-not-a-weapon/.

11. University of Arkansas School Choice Demonstration Project, Louisiana Scholarship Program Evaluation, https://scdp.uark.edu/louisiana-scholarship-program-evaluation/; Corey A. DeAngelis and Patrick J. Wolf, "Private School Choice and Character: More Evidence from Milwaukee," *Journal of Private Enterprise* 35, no. 3 (2020), http://journal.apee.org/index.php/Parte3_2020_Journal_of_Private_Enterprise_Vol_35_No_3_Fall.

12. Barnum, "Betsy DeVos's Explanation"; Matt Barnum, "School Choice Supporters Downplay New Voucher Research, Saying Schools Are More Than a Test Score," Chalkbeat, May 25, 2017, https://www.chalkbeat.org/2017/5/24/21107273/school-choice-supporters-downplay-new-voucher-research-saying-schools-are-more-than-a-test-score.

13. Nelson, *Shadow Network*.

14. Nancy MacLean, "How Milton Friedman Exploited White Supremacy to Privatize Education" (working paper series no. 161, Institute for New Economic Thinking, September 2021), https://papers.ssrn.com/sol3/papers.cfm?abstract_id=3932454.

15. American Enterprise Institute Profiles: John R. Bolton, https://www.aei.org/profile/john-r-bolton/; Michael Barone, https://www.aei.org/profile/radley-barone/; Glenn Hubbard, https://www.aei.org/profile/r-glenn-hubbard/; Rob Portman, https://www.aei.org/profile/rob-portman/; American Enterprise Institute Events: Ryan, https://www.aei.org/events/modernizing-americas-health-care-a-conversation-with-speaker-paul-ryan-r-wi-and-the-speakers-task-force-on-health-care-reform/; Cheney, https://www.aei.org/events/the-nuclear-deal-with-iran-and-the-implications-for-us-security-a-speech-by-former-vice-president-richard-b-cheney/.

16. American Enterprise Institute Profile: Charles Murray, https://www.aei.org/profile/radley-murray/.

17. George Packer, *The Assassins' Gate: America in Iraq* (New York: Farrar, Straus and Giroux, 2005), 111–12.

18. Heritage Foundation: Jay W. Richards, PhD Director of the DeVos Center for Life, Religion and Family, https://www.heritage.org/staff/jay-w-richards-phd; Rick Hess, "Betsy DeVos and the Manichean Impulse," Education Week, January 17, 2017, https://www.edweek.org/policy-politics/opinion-betsy-devos-and-the-manichean -impulse/2017/01.

19. Michael Barone, "Can Betsy DeVos's Good Work Be Saved from 'the Blob?'" American Enterprise Institute, January 11, 2021, https://www.aei.org/op-eds/can-betsy-devoss-good -work-be-saved-from-the-blob/; Rick Hess, "An Exit Interview with Secretary of Education Betsy DeVos," Education Week, December 15, 2020, https://www.edweek.org/policy -politics/opinion-an-exit-interview-with-secretary-of-education-betsy-devos/2020/12.

20. Jim Blew, "What Conservatives Could Learn from Betsy DeVos," American Enterprise Institute, May 13, 2021, https://www.aei.org/wp-content/uploads/2021/05/What -Conservatives-Could-Learn-from-Betsy-DeVos.pdf?x91208; The Federalist Society, Contributors: Jim Blew https://fedsoc.org/contributors/jim-blew.

21. American Enterprise Institute Events, The Fight for American Education: Betsy DeVos on Her Tenure as U.S. Secretary of Education, https://www.aei.org/events/the-fight-for -american-education-betsy-devos-on-her-tenure-as-secretary-of-education/. American Enterprise Institute Profile: Frederick M. Hess, https://www.aei.org/profile/radleyk-m -hess/.

22. Rick Hess, "The 2023 Edu-Scholar Public Influence Rankings" Education Week, January 5, 2023, https://www.edweek.org/policy-politics/opinion-the-2023-rhsu-edu -scholar-public-influence-rankings/2023/01.

23. Rick Hess, "The 2022 Edu-Scholar Public Influence Scoring Rubric," Education Week, January 4, 2023, https://www-edweek-org.proxy1.cl.msu.edu/policy-politics/opinion -the-2022-rhsu-edu-scholar-public-influence-scoring-rubric/2022/01.

24. American Enterprise Institute, Education Policy Program, email message to author, January 29, 2020.

25. Dan Mangan, "Former White House Obama Aide Seth Andrew Sentenced to Year in Prison for Charter School Theft Scheme," CNBC, July 29, 2022, https://www.cnbc.com /2022/07/28/former-obama-white-house-aide-seth-andrew-sentenced-for-school-theft .html.

26. The Lynde and Harry Bradley Foundation, Bradley Fellows, https://www.bradleyfdn.org /radley-fellows.

27. As an example, as part of my contract to found the Education Policy Innovation Collaborative at Michigan State University, in 2016, I secured roughly $1.9 million in seed funding from the education reform-oriented group, the Laura and John Arnold Foundation. That funding was conditional on securing another or $600,000 in matching funds from other sources. This is a common arrangement for education research centers across the country.

28. Roger Sollenberger, "Conservative Group Accidently Reveals Its Secret Donors," The Daily Beast, November 22, 2023, https://www.thedailybeast.com/conservative-group -accidentally-reveals-its-secret-donors-some-of-them-are-liberal-orgs.

29. 15–577 Trinity Lutheran Church of Columbia, Inc. v. Comer, 582 US (2017). https:// www.supremecourt.gov/opinions/16pdf/15-577_khlp.pdf; 18–1195 Espinosa v. Montana

Department of Revenue (2019), https://www.supremecourt.gov/opinions/19pdf/18 -1195_g314.pdf.

30. Linda Greenhouse, *Justice on the Brink: The Death of Ruth Bader Ginsburg, the Rise of Amy Coney Barrett, and Twelve Months That Transformed the Supreme Court* (New York: Random House, 2023), 218.

31. Libby Nelson, "Betsy DeVos Was Asked a Basic Question About Education Policy—And Couldn't Answer," Vox, January 17, 2017, https://www.vox.com/2017/1/17/14304692 /devos-confirmation-hearing-education; Alastair Jamieson, "Betsy DeVos Cites Grizzly Bears During Guns-in-Schools Debate," NBC News, January 18, 2017, https://www .nbcnews.com/news/us-news/betsy-devos-schools-might-need-guns-due-potential -grizzlies-n708261.

32. "Sketch: Sean Spicer Press Conference," *Saturday Night Live,* Aired February 5, 2017, on NBC, https://www.youtube.com/watch?v=UWuc18xISwI.

33. US Senate, Donald J. Trump Cabinet Nominations, n.d., https://www.senate.gov /legislative/nominations/Trump_cabinet.htm.

34. "DeVos to Speak at Harvard Conference on School Choice," *Boston Globe*, September 28, 2017, https://www.boston.com/news/local-news/2017/09/28/devos-to-speak-at -harvard-conference-on-school-choice/.

35. "Harvard Students Taunt Betsy DeVos," Aired September 29, 2017, on CNN. https:// www.cnn.com/videos/politics/2017/09/29/betsy-devos-speech-protesters-orig-vstan.cnn.

36. "Harvard Students Taunt Betsy DeVos."

37. Harvard University, "A Conversation on Empowering Parents with Betsy DeVos," Institute of Politics, September 28, 2017, https://iop.harvard.edu/events/conversation -empowering-parents-secretary-betsy-devos.

38. Graham Vyse, "Betsy DeVos Is Headlining Harvard's Koch-Backed Conference on School Choice—With No Critics of School Choice," *New Republic*, September 25, 2017, https://newrepublic.com/article/144980/betsy-devos-headlining-harvards-koch-backed -conference-school-choicewith-no-critics-school-choice; "Grant Agreement," Charles M. Koch Foundation, July 1, 2020, https://charleskochfoundation.org/app /uploads/2021/12/Harvard-University-Grant-Agreement-2020.pdf.

39. Vyse, "Betsy DeVos Is Headlining."

40. Annual Report, Harvard University, Program on Education Policy and Governance, 2017, https://www.hks.harvard.edu/sites/default/files/Taubman/PEPG/annual-reports /2017-pepg-annual-report.pdf; Annual Report, Harvard University Program on Education Policy and Governance, 2018; https://www.hks.harvard.edu/sites/default/files /Taubman/PEPG/annual-reports/2018-pepg-annual-report.pdf.

41. Annual Report, Harvard University, 2017, 8.

42. Charles M. Koch Foundation, "Grant Agreement," 3.

43. Charles M. Koch Foundation, "Grant Agreement," 4.

44. Paul E. Peterson, "In New Book, Education Secretary Betsy DeVos Emerges as a Modern 'Aloysha,'" *Education Next*, 24, no. 4: 72–74. https://www.educationnext.org/hostages -no-more-school-choice-advances-farther-than-anticipated/.

45. Nelson, *Shadow Network*.

46. The phrase "boots on the ground" to describe ADA comes from Anne Nelson, *Shadow Network*, 142.

47. Nelson, *Shadow Network*, 140–2.

48. Nelson, 71.

49. The Center for Media and Democracy's SourceWatch project: "Contributions of the Bradley Foundation," a compilation of annual IRS 990 forms from 1998–2021; Nelson, *Shadow Network*, 142.

50. Annual Report, Harvard University, Program on Education Policy and Governance, 2022, https://www.hks.harvard.edu/sites/default/files/Taubman/PEPG/annual-reports /2022-pepg-annual-report.pdf; Nelson, *Shadow Network*, 142.

51. Heritage Foundation Staff: Edwin Meese, https://www.heritage.org/staff/the-hon-edwin -meese-iii; Paul E. Peterson and Michael W. McConnell, eds. *Scalia's Constitution: Essays on Law and Education* (Cham, Switzerland: Palgrave MacMillan, 2018).

52. Posner, *Unholy*.

53. Posner, chapter 7.

54. Jeff Sessions, "Memorandum for All Executive Departments and Agencies," Department of Justice, October 6, 2017, 1, https://www.justice.gov/media/917256/dl?inline.

55. Posner, *Unholy*, 169.

56. Jeff Sessions, "Memorandum for All Executive Departments and Agencies," 2.

57. Posner, *Unholy*, 174.

58. Posner, 180.

59. Posner, chapter 7.

60. Emma Brown and Peter Jamison, "The Christian Home-Schooler Who Made 'Parental Rights' a GOP Rallying Cry," *Washington Post*, August 29, 2023, https://www .washingtonpost.com/education/2023/08/29/michael-farris-homeschoolers-parents -rights-ziklag/.

61. Betsy DeVos, "Religious Liberty in Our Schools Must Be Protected," *USA Today*, January 17, 2020, https://www.usatoday.com/story/opinion/2020/01/17/betsy-devos -religious-liberty-schools-protected-first-amendment-column/4488287002/.

62. Posner, *Unholy*.

63. Frederick M. Hess, "Does School Choice 'Work'?" *National Affairs*, Fall 2010, https:// www.nationalaffairs.com/publications/detail/does-school-choice-work.

64. Bella DiMarco and Liz Cohen, "The New Wave of Public Funding of Private Schooling, Explained," FutureEd, March 9, 2023, https://www.future-ed.org/the-new-wave-of -public-funding-of-private-schools-explained/.

65. DiMarco and Cohen, "New Wave of Public Funding."

66. See the catalog on the School Choice Demonstration Project's list of reports, particularly from Louisiana, Milwaukee, and Washington, D.C., for this kind of flood-the-zone style of report dissemination: School Choice Demonstration Project, University of Arkansas, https://scdp.uark.edu/.

67. The Center for Media and Democracy's SourceWatch project, "Moving Picture Institute," https://www.sourcewatch.org/index.php/Moving_Picture_Institute; Nelson, *Shadow Network*; "A Big Close-up for Educational Opportunities," Philanthropy Roundtable, https://www.philanthropyroundtable.org/magazine/a-big-close-up-for -educational-opportunities/.

68. EdChoice 2021 Annual Report, 9, https://www.edchoice.org/wp-content/uploads/2022 /05/EdChoice-Annual-Report-041222.pdf.

69. A Big Close-up for Educational Opportunities," Philanthropy Roundtable. For the Koch contributions to Institute for Justice, see Mayer, *Dark Money*, 146.

70. Frank E. Lockwood, "Backer of School Choice Saluted: Arkansan Helped Start D.C. Awards," *Northwest Arkansas Times*, January 27, 2019, https://www.nwaonline.com /news/2019/jan/27/backer-of-school-choice-saluted-2019012/.

71. Lockwood, "Backer of School Choice."

72. Lockwood.

73. Spencer S. Hse, "How Vouchers Came to D.C.," *Education Next*, June 30, 2006, https://www.educationnext.org/howvoucherscametodc/.

Chapter 7

1. Samuel J. Robinson, "Betsy DeVos Says Ballot Petition Would Let Parents 'Take Control' of Michigan Education," Mlive.com, February 2, 2022, https://www.mlive.com/public -interest/2022/02/betsy-devos-says-ballot-initiative-would-let-parents-take-control-of -michigan-education.html.

2. Erin Einhorn, "Betsy DeVos Fought for Private School Vouchers for Decades. She May Finally Get Her Wish," NBC News, March 26, 2022, https://www.nbcnews.com/news /education/betsy-devos-private-school-vouchers-michigan-rcna21384.

3. Marc LeBlond and Ed Tarnowski, "Educational Freedom and Choice Hits Escape Velocity: End of Session Wrap-Up," EdChoice, July 19, 2023, https://www.edchoice.org /engage/educational-freedom-and-choice-hits-escape-velocity-end-of-session-wrap/.

4. Bella DiMarco and Liz Cohen, "The New Wave of Public Funding of Private Schooling, Explained," FutureEd, March 9, 2023, https://www.future-ed.org/the-new-wave-of -public-funding-of-private-schools-explained/.

5. Joshua Cowen, "Research on School Vouchers Suggests Concerns Ahead for Education Savings Accounts," Brookings Institution, August 15, 2023, https://www.brookings.edu /articles/research-on-school-vouchers-suggests-concerns-ahead-for-education-savings -accounts/.

6. Monica Potts and Mary Radcliffe, "Politicians Want Universal Vouchers. But What About the Public?" FiveThirtyEight, March 29, 2023, https://fivethirtyeight.com/features /politicians-want-universal-school-vouchers-but-what-about-the-public/.

7. See Yue Stella Yu, "Michigan Proposal 3 Fact Check: No, Masseuses Won't Give Abortions to Minors," Bridge Michigan, October 3, 2022, https://www.bridgemi.com /michigan-government/michigan-proposal-3-fact-check-no-masseuses-wont-give -abortions-minors; Robin Erb and Yu Stella Yu, "Abortion Locked into Michigan Constitution. What Comes Next," Bridge Michigan, November 9, 2022, https://www .bridgemi.com/michigan-health-watch/abortion-locked-michigan-constitution-what -comes-next; Jonathan Oosting, "Betsy DeVos's Let MI Kids Learn Scholarship Plan to Submit Signatures," Bridge Michigan, August 9, 2022, https://www.bridgemi.com /michigan-government/betsy-devos-let-mi-kids-learn-scholarship-plan-submit -signatures.

8. Zach Montellaro, "The GOP's Messiest Primary" *Politico*, July 26, 2022, https://www .politico.com/news/2022/07/26/gop-messiest-primary-michigan-00047790.

9. Jon King, "Dixon Opposes Abortion for Rape Victims Because There's 'Healing Through That Baby,'" Michigan Advance, August 21, 2022, https://michiganadvance .com/2022/08/21/dixon-opposes-abortion-for-rape-victims-because-theres-healing -through-the-baby/.

10. Allison Donahue, "Dixon Demands Action on Book Bans, 'Grooming' and More—But She's Quiet on the Details," Michigan Advance, October 3, 2022; https://michigan advance.com/2022/10/03/dixon-demands-action-on-book-bans-grooming-and-more -but-shes-quiet-on-the-details/.

11. Emma Stein, "Book Bans Spreading Across Michigan: What's Driving Them?" *Detroit Free Press*, October 11, 2022, https://www.freep.com/story/news/local/michigan/2022 /10/11/book-bans-michigan-lgbtq/69541902007/; Betsy DeVos, *Hostages No More: The Fight for Education Freedom and the Future of the American Child* (Nashville, TN: Center Street, 2022).

12. Christopher F. Rufo, "Concealing Radicalism," *Substack*, September 14, 2022, https:// christopherrufo.com/p/concealing-radicalism; Pro-Publica, "Non-Profit Explorer," IRS Form 990, Moving Picture Institute, https://projects.propublica.org/nonprofits /organizations/203237801.

13. Benjamin Wallace-Wells, "How a Conservative Activist Invented the Conflict Over Critical Race Theory," *New Yorker*, June 18, 2021, https://www.newyorker.com/news/annals-of -inquiry/how-a-conservative-activist-invented-the-conflict-over-critical-race-theory.

14. The Center for Media and Democracy's SourceWatch Project, "Contributions of the Bradley Foundation," a compilation of annual IRS 990 forms from 1998–2021, https://www.sourcewatch.org/index.php/Lynde_and_Harry_Bradley_Foundation.

15. DeVos, *Hostages No More*, 253–260.

16. Chris Rufo, "Laying Siege to the Institutions," Hillsdale College, April 5, 2022, https://www.youtube.com/watch?v=W8Hh0GqoJcE&t=2087s.

17. Southern Poverty Law Center, "The Council for National Policy: Behind the Curtain," https://www.splcenter.org/hatewatch/2016/05/17/council-national-policy-behind-curtain.

18. Domenico Montanaro, "Republicans Can't Stop Using the Word 'Woke,' But What Does It Mean?" NPR, July 21, 2023, https://www.npr.org/2023/07/21/1189016049/woke -desantis-trump-black-culture; Moira Donean, "Florida's Attacks on Academic Freedom Just Got Worse," *The Guardian*, August 16, 2023, https://www.theguardian .com/commentisfree/2023/aug/16/florida-ron-desantis-academic-freedom.

19. Office of Governor Ron DeSantis, "Governor DeSantis Announces Legislative Proposal to Stop W.O.K.E. Activism and Critical Race Theory in Schools and Corporations," December 15, 2021, https://www.flgov.com/2021/12/15/governor-desantis-announces -legislative-proposal-to-stop-w-o-k-e-activism-and-critical-race-theory-in-schools-and -corporations/.

20. Ed Mazza, "DeSantis Mocked After 'Buzzword Diarrhea of the Mouth" Rant Against 'Woke,'" Yahoo Life, April 20, 2023, https://www.yahoo.com/lifestyle/ron-desantis -mocked-buzzword-diarrhea-083928815.html.

21. John Kennedy and Nirvi Shah, "DeSantis Signs Major Private School Voucher Expansion in Florida," *USA Today*, March 28, 2023, https://www.usatoday.com/story/news /nation/2023/03/28/desantis-signs-floridas-biggest-school-voucher-program-expansion /11556334002/.

22. Danielle Prieur, "Florida Policy Institute Asked for School Voucher Data, Here's What Step Up for Students Provided," WMFE, September 14, 2023, https://www.wmfe.org /education/2023-09-14/florida-policy-institute-school-voucher-data-step-up-for -students; Jeffrey Solochek, "Florida's School Vouchers Can Pay for TVs, Kayaks, and

Theme Parks; Is That OK?" *Tampa Bay Times*, September 1, 2023, https://www.tampabay
.com/news/education/2023/09/01/florida-school-vouchers-can-pay-tvs-kayaks-theme
-parks-is-that-ok/; Step Up For Students, "Transparency in Scholarship Programs," n.d.,
https://drive.google.com/file/d/1yyl80Jbs9mU6GlV1ktA6zZg8GUjLnsP4/view.

23. Jordan Valinksy, "Major Bank Pulls Support for Florida Voucher Program After LGBT
Discrimination Report," CNN, January 29, 2020, https://www.cnn.com/2020/01/29
/business/fifth-third-bank-florida-voucher-trnd/index.html.

24. Andrew DeMillo, "Arkansas Gov. Sanders Signs Bill Creating School Vouchers,"
Associated Press, March 8, 2023, https://apnews.com/article/huckabee-sanders
-vouchers-schools-lgbtq-education-teachers-bd56e89399d401ea44018cc92a5116ee;
Office of Gov. Kim Reynolds, "Gov. Reynolds Signs Students First Act Into Law,"
https://governor.iowa.gov/press-release/2023-01-24/gov-reynolds-signs-students-first
-act-law; Kate Lobosco, "New Iowa Law Restricts Gender Identity Education, Bans
Books With Sexual Content," CNN, May 17, 2023, https://www.cnn.com/2023/05/27
/politics/iowa-law-gender-identity-book-ban/index.html.

25. Robert Downen, "Texas Families Would Get $8000 in Tax Dollars to Send Students to
Private School in Sweeping 'Parental Rights' Bill Backed by Lieutenant Governor," *Texas
Tribune*, March 10, 2023, https://www.texastribune.org/2023/03/10/gender-sexual
-orientation-vouchers-texas-senate-bill/.

26. Tyler Kingkade, "A Betsy DeVos-Backed Group Helps Fuel a Rapid Expansion of Public
Money for Private Schools," NBC News, March 30, 2023, https://www.nbcnews.com
/politics/politics-news/betsy-devos-american-federation-children-private-school
-rcna76307.

27. Andrew Prokop, "A Conservative Push for School Choice Has Had Its Most Successful
Year Ever," Vox, September 11, 2023, https://www.vox.com/politics/23689496/school
-choice-education-savings-accounts-american-federation-children.

28. Kingkade, "Betsy DeVos-Backed Group."

29. Kingkade.

30. Bella DiMarco, "Legislative Tracker: 2023 Parent-Rights Bills in the States," FutureEd,
https://www.future-ed.org/legislative-tracker-2023-parent-rights-bills-in-the-states;
Jonathan Friedman, Jeffrey Sachs, Jeremy C. Young, and Samantha LeFrance, "Educational Censorship Continues: the 2023 Legislative Sessions So Far," Pen America,
February 16, 2023, https://pen.org/educational-censorship-continues-in-2023/.

31. Step Up For Students, "Transparency in Scholarship Programs"; Jay P. Greene and Jason
Bedrick, "School Choice Primarily Benefits Students Who Weren't Already in Private
School," Heritage Foundation, March 21, 2023, https://www.heritage.org/education
/commentary/school-choice-primarily-benefits-students-who-werent-already-private
-schools; Talia Richman and Allie Morris, "Who Would Texas' ESAs Benefit? Tension
Emerges Over Who Would Get Money for Private School" *Dallas Morning News*,
March 24, 2023, https://www.dallasnews.com/news/education/2023/03/24/who-would
-texas-education-savings-accounts-be-for-a-divide-over-homeschoolers-emerges/.

32. Jason Bedrick, Jay P. Greene, and Lindsey Burke, "Does School Choice Affect Private
Tuition?" Heritage Foundation, August 31, 2023, https://www.heritage.org/education
/report/does-school-choice-affect-private-school-tuition.

33. Heritage Foundation, *Education Freedom Report Card: State Rankings for Parents*,
https://www.heritage.org/educationreportcard/index.html.

34. 20–1088 Carson v. Makin, 596 US Supreme Court, June 21, 2022, https://www
.supremecourt.gov/opinions/21pdf/20-1088_dbfi.pdf; Linda Greenhouse, *Justice on the Brink: The Death of Ruth Bader Ginsburg, the Rise of Amy Coney Barrett, and Twelve Months That Transformed the Supreme Court* (New York, Random House, 2021).
35. Greenhouse, *Justice on the Brink*, 220.
36. Anthony Izaguirre, "DeSantis Signs Florida GOP's 6-Week Abortion Ban into Law," Associated Press, April 14, 2023, https://apnews.com/article/florida-abortion-ban
-approved-c9c53311a0b2426adc4b8d0b463edad1.
37. Mary Kekatos and Kendall Ross, "Iowa Gov. Reynolds Signs New 6-Week Abortion Ban into Law," ABC News, July 14, 2023, https://abcnews.go.com/US/iowa-gov-kim-reynolds
-signs-new-6-week/story?id=101082504.
38. Tess Vrbin, "Lawmakers Reject Two Proposed Exceptions to Arkansas' Abortion Ban," *Arkansas Advocate*, March 30, 2023, https://arkansasadvocate.com/2023/03/30
/lawmakers-reject-two-proposed-exceptions-to-arkansas-abortion-ban/; Associated Press, "A New Arkansas Law Allows an Anti-Abortion Monument Near the State Capitol," National Public Radio, March 19, 2023, https://www.npr.org/2023/03/19
/1164614996/arkansas-abortion-monument-sanders.
39. Alexandra Marquez, "Almost Half of States Have Restricted Abortion Access Since Dobbs," NBC News, June 21, 2023, https://www.nbcnews.com/meet-the-press
/meetthepressblog/almost-half-states-restricted-abortion-dobbs-rcna90409; LeBlond and Tarnowski, "Educational Freedom and Choice."
40. See Greenhouse, *Justice on the Brink*; Katherine Stewart, *The Power Worshippers: Inside the Dangerous Rise of Religious Nationalism* (New York: Bloomsbury Publishing, 2019); Sarah Posner, *Unholy: Why White Evangelicals Worship at the Alter of Donald Trump* (New York: Random House, 2020); Anne Nelson, *Shadow Network: Media, Money and the Secret Hub of the Radical Right* (New York: Bloomsbury Publishing, 2019).
41. Anya Kamenetz, "DeVos Family Money Is All Over the News Right Now," NPR, August 2, 2018, https://www.npr.org/2018/08/02/630112697/devos-family-money-is-all
-over-the-news-right-now.
42. Posner, *Unholy*.
43. Cory Turner, "Asked About Discrimination, Betsy DeVos Said This 14 Times," NPR, June 7, 2017, https://www.npr.org/sections/ed/2017/06/07/531783226/asked-about
-discrimination-betsy-devos-said-this-14-times; Posner, *Unholy*.
44. Mary Emily O'Hara, "This Law Firm Is Linked to Anti-Transgender Bathroom Bills Across the Country," NBC News, April 8, 2017, https://www.nbcnews.com/feature/nbc
-out/law-firm-linked-anti-transgender-bathroom-bills-across-country-n741106.
45. Mark Joseph Stern, "It Wasn't About Bathrooms, and It Isn't About Women's Sports" *Slate*, April 7, 2021, https://slate.com/news-and-politics/2021/04/transgender-rights
-bathrooms-sports-alliance-defending-freedom.html.
46. Andrew Kaczynski, "Before He Became a Politician, House Speaker Mike Johnson Partnered With an Anti-Gay Conversation Therapy Group," CNN.com, November 1, 2023; https://www.cnn.com/2023/11/01/politics/mike-johnson-kfile-invs/index
.html.
47. Alliance Defending Freedom, "Fully two-thirds of American voters oppose biological males who identify as women from competing in women's athletics," Twitter, September 15, 2023, https://twitter.com/ADFLegal/status/1702674884596224407.

48. Betsy DeVos, "We can, we must, we will #SaveWomensSports and #ProtectTitleIX!" Twitter, September 15, 2023, https://twitter.com/BetsyDeVos/status/170268521833 7927480.

49. Alliance Defending Freedom, "'By repeatedly and unlawfully removing critical safeguards in the chemical abortion regimen, the FDA has failed to protect the safety of women and girls.'-ADF's Erik Baptist," Twitter, September 15, 2023, https://twitter.com /ADFLegal/status/1702773785298940247; Alliance Defending Freedom, "Bigotry cannot be defeated by more bigotry, but the Albemarle County School Board's policy forces students to judge everyone and everything through the lens of race," Twitter, September 15, 2023, https://twitter.com/ADFLegal/status/1702743835917357531.

50. Emma Brown and Peter Jamison, "The Christian Home-Schooler Who Made 'Parental Rights' a GOP Rallying Cry," *Washington Post*, August 29, 2023, https://www .washingtonpost.com/education/2023/08/29/michael-farris-homeschoolers-parents -rights-ziklag/; Betsy DeVos, "Religious Liberty in Our Schools Must Be Protected," *USA Today*, January 17, 2020, https://www.usatoday.com/story/opinion/2020/01/17 /betsy-devos-religious-liberty-schools-protected-first-amendment-column/4488287002/.

51. Gregory Krieg, "How Moms for Liberty Grew Into a 2024 Player," CNN, June 30, 2023, https://www.cnn.com/2023/06/30/politics/moms-for-liberty-2024/index.html; Tyler Kingkade, "GOP Presidential Candidates Want the Moms for Liberty Vote in Pennsylvania After Local Victories," NBC News, June 28, 2023, https://www.nbcnews.com /politics/politics-news/moms-liberty-pennsylvania-2024-election-republican-president -votes-rcna91339.

52. Krieg, "How Moms for Liberty Grew."

53. Moms for Liberty Event Site, "Moms for Liberty Presents Fearless: An Evening with Megyn Kelly," June 21, 2021, https://web.archive.org/web/20210519234546/https: /momsforliberty.ticketspice.com/fearless-with-megyn-kelly.

54. Moms for Liberty Event Site, "Moms for Liberty National Summit 2022," July 14–17, 2022, https://www.momsforliberty.org/summit22/.

55. Moms for Liberty Event Site, "Joyful Warriors: National Summit," https://web.archive .org/web/20220530110816/https://www.momsforliberty.org/summit22-sponsors/; Kathryn Varn, "Moms for Liberty to Host Inaugural Summit Amid Rapid Growth in Membership—And Notoriety," *Tallahassee Democrat*, July 13, 2022, https://www .tallahassee.com/story/news/politics/2022/07/13/moms-liberty-inaugural-summit -tampa-feature-florida-gov-ron-desantis/10029086002/; Anne Nelson, "A Rare Peak Inside the Vast Right Wing Conspiracy," *New Republic*, August 26, 2022, https:// newrepublic.com/article/167002/council-national-policy-documents-right-wing -conspiracy.

56. Parents Defending Education, "Coalition of 22 Organizations Send Letter to Secretary of Education Miguel Cordona Expressing Concerns with Proposed Grant Program," May 19, 2021, https://defendinged.org/press-releases/coalition-of-22-organizations-send -letter-to-secretary-of-education-miguel-cardona-expressing-concerns-with-proposed -grant-program/; Adam Gabbatt, "U.S. Conservatives Linked to Rich Donors Wage Campaign to Ban Books from Schools," *The Guardian*, January 24, 2022, https://www .theguardian.com/us-news/2022/jan/24/us-conservatives-campaign-books-ban -schools.

57. Parents Defending Education, "Our Team," https://defendinged.org/about/.

58. Krieg, "How Moms for Liberty Grew"; Moms for Liberty Event Site, "Summit Speakers," https://www.momsforliberty.org/summit23/?page=1.

59. Moms for Liberty Event Site, "Education Panel," July 10, 2023, https://www .momsforliberty.org/news/summit23-education-panel/; "Kevin Roberts," July 11, 2023, https://www.momsforliberty.org/news/summit23-kevin-roberts/. For more on Roberts' role in the CNP, see Anne Nelson, "A Rare Peak Inside the Vast Right Wing Conspiracy."

60. Moms for Liberty Event Site, "Education Panel."

61. Carly Sitrin and Dale Mezzacappa, "Trump, DeSantis, and Moms for Liberty Come to Philadelphia to Promote Education Agenda," Chalkbeat Philadelphia, https:// philadelphia.chalkbeat.org/2023/6/30/23780585/philadelphia-pennsylvania-moms-for -liberty-republican-education-agenda-trump-desantis.

62. Moms for Liberty Event Site, "Florida Governor Ron DeSantis," July 10, 2023, https:// www.momsforliberty.org/news/summit23-ron-desantis/.

63. Lisa Lerer and Patrica Mazzei, "Florida Sex Scandal Shakes Moms for Liberty, as Group's Influence Wanes," *New York Times*, December 16, 2023, https://www.nytimes .com/2023/12/16/us/politics/moms-for-liberty-sex-scandal.html Retrieved December 18, 2023.

64. Stewart, *Power Worshippers*.

65. See Cara Fitzpatrick, *The Death of Public School: How Conservatives Won the War over Education in America* (New York: Basic Books, 2023), 210.

66. See George Packer, *The Assassins' Gate: America in Iraq* (New York: Farrar, Straus and Giroux, 2005) for the role that the American Enterprise Institute played in making the case for the Iraq invasion.

67. Patrick Keefe, *Empire of Pain: The Secret History of the Sackler Dynasty* (New York: Doubleday, 2021), 183.

68. John E. Chubb and Terry M. Moe, "America's Schools: Choice *Is* a Panacea," *Brookings Review* 8, no. 3 (Summer 1990): 4–12.

Epilogue

1. Josh Dawsey and Amy Gardner, "Top GOP Lawyer Decries Ease of Campus Voting in Private Pitch to RNC," *Washington Post*, April 20, 2023, https://www.washingtonpost .com/nation/2023/04/20/cleta-mitchell-voting-college-students/.

2. Heidi Przybyla, "RNC Links Up With 'Stop the Steal' Advocates to Train Poll Watchers," *Politico*, August 2, 2022, https://www.politico.com/news/2022/08/02/rnc-stop-the -steal-advocates-poll-workers-00049109.

3. Dawsey and Gardner, "Top GOP Lawyer"; Select Committee to Investigate the January 6th Attack on the United States Capitol, Final Report, December 22, 2022, https://www.govinfo.gov/content/pkg/GPO-J6-REPORT/pdf/GPO-J6-REPORT.pdf.

4. Lynde and Harry Bradley Foundation, "Our People: Cleta Mitchell," https://www .bradleyfdn.org/our-people/cleta-mitchell.

5. Jane Mayer, "The Big Money Behind the Big Lie," *New Yorker*, August 2, 2021, https:// www.newyorker.com/magazine/2021/08/09/the-big-money-behind-the-big-lie.

6. Anne Nelson, "A Rare Peak Inside the Vast Right-Wing Conspiracy," *New Republic*, August 26, 2022, https://newrepublic.com/article/167002/council-national-policy -documents-right-wing-conspiracy.

7. See, for example, Derek Black, "America's Founders Recognized the Need for Public Education; Democracy Requires Maintaining That Commitment," *Time*, September 22, 2020, https://time.com/5891261/early-american-education-history/.

8. Ingrid Jacques, "Betsy DeVos: Trump's Actions on January 6 Were 'Line in the Sand' That Led to Resignation," *USA Today*, June 9, 2022, https://www.usatoday.com/story/opinion/columnist/2022/06/09/devos-trump-why-i-quit/7529651001/?gnt-cfr=1; Fin Gomez, "Koch-Backed Group Plans to Help Trump's Rivals in 2024," CBS News, February 6, 2023, https://www.cbsnews.com/news/charles-koch-opposing-donald-trump-2024-election-americans-for-prosperity/.

9. Anne Nelson, *Shadow Network: Media, Money and the Secret Hub of the Radical Right* (New York: Bloomsbury Publishing, 2019); Jane Mayer, "State Legislatures Are Torching Democracy," *New Yorker*, August 6, 2022, https://www.newyorker.com/magazine/2022/08/15/state-legislatures-are-torching-democracy.

10. Jeremiah Poff, "School Choice Group Launches New Super PAC to Target State Lawmakers," *Washington Examiner*, September 25, 2023, https://www.washingtonexaminer.com/policy/education/school-choice-group-launches-super-pac-target-states; American Federation for Children Press Release, "AFC Announces Launch of Affiliated 'AFC Victory Fund Super PAC,'" September 25, 2023, https://www.federationforchildren.org/afc-announces-launch-of-affiliated-afc-victory-fund-super-pac/.

11. American Federation for Children Slide Deck, "AFC Is the Most Successful Force for Education Freedom in America," obtained by author, December 2023.

12. See Daniel Lippman, "SCOOPLET: Kevin Roberts, the president of the Heritage Foundation, has been also named president of Heritage Action for America, he just told an all-hands staffer meeting," Twitter, September 25, 2003, https://twitter.com/dlippman/status/1706372956379554075?s=42&t=ohXgTlSXyYFmA0RRo2t1wQ.

13. Nelson, "Rare Peak Inside"; Kathryn Varn, "Moms for Liberty to Host Inaugural Summit Amid Rapid Growth in Membership—And Notoriety," *Tallahassee Democrat*, July 13, 2022, https://www.tallahassee.com/story/news/politics/2022/07/13/moms-liberty-inaugural-summit-tampa-feature-florida-gov-ron-desantis/10029086002/.

14. Brendan Fischer and Ed Pilkington, "Right-Wing Group Pours Millions in 'Dark Money' into US Voter Suppression Bid," *The Guardian*, January 13, 2023, https://www.theguardian.com/us-news/2023/jan/13/heritage-foundation-voter-suppression-lobbying-election-action-plan.

15. Jonathan Swan, Charlie Savage, and Maggie Haberman, "Trump and Allies Forge Plans to Increase Presidential Power in 2025," *New York Times*, July 17, 2023, https://www.nytimes.com/2023/07/17/us/politics/trump-plans-2025.html.

16. Lindsey M. Burke, "Department of Education," Project 2025 (Washington, DC: The Heritage Foundation, January 2023), https://www.project2025.org/policy/.

17. Frederick M. Hess, "What Would It Mean to Abolish the U.S. Department of Education?" *American Enterprise Institute*, September 7, 2023, https://www.aei.org/op-eds/what-it-would-mean-to-abolish-the-u-s-department-of-education/.

18. See Katherine Stewart, *The Power Worshippers: Inside the Dangerous Rise of Religious Nationalism* (New York: Bloomsbury Publishing, 2019); Sarah Posner, *Unholy: Why White Evangelicals Worship at the Altar of Donald Trump* (New York: Random House, 2020).

19. See, for example, The Badger Institute, "Give Every Wisconsin Family the Power to Choose the Best Education," September 27, 2022, https://www.badgerinstitute.org/give -every-wisconsin-family-the-power-to-choose-the-best-education/; The Buckeye Institute, "Buckeye Institute Calls for School Choice for Every Child, Every Family, Every Community," March 30, 2023, https://www.buckeyeinstitute.org/research/detail /the-buckeye-institute-calls-for-school-choice-for-every-child-every-family-every -community; The Cardinal Institute, "More Hope Information," https:// cardinalinstitute.com/hope-info/; The Commonwealth Institute, "School Choice Report," https://www.commonwealthfoundation.org/school-choice-report/; The Goldwater Institute, "States Winning on School Choice; Tee Up Academic Transparency," March 8, 2023, https://www.goldwaterinstitute.org/states-winning-on-school -choice-tee-up-academic-transparency/; Texas Public Policy Foundation, "Issues: Education," https://www.texaspolicy.com/issues/?issues=k-12-education.

20. The Center for Media and Democracy's SourceWatch Project, "Contributions of the Bradley Foundation," a compilation of annual IRS 990 forms from 1998–2021, https://www.sourcewatch.org/index.php/Lynde_and_Harry_Bradley_Foundation.

21. David Armiak, "Bradley Funneled $86 Million to Right-Wing Litigation, Policy, Media, Youth Groups, and Higher Education in 2022," *Center for Media and Democracy: Exposed by CMD*, December 13, 2023, https://www.exposedbycmd.org/2023/12/13 /bradley-funneled-86-million-to-right-wing-litigation-policy-media-youth-groups-and -higher-education-in-2022/.

22. The Center for Media and Democracy's SourceWatch project: "Contributions of the Bradley Foundation"; Anne Nelson, *Shadow Network*, 142; Harvard University, "Annual Report," *Program on Education Policy and Governance*, 2022, https://www.hks.harvard .edu/sites/default/files/Taubman/PEPG/annual-reports/2022-pepg-annual-report.pdf.

23. See, for example, Garrett Ballengee, "Passing Universal Education Savings Accounts Is Base Camp, Don't Mistake It for the Peak," *Education Next*, June 8, 2023, https://www .educationnext.org/passing-universal-education-savings-accounts-is-the-base-camp -dont-mistake-it-for-the-peak/; Robert Enlow, "Success of Educational Choice Laws Will Depend on Implementing Them with Excellence," *Education Next*, June 12, 2023, https://www.educationnext.org/success-of-educational-choice-laws-will-depend-on -implementing-them-with-excellence/; Adam Peshak, "Surge in Education Savings Accounts Was Decades in the Making," Education Next, March 9, 2023, https://www .educationnext.org/surge-in-education-savings-accounts-was-decades-in-the-making/; Nicole Stelle Garnett, "As Private School Choice Spreads, Implementation Is Imperative," Education Next, March 21, 2023, https://www.educationnext.org/private-school -choice-spreads-implementation-is-imperative-excessive-eligibility-restrictions -undercut-effectiveness/; see also Caroline Hendrie, "As Many More States Enact Education Savings Accounts, Implementation Challenges Abound," Education Next, 23(4): 8–16, 2023; For Education Next funding, see The Center for Media and Democracy's SourceWatch project "Contributions of the Bradley Foundation," a compilation of annual IRS 990 forms from 1998–2021, https://www.sourcewatch.org/index.php/Lynde _and_Harry_Bradley_Foundation; Charles M. Koch Foundation, "Grant Agreement," July 1, 2020, https://charleskochfoundation.org/app/uploads/2021/12/Harvard -University-Grant-Agreement-2020.pdf.

24. Nicole Stelle Garnett and Michael McShane, "Implementing K-12 Savings Accounts," Manhattan Institute, June 22, 2023, https://manhattan.institute/article/implementing-k -12-education-savings-accounts.

25. Heritage Foundation, "Matthew Ladner Joins Heritage to Lead Work on Education Choice Implementation," July 19, 2023, https://www.heritage.org/press/matthew-ladner -joins-heritage-lead-work-education-choice-implementation; American Legislative Exchange Council, "Dr. Matthew Ladner," https://alec.org/person/matthew-ladner/.

26. Alliance for Catholic Education, "Nicole Stelle Garnett," https://ace.nd.edu/people /nicole-stelle-garnett.

27. Nicole Stelle Garnett, "Oklahoma's Approval of America's First-Ever Religious Charter School is Cause for Celebration," *Education Next*, June 7, 2023, https://www .educationnext.org/oklahomas-approval-of-americas-first-ever-religious-charter-school -is-cause-for-celebration/.

28. Lucien Brugemann, "'Inside Baseball:' Critics Say Academia Has 'Troubling' Influence with the Supreme Court," ABC News, April 27, 2023, https://abcnews.go.com/US/inside -baseball-critics-academia-troubling-influence-supreme-court/story?id=98849111.

29. Joshua Kaplan, Justin Elliott, and Alex Mierjeski, "Clarence Thomas Secretly Participated in Koch Network Donor Events," ProPublica, September 22, 20–23, https://www .propublica.org/article/clarence-thomas-secretlyattended-koch-brothers-donor-events -scotus; Nicole Stelle Garnett, "I've known Justice Thomas for over 25 years. He is the rare person whose goodness matches his greatness. It breaks my heart that so many are willing to go so far to attack a good, and great, man for political gain," Twitter, April 12, 2023, https://twitter.com/nsgarnett/status/1646641178312310791.

30. Nicole Stelle Garnett, "Incredibly proud of my former student @josephjconnor. Mission-focused entrepreneurs like Joe are critical to the success of parental choice as states implement ESAs," Twitter, July 25, 2023, https://twitter.com/nsgarnett/status /1683929822995656707?s=46&t=IlXtom7CfHEK0AiwKuzm3w; "Odyssey, a Company Founded and Led by Joseph Connor '16 J.D., Is Enabling Parents to Use Education Savings Accounts on a Vast Scale," University of Notre Dame Law School, https://law.nd .edu/news-events/news/alumni-joseph-connor-16-j-d-founder-ceo-of-odyssey/.

31. US House of Representatives, Corey DeAngelis, curricula vitae, June 27, 2020, https:// docs.house.gov/meetings/IF/IF17/20210311/111298/HHRG-117-IF17-Bio-DeAngelisC -20210311.pdf; Center for Media and Democracy SourceWatch: The Reason Foundation, https://www.sourcewatch.org/index.php/Reason_Foundation.

32. Corey DeAngelis, "Legalizing Discrimination Would Improve the Education System," Foundation for Economic Education, September 29, 2016, https://fee.org/articles /legalizing-discrimination-would-improve-the-education-system/.

33. Andrew Prokop, "The Conservative Push for 'School Choice' Has Had Its Most Successful Year Ever," Vox, https://www.vox.com/politics/23689496/school-choice -education-savings-accounts-american-federation-children.

34. Conservative Political Action Committee, "Confirmed Speaker, Dr. Corey DeAngelis Will Be Speaking at CPAC DC," Facebook, March 1, 2023, https://www.facebook.com /CPAC/videos/confirmed-speaker-dr-corey-deangelis-will-be-speaking-at-cpac-dc -2023march-1st-4/1387344582023565/; Rekha Basu, "Your Tax Dollars for Their Private School? More and More States Are Saying Yes," *Los Angeles Times*, February 12, 2023, https://www.latimes.com/opinion/story/2023-02-12/school-vouchers-private-public

-school-iowa-kim-reynolds-lgbtq-parental-rights; Christopher F. Rufo, "Winning the Language War," March 23, 2023, https://christopherrufo.com/p/winning-the-language -war.

35. The LEARNS acronym stands for "learning, empowerment, accountability, readiness, networking, school safety." See State of Arkansas, Office of the Governor, "WTAS Statements in Support of LEARNS," https://governor.arkansas.gov/news_post/wtas -statements-of-support-for-arkansas-learns/, n.d.; Austin Bailey, "Pro-Voucher Politicians Attack Public Educators for Putting Up a Fight," *Arkansas Times*, February 23, 2023, https://arktimes.com/arkansas-blog/2023/02/23/pro-voucher-politicians -attack-public-school-educators-for-putting-up-a-fight.

36. Moms for Liberty Event Site, "Education Panel," July 10, 2023, https://www.momsfor liberty.org/news/summit23-education-panel/.

37. Samantha Boyd, "Arkansas Department of Education Report Details Students Using Education Freedom Accounts to Attend Private Schools," KARK.com, October 19, 2023, https://www.kark.com/news/education/arkansas-department-of-education-report -details-students-using-education-freedom-accounts-to-attend-private-schools/.

38. David Ramsey, "Christian School Promoted by State Education Department Does Not Allow LGBT Students," *Arkansas Times*, November 21, 2023, https://arktimes.com /arkansas-blog/2023/11/21/christian-private-school-promoted-by-state-education -department-does-not-allow-lgbt-students.

39. Frank E. Lockwood, "Backer of School Choice Saluted: Arkansan Helped Start D.C. Awards," *Northwest Arkansas Times*, January 27, 2019, https://www.nwaonline.com /news/2019/jan/27/backer-of-school-choice-saluted-2019012/.

40. Independent Women's Forum, "The School Choice Journey," *Students Over Systems Podcast*, July 11, 2023, https://www.iwf.org/2023/07/11/patrick-wolf-the-school-choice -journey/; Center for Media and Democracy SourceWatch, "Independent Women's Forum," https://www.sourcewatch.org/index.php/Independent_Women%27s_Forum. For more on the IWF and its ties to the Koch Network, see Nelson, *Shadow Network* and Jane Mayer, *Dark Money: The Hidden History of the Billionaires Behind the Rise of the Radical Right* (New York: Doubleday, 2016).

41. Patrick J. Wolf, "The Comprehensive Longitudinal Evaluation of the Milwaukee Parental Choice Program: Summary of Baseline Reports" University of Arkansas, Department of Education Reform, 2008, 2, https://scdp.uark.edu/the-comprehensive-longitudinal -evaluation-of-the-milwaukee-parental-choice-program-summary-of-baseline-reports/.

42. For a comprehensive review, see Joshua Cowen, "Apples to Outcomes? Revisiting the Achievement v. Attainment Differences in School Voucher Studies," Brookings Institution, September 1, 2022, https://www.brookings.edu/articles/apples-to-outcomes -revisiting-the-achievement-v-attainment-differences-in-school-voucher-studies/.

43. For an overview, see Terry M. Moe, *Special Interest: Teachers Unions and America's Public Schools* (Washington, D.C., Brookings Institution Press, 2011).

44. Launch Michigan, "Launch Michigan Publicly Releases Framework, Sets Foundation For Work Ahead to Transform Public Education" June 23, 2022, https://www .launchmichigan.org/news/launch-michigan-publicly-releases-framework-sets -foundation-for-work-ahead-to-transform-public-education.

45. Ron French and Isabel Lohman, "A Supergroup Was to Reform Michigan Schools, Then the Schools Dropped Out," Bridge Michigan, July 5, 2022, https://www.bridgemi.com

/talent-education/supergroup-was-reform-michigan-schools-then-schools-dropped
-out.

46. See US Department of Education, "What Works Clearinghouse," https://ies.ed.gov/ncee
    /wwc/.
47. See Eric A. Hanushek, Ludger Woessmann, and Stephen J. Machin, *Handbook of the
    Economics of Education* (Amsterdam, Elsevier, 2023), https://www.sciencedirect.com
    /handbook/handbook-of-the-economics-of-education/vol/6/suppl/C; Matt Barnum,
    "An Economist Spent Decades Saying Money Wouldn't Help Schools; Now His Research
    Says Otherwise," Chalkbeat, May 16, 2023, https://www.chalkbeat.org/2023/5/16
    /23724474/school-funding-research-studies-hanushek-does-money-matter.
48. For an academic summary see C. Kirabo Jackson and Claire L. Mackevicius, "What
    Impacts Can We Expect from School Spending Policy? Evidence from Evaluations in
    the US," *American Economic Journal: Applied Economics*, 2023, https://www.aeaweb.org
    /articles?id=10.1257/app.20220279; for comprehensive media coverage of these results,
    including links to papers and reports, see Matt Barnum, "Does Money Matter for
    Schools? Why One Researcher Says the Debate Is 'Essentially Settled,'" Chalkbeat,
    December 17, 2018, https://www.chalkbeat.org/2018/12/17/21107775/does-money
    -matter-for-schools-why-one-researcher-says-the-question-is-essentially-settled; Matt
    Barnum, "4 New Studies Bolster the Case: More Money for Schools Helps Low-Income
    Children," Chalkbeat, August 13, 2019, https://www.chalkbeat.org/2019/8/13/21055545
    /4-new-studies-bolster-the-case-more-money-for-schools-helps-low-income-students.
49. Rucker C. Johnson and C. Kirabo Jackson, "Reducing Inequality Through Dynamic
    Complementarity: Evidence from Head Start and Public School Spending," *American
    Economic Journal: Economic Policy* 11, no. 4 (2019): 310–49.
50. Johnson and Jackson, "Reducing Inequality."
51. Johnson and Jackson; E. Jason Baron, Joshua M. Hyman, Brittany M. Vasquez, "Public
    School Spending, School Quality and Adult Crime" (National Bureau of Economic
    Research working paper no. 29855, March 2022), https://www.nber.org/papers/w29855.
52. Barbara Biasi, "School Finance Equalization Increases Intergenerational Mobility,"
    Journal of Labor Economics 41 no. 1 (2023): 1–38.
53. C. Kirabo Jackson, Cora Wigger, and Heyu Xiong, "Do School Spending Cuts Matter?
    Evidence from the Great Recession," *American Economic Journal: Economic Policy* 13,
    no. 2 (2021): 304–35.
54. David Figlio and Cassandra M. D. Hart, "Competitive Effects of Means-Tested School
    Vouchers," *American Economic Journal: Applied Economics* 6, no. 1 (2014): 133–56.
55. Biasi, "School Finance Equalization Increases Intergenerational Mobility."
56. See, for example, Bruce D. Baker, *Educational Inequality and School Finance: Why
    Money Matters for America's Students* (Cambridge, MA: Harvard Education Press,
    2021).
57. Kahlil Gibran, *On Children* (Knopf, 1923).
58. Benjamin Wermund, "Trump's Education Pick Says Reform Can 'Advance God's
    Kingdom,'" *Politico*, December 2, 2016, https://www.politico.com/story/2016/12/betsy
    -devos-education-trump-religion-232150.

Acknowledgments

Any book written by one author is still a collection of lessons and experiences created by many other people.

I thank the doctoral students, postdocs, early career researchers, and my coauthors and departmental colleagues past and present. I assure you I have learned as much from you as you ever did from me. Thank you to guidepost mentors who at different crossroads helped to show me the way: Ann Austin, Paul Begala, Adam Gamoran, Sue Dynarski, Doug Harris, Ed Jennings, Genia Toma, and John Witte. Thanks especially to Sheneka Williams for all your support and friendship.

Thank you to Anne Nelson, Diane Ravitch, and Katherine Stewart for inspiring me at various points to take this project on. Thank you to Shannon Davis, the whole team at Harvard Education Press, and to Angela Baggetta, for seeing it through with me.

I am grateful for my Michigan community: the 508 Allstars, the Cunninghams, the Eggerts, the Gielczyks, Peter Spadafore, Amanda Stitt, the local journalists whose reporting has helped me grow as a writer, and the "concerned neighbors of Glencairn."

Blessings in my life come from friends and family, old and new—those I have grown with and those who helped me grow: Johannes and Walt; Jen, Tory, Nick, Erin, Emily W-T, and a special gratitude to Brendon, Brian, and Leah; the Katakowskis; the Lindbloms; the Walshes; the Eric and Tami Cowens; Jocelyn and the Haywards; my bonus boys, Henry and George;

Stephen, David, Caroline, and their families; my mom, Ginny, and a special thank you to my dad, Mark, for teaching me that fatherly love can be tender as much as it is strong.

Thank you to my wife, Emily Laidlaw, who shows me new meanings of companionship and love every day.

This book is dedicated with love to and in thanksgiving for Nora, Clare, and James. Being their parent has always been far more of a privilege than it will ever be a right.

About the Author

Josh Cowen is a professor of education policy at Michigan State University and an author on topics related to education politics, school choice, and culture wars in the United States. In addition to all of the major academic outlets in his research field, his popular writing has appeared in outlets such as the *Dallas Morning News*, the *Detroit Free Press*, the *Hechinger Report*, the *Houston Chronicle*, the *New Republic*, the *Philadelphia Inquirer*, *Slate*, *Time Magazine*, *The Tennessean*, the *Washington Spectator*, and more. He lives in mid-Michigan with his family.

Index